Introduction to Linguistic Philosophy

This book is dedicated to Palma.

I. E. Mackenzie

Introduction to Linguistic Philosophy

SAGE Publications
International Educational and Professional Publisher
Thousand Oaks   London   New Delhi

For information:

SAGE Publications, Inc.
2455 Teller Road
Thousand Oaks, California 91320
E-mail: order@sagepub.com

SAGE Publications Ltd.
6 Bonhill Street
London EC2A 4PU
United Kingdom

SAGE Publications India Pvt. Ltd.
M-32 Market
Greater Kailash I
New Delhi 110 048 India

Printed in the United States of America

Library of Congress Cataloging-in-Publication Data

Mackenzie, I. E.
    Introduction to linguistic philosophy / author, I. E. Mackenzie.
       p.   cm.
    Includes bibliographical references and index.
    ISBN 0-7619-0174-4. — ISBN 0-7619-0175-2 (pbk.)
       1. Language and languages—Philosophy.   I. Title.
    P106.M27 1997
    410'.1—dc21   97-4608

97 98 99 00 01 02 03 10 9 8 7 6 5 4 3 2 1

Acquiring Editor:	Catherine Rossbach
Editorial Assistant:	Kathleen Derby
Production Editor:	Diana E. Axelsen
Production Assistant:	Denise Santoyo
Typesetter/Designer:	Christina M. Hill
Indexer:	Virgil Diodato
Cover Designer:	Ravi Balasuriya
Print Buyer:	Anna Chin

Contents

Introduction   ix
   The Scope of This Book   ix
   Some Important Terms   x
   The Structure of the Book   xii

Acknowledgments   xv

PART I. FOUNDATIONAL ISSUES

1. Meaning and the Nature of Language   3

   1.1. What Is Meaning?   3
   1.2. Does the Structure of Language Reflect
        the Structure of the World?   16
   1.3. Summary   29

2. The Semantic Conception of Truth   31

   2.1. No Absolute Truth   31
   2.2. The Semantic Conception of Truth   34
   2.3. Summary   49

3. Logical Truth and Analyticity   50

   3.1. Unconditional and Contingent Truths   50
   3.2. Logical Truth   52
   3.3. Analyticity   61
   3.4. Summary   66

Part I: Further Reading   67

PART II. NAMING

4. Names, Sense, and Nominatum   71

   4.1. The Name Relation   71
   4.2. The Paradox of the Name Relation   73
   4.3. Solution to the Paradox of the Name Relation   74
   4.4. Summary   86

5. The Causal Theory of Names   88

   5.1. Ordinary Proper Names   88
   5.2. Modal Sentences   91
   5.3. Epistemic Sentences   92
   5.4. Names of Natural Kinds   95
   5.5. Summary   100

Part II: Further Reading   102

PART III. DEFINITE DESCRIPTIONS

6. Description and Analysis   105

   6.1. Russell's Theory of Descriptions   105
   6.2. The Acquisition of the Referential Function   115
   6.3. Three Additional Puzzles Solved by Russell   120
   6.4. Scope   125
   6.5. Wittgenstein   127
   6.6. Summary   138

7. Descriptions as Names   140

    7.1. The Fregean Theory   140
    7.2. Referential Descriptions   151
    7.3. Summary   162

Part III: Further Reading   162

PART IV. NONEXTENSIONAL CONTEXTS

8. Modality   167

    8.1. What Is Logical Modality?   167
    8.2. Interchangeability and Existential Generalization 169
    8.3. Necessity as a Semantic Predicate   172
    8.4. Kripke: Essentialism   174
    8.5. Frege-Kaplan: The Middle Way   177
    8.6. The Method of Extension and Intension   180
    8.7. Summary   182

9. Propositional Attitudes   183

    9.1. What Are Propositional Attitudes?   183
    9.2. Interchangeability and Quantifying In   184
    9.3. Quine   186
    9.4. Kaplan: Cognitive Fixes   193
    9.5. Individuating Attitude Objects   198
    9.6. Summary   202

Part IV: Further Reading   203

PART V. GENERALITY

10. Indefinite Noun Phrases, Fregean Quantifiers,
    and Class Theory   207

    10.1. Indefinite Noun Phrases   207
    10.2. Scope Ambiguities Concerning Indefinite
        Noun Phrases   210
    10.3. Logical Analysis of Indefinite Noun Phrases   212

10.4. Numerically Definite Quantifiers 221
10.5. Expanding the Theory 224
10.6. Summary 229

Part V: Further Reading 230

References 231

Index 235

About the Author 245

Introduction

The Scope of This Book

Linguistics is the empirical study of natural languages. Philosophy of language is concerned with the *underlying nature* of the phenomena that linguists study. And linguistic philosophy is an approach to the philosophy of language. This approach is perhaps exemplified best by Wittgenstein's *Philosophical Investigations,* which stresses the importance of always seeing how language is *used* rather than assuming it to conform to some preexisting logical structure.

This book is about philosophy of language in general, but the conception of meaning that emerges is fundamentally Wittgensteinian in inspiration. It is designed above all for linguists with an interest in the deeper issues of their science, although it may well be of interest to anyone of a philosophical disposition. It presupposes no prior acquaintance either with the philosophy of language or with linguistic theory.

The book's aim is to give the reader a solid foundation in the field. As a consequence, it is concerned primarily with the grandees of linguistic analysis: Frege, Russell, Wittgenstein, Carnap, Quine, and so on. Anyone who has read and understood the book should feel equipped to deal with advanced work on most topics in semantics and philosophy of language.

Some Important Terms

Although this book does not presuppose any technical knowledge, there are a number of terminological distinctions that are made so frequently that some acquaintance with them is essential.

Sentence and Utterance

A sentence is an abstract unit constructed according to appropriate syntactic rules. For example, of the following two expressions,

(1)   Smith is raking the leaves,

(2)   Raking the leaves,

only (1) counts as a sentence in English.

Sentences are realized in discourse through utterances. For example, all performances of *Hamlet* begin with the same sentence but a different utterance.

The term 'utterance' is actually ambiguous, because it denotes both the act of uttering something, as in

(3)   His utterance of those words provoked much amusement,

and the product of this act, as in

(4)   That was a rather objectionable utterance.

Some linguists disambiguate between the two senses, employing the expressions 'utterance act' and 'utterance signal', respectively. In this book, the single term 'utterance' is used because the context is generally sufficient for disambiguation.

Sentence and Proposition

A proposition is taken to be what is expressed by a declarative sentence (used with assertoric force). From that perspective, the proposition expressed by a sentence *p* in English is identical to the proposition expressed by any sentence, in any language, that is synonymous with *p*.

Propositions are often identified with the objects of belief, assertion, and so on in sentences such as these:

(5)   Amanda believes that England will never win the football world cup.

(6)   John said that a gale was blowing.

The subordinate clause in these and similar sentences is often held to designate a proposition.

Use and Mention

A linguistic expression may be used to make a statement, ask a question, issue a command, and so on, but it may also be mentioned. Consider the name 'London' in the following sentences:

(7)   London is the capital of Great Britain.

(8)   'London' contains six letters.

In (7), the word 'London' is a name of the city London. That is to say, the sentence is about London. In this case, the name 'London' has simply been *used,* in accordance with the general conventions governing its application. Sentence (8), on the other hand, is about the *name* 'London': It does *not* assert that the city London contains eight letters. Thus, in sentence (8), the expression 'London' is not used but *mentioned,* which is why it appears between inverted commas or single quotation marks.

The distinction between use and mention can be generalized into a distinction between object languages and metalanguages. An object language is a language viewed as an object of study or semantic analysis.

The metalanguage is the language in which statements about the object language are made. Thus (8) is a *metalinguistic* sentence.

Extensional and Nonextensional

Normally, any two expressions standing for the same object can be exchanged one for the other without altering the truth-value of the containing sentence. For example, the two descriptions 'the capital of Peru' and 'the south American city with the oldest university' both designate the same thing, namely, Lima; so just as the sentence

(9)   The capital of Peru is on the River Rímac

is true, so is

(10)   The south American city with the oldest university is on the River Rímac.

The principle just illustrated follows naturally enough from the idea that if one thing is identical to another, anything that is true of the one must be true of the other; this principle holds good for a very large number of cases. The contexts in which it holds are called *extensional* contexts. Contexts where it does not hold are called, unsurprisingly, *nonextensional* contexts. Sentence (11) below exhibits a nonextensional context,

(11)   Jones thinks that Isaac Newton died in 1727,

for the truth of (11) does not secure the truth of

(12)   Jones thinks that the author of *Opticks* died in 1727,

despite the fact that Newton and the author of *Opticks* are one and the same.

The Structure of the Book

The philosophical study of language is not a systematic program. Rather, particular aspects of language have received substantial treatment because they are considered to be of fundamental conceptual significance. The structure of this book reflects this circumstance and contains discussions only of those areas of language that are of genuine philosophical interest.

The book is divided into five sections. The first is concerned with foundational issues, such as truth, meaning, and the nature of language. The other four deal with the specific linguistic phenomena that have attracted the most philosophical attention, that is, names, descriptions, nonextensional contexts, and quantification. There is no "core" to the book, in the sense of one or more chapters being more important than the others. Nor is it absolutely necessary to start at the beginning. Thus Chapter 10 may be attempted before Chapter 6 and so on. Where a chapter presupposes an understanding of something that is explained elsewhere in the book, a specific cross-reference is always given.

Acknowledgments

I wish to acknowledge the help of the following people: Jenny Saul, Nigel Armstrong, Andrew Linn, Alex Schwartz, Jim Hurford, and my parents. Any remaining errors are entirely my responsibility.

PART I

FOUNDATIONAL ISSUES

1

Meaning and the
Nature of Language

1.1. What Is Meaning?

1.1.1. Wittgenstein's Paradox

Arithmetic, logic, and language—indeed, any form of conceptual knowledge—find expression in symbolic systems. The spoken words of the English language, for example, are symbols that happen to have an acoustic form. Now, it is readily seen that whenever we use symbols meaningfully, we follow rules at every turn. For example, figurative uses apart, if someone employs the word 'table' in accordance with its meaning, he or she will use the word for some things and withhold it from others, and a certain regularity will be apparent in the linguistic behavior. From this we can infer that the person is following, tacitly or otherwise, a rule that governs how the word is to be employed. Notice that a rule does not determine how a word *will* be used but how it *should* be used: There is always the possibility of a performance error.

The same observations apply in the case of arithmetic. For example, if you are instructed to add (manually) 236 and 197, you don't just say whatever number comes into your head but, instead, you follow a series of rules that seem to guide you to the correct answer: You might, for example, write '236' above '197' and then add up each column (6 + 7 and so on) in succession, carrying over the excess from the preceding column.

So it seems to be a patent truism that all meaningful language use—indeed, all concept formation—involves following rules. Given that rules are so fundamental, we can ask ourselves how rules can be made explicit. Let us consider an example. As everybody knows, the symbols '×', ÷, '+', and '–' designate the following mathematical operations, respectively: multiplication, division, addition, and subtraction. In other words, we have a rule that associates each symbol with a specific operation, and this rule can be expressed or represented in tabular form, as in Table 1.1.

Assume, for example, that the person for whom the table is intended understands the words 'multiplication', 'division', and so on but has not yet learned the corresponding symbols. Common sense tells us that what Table 1.1 expresses is that '×' is the symbol for multiplication, ÷ the symbol for division, and so on. But this is not stated explicitly. Instead, the intended interpretation of Table 1.1 relies on a tacit convention, namely, one according to which items in the same row are to be matched up with each other. As Wittgenstein puts it (*Philosophical Investigations*, I, §86), we trace an imaginary line from left to right. So, to be more explicit, Table 1.1 stands in need of a supplementary interpretation rule, which we might represent as in Table 1.2.

The arrows are intended to indicate which symbol goes with which operation; for example, '×' goes with multiplication, ÷ goes with division, and so on. But Table 1.2, although *more* explicit than Table 1.1, is still not *completely* explicit, for it too relies on a tacit convention, namely, one that tells us what we are to make of the '→' shape. It is not inconceivable that someone who had never seen an arrow would simply view a '→' as a meaningless configuration of three lines. So, like Table 1.1, Table 1.2 also stands in need of an interpretation rule, some rule that would make clear how we are supposed to respond to the presence of the shape we call an arrow. However, it is readily seen that, like Table 1.1 and Table 1.2, our representation of *that* rule would not be fully

Table 1.1   Rule Associating Certain Symbols
With Mathematical Operations

Symbol	Operation
×	multiplication
÷	division
+	addition
−	subtraction

Table 1.2   Rule for Interpreting Table 1.1

Symbol		Operation
×	→	multiplication
÷	→	division
+	→	addition
−	→	subtraction

explicit either. It would rely on further symbols, possibly words, that might in principle stand in need of definition or explanation, and *that* definition/explanation might require an auxiliary definition/explanation, and so might *that* definition/explanation, and so on. The moral is this: *In attempting to be completely explicit in our expression of a rule, we embark on an infinite regress.* (See *Philosophical Investigations*, I, §§86, 163.)

One consequence of this circumstance is that no expression for a rule ever excludes unwanted interpretations. This is true for all rules but is most easily exemplified in the case of rules for mathematical series, and the classic exposition is in *Philosophical Investigations* (I, §§185-187). Let us suppose we have taught someone to build up series of the form '0, *n*, 2*n*, 3*n*, 4*n* . . .' when presented with the instruction 'Add *n*'. For instance, when presented with the instruction 'Add 1', our pupil produces the series '0, 1, 2, 3, 4 . . .' and, when given the instruction 'Add 2', he or she writes down '0, 2, 4, 6 . . .'. Now imagine that our pupil has been taught and tested for series up to 1000 and has always performed as required, and that now, when asked to complete the series 0, 2, 4, 6 . . . *beyond* 1000, he or she writes down '1000, 1004, 1008,

10012'. Absurd as it sounds, there is a sense in which our pupil's behavior is not in conflict with our teaching. For, when we instructed the pupil in the meaning of 'Add *n*', although we used various techniques—exemplification, drilling, and so on—one thing we are assuming we did not do was consider any cases beyond 1000 and, as any mathematician knows, every finite series of numbers can be continued in an infinite number of different ways. If we were presented with the series '994, 996, 998, 1000 . . .' in an elementary intelligence test, we would no doubt be expected to follow a rule that can be expressed as '$y = x + 2$', where y is the next number in the series and x is its predecessor. Strictly speaking, however, the rule could equally well be one that can be expressed as

(1) $y = x + 2$, if $x < 1000$; otherwise $y = x + 4$,

which represents the way our pupil has interpreted our teaching. Counterintuitive though our pupil's behavior would be, we could not fault his or her arithmetic. As Wittgenstein puts it (*Philosophical Investigations*, I, §185), "Such a case would present similarities with one in which a person naturally reacted to the gesture of pointing with the hand by looking in the direction of the line from finger-tip to wrist, not from wrist to finger-tip."

Notice that even if we actually make specific reference to the algebraic formula '$y = x + 2$' when we teach the rule for the series 0, 2, 4, 6 . . . , we still encounter the same problem. This can be shown as follows. To understand '$y = x + 2$', the pupil needs to understand the symbol '+'. To teach what '+' means, we might start off with small piles of tokens x and y. We might count up x and y and then combine them into a single pile z. We would then say that the total number of tokens in z is the result of $x + y$. Exposure to many such examples, together with practice and guidance from the teacher, would normally lead our pupil to associate some specific operation with the symbol '+'. But, of course, we would only be able to employ a finite number of examples in our teaching. Let us assume that our pupil has never seen or performed an addition involving a number greater than 999. In that case, our pupil will never have received any specific instruction about how to add two numbers when one of them is equal to or greater than 1000; hence nothing he or she has encountered up till now rules out the possibility that the symbol '$a + b$' designates not what *we* understand as the sum of a and b but, instead, what *we* would express as

(2) $a + b$, if $a, b < 1000$; otherwise $a + (2 \times b)$.

If '$a + b$' is understood as in (2), our pupil's interpretation of the formula '$y = x + 2$' will be such that he or she continues the series 0, 2, 4, 6 . . . beyond 1000 by writing: '1004, 1008, 1012 . . .'. The point is that, analogously to the case of Table 1.1 and Table 1.2 above, "We can think of more than *one* application of an algebraic formula; and every type of application can in turn be formulated algebraically; but naturally this does not get us any further" (*Philosophical Investigations*, I, §146).

Similarly with words: Imagine, for example, that someone asks me to explain the rule governing how I use the proper name 'Moses' (*Philosophical Investigations*, I, §87). I might say that I use this word to refer to the man who is thought by many to have led the Israelites out of Egypt. But this explanation does not suffice, because, as Wittgenstein puts it,

> Similar doubts to those about "Moses" are possible about the words of this explanation (what are you calling "Egypt", whom the "Israelites" etc.?). Nor would these questions come to an end when we got down to words like "red," "dark," "sweet."

Thus an explanation, although it may serve to remove *some* doubts or to avoid *some* misunderstandings, can never eliminate *every possible* doubt. As Wittgenstein famously put it (*Philosophical Investigations*, I, §201), "This was our paradox: no course of action could be determined by [an expression for] a rule, because every course of action can be made out to accord with the rule."

Lest the reader think that the previous example is somehow undermined because 'Moses' is a proper name, it can easily be shown that Wittgenstein's problem applies generally. Consider the English word 'green'. Asked to define this word for the benefit of someone who does not understand it, you might point to a green leaf and say, 'That is green'. But that (ostensive) definition lets in the possibility that your audience will take the leaf to be a sample of a leaf shape rather than a sample of green. Thus you need to be able to use a word such as 'color', you need to be able to say, 'That color is green'. Again, *that* definition presupposes an understanding of the word 'color', and in any explanation of *that* word there would likewise be the possibility of a misunderstanding.

The point is that each time one doubt is eliminated, a new one can spring up. Eventually, if the teaching of the word is successful, the pupil just *catches on,* the *penny drops.* But the actual definition of the word can never be completely self-sufficient. (Compare *Philosophical Investigations,* I, §§73-74, 82.)

1.1.2. Do Rules Correspond to Concrete Facts?

1.1.2.1. Rule following is not causal. If someone knows how to use a word, apply an algebraic formula, and the like, correctly, we feel that that person "has a proper understanding of the rule." But if rules can never be made completely explicit, in what can this understanding be said to consist? Can following a rule be explained in terms of any *fact,* psychological or otherwise, about a person?

Before considering various candidates for such a fact, we need to stress that we are *not* looking for a fact that *causally* determines that an individual *will* use a word, apply a formula, and so on in a specific way. Let us consider the case of word use. The difference between, on the one hand, a word's being used in accordance with a rule and, on the other, a word's being used as the result of some causal chain is best illustrated by an example.

Most word-processing programs enable users to create miniprograms whereby, for example, a frequently used expression appears on the screen at the touch of some previously designated key or combination of keys. Let us imagine that I have set things up so that the word 'table' appears on my screen when I simultaneously press the Shift, Control, and 'T' keys. We can then say that I *cause* the word 'table' to occur or be used whenever I touch the relevant keys. To say that there is some fact about Smith that *causally* determines his use of the word 'table' is to postulate some physical mechanism in his brain whose functioning, like that of the miniprogram in my computer, issues in the production of the word 'table' whenever certain physical conditions are fulfilled. The fundamental difference between a causal account of

Smith's language use and an account based on the idea of following a rule (tacitly or otherwise) is that the idea of rule following presupposes some notion of *correct and incorrect usage,* whereas the causal explanation accounts only for what Smith actually *does,* and so makes no reference to a norm in terms of which Smith's use of the word 'table' can be adjudged right or wrong.

So we see that any causal explanation of Smith's use of the word 'table' would not be our concern; we are interested in what Waismann (1965:124) called "the geometry of language; not the physics." Note that the term 'causal' is being used here without any commitment to the theory of the causal nexus (causal chain). What is meant by the term 'causal nexus' is an alleged *objective* connection between a cause and effect. We often say, 'Event *x* caused event *y*', but does this form of words say anything more than 'Event *y* followed event *x* and there exists a regularity according to which events *like y* follow events *like x*'? As in Wittgenstein's *Tractatus Logico-Philosophicus* (5.135-5.1361), the view is taken here that belief in a causal nexus is little more than superstition. Thus turns of phrase such as '*X* caused *Y*' or '*X* is causally determined by *Y*', although use is made of them here, should not be interpreted as implying that causal connections are objectively given entities.

1.1.2.2. The dispositional explanation. It is sometimes argued that, for example, to mean addition by '+' or to mean what is *normally* meant by 'table' is to be *disposed* to use the symbol '+' or the word 'table' in a specific way. The assertion that *X* is disposed to do *Y* can be understood in two ways. First, it can be seen simply as a turn of phrase, equivalent in meaning to the assertion that *X* would do *Y* in appropriate circumstances. In that sense, the idea of a disposition does not really explain anything; it merely shifts the burden to the '*X* would do *Y* if . . .' type of construction. On the other hand, some have seen *X*'s disposition to do *Y* as a kind of *fact* about *X,* as, in Quine's words (1960:33-34), "some subtle structural condition, like an allergy and like solubility" or, in the more specific case of a disposition to use or respond to a linguistic expression in a particular way, "some subtle neural condition, induced by language-learning" (1960:223). In other words, when not vacuous, a dispositional account of language use, and of rule following in general, is essentially a causal account that invokes the concept of a mental mechanism. As such, it fails to capture the normative aspect mentioned just now. As Kripke (1982:24) puts it, "The dispositional view [is] simply an equation of performance and correctness."

Wittgenstein himself implicitly takes this man-as-machine idea to task in §§193-195 of *Philosophical Investigations*. There he distinguishes between a machine as a concrete object and a machine as a symbol of what it has been designed to do. It is not immediately obvious what Wittgenstein means by a machine-as-symbol (*der Maschine als Symbol*), but the idea can be explained as follows. When we look at an unfamiliar machine at rest, we can perhaps imagine what it is supposed to do, how it is supposed to work. In this way, we extrapolate the intended functioning of the active machine from its inert form, which can thus be viewed as a kind of symbol. The machine-as-symbol is, in essence, the expression of a rule governing what the machine is *supposed* to do. It is like a definition that is intended to regulate how a word is to be used. The point Wittgenstein makes is that the machine *qua mechanical contraption,* unlike the machine-as-symbol, cannot be said to embody any rule, because it will not necessarily perform as intended; for example, there could be a mechanical fault: "The movement of the machine-as-symbol is predetermined in a different sense from that in which the movement of any given actual machine is predetermined" (§193). Similarly, whatever electrochemical mechanisms exist in the human brain, none of these can be said to embody any rules governing how linguistic expressions are to be used. The functioning of a mechanism is a *causal* matter, whereas the observance (tacit or otherwise) of a rule is not.

1.1.2.3. Qualitative mental states. A once popular idea, which originates in the thought of the eighteenth-century Scottish philosopher Hume, was that meaning something (hence rule following in general) consisted in an irreducible mental experience, characterized by a specific quality. According to that view, to mean whatever it is that the word 'red' means would consist in experiencing a red image (or some other qualitative mental state) every time one heard or used this word. Wittgenstein attacks this sort of idea on two fronts.

First, he shows that, in fact, if we do have inner experiences when we follow a rule, it is never the case that to one rule corresponds one and only one experience. One case of rule following that Wittgenstein uses in *Philosophical Investigations* to illustrate this point is reading out loud, understood in the sense of a transition from written marks to spoken sounds, leaving aside the question of understanding what is written (I, §§156-178). Wittgenstein asks us to compare the cases of someone who has been taught to read and someone who is learning. The learner might say some of the written words correctly, by guessing or because, having rehearsed the passage so many times, he or she knows it by heart. Now, as Wittgenstein says (I, §156), we assume all too naturally that what goes on in the learner and the practiced reader when they 'read' the same word cannot be the same thing, that they cannot both undergo the same mental experience. But, on reflection, we see that this is not so, that both may feel nothing or anything. Also, if being able to read can be explained in terms of some determinate mental experience or state, there ought to come a moment in the learning process at which the learner suddenly feels: "Yes, *now* I am reading." But, although some learners may experience such a feeling, most probably do not: Learning to read is a gradual process and there is no clear-cut boundary between being able to read and not being able to.

Much the same applies to the case of 'grasping' a mathematical rule (I, §§151-154). *A* watches *B* write down a series of numbers, trying to work out what the rule is. At some point *A* cries out: "Now I understand! I know how to go on." We might imagine that *A*'s grasping the rule had some determinate psychological correlate, that *A*'s knowing how to continue the series consisted in some mental state or process. But, again, this is not so. *A* might experience anything, a mental picture of the algebraic formula, a sense of tension, a string of unrelated thoughts, the sensation "that's easy," or whatever. Alternatively, he might experience nothing at all.

The second, and most damaging, point that Wittgenstein makes against the qualitative-mental-states explanation of meaning (and rule following) is that such states could not, in any case, cast light on the *nature* of meaning. Imagine, for example, that we discovered that when we used the word 'cube', an image of a cube always passed before our mind (see §139). We might then say that we use the word correctly whenever the thing for which we use it fits the mental image, and incorrectly otherwise. For instance, it seems that if we used the word 'cube' for a triangular prism, our use would not fit the mental picture. However, as Wittgenstein points out, the mental image of the cube *could* be projected in such a way that it *did* fit the triangular prism; that is, as

Kripke (1982:42) puts it, "The image [could] be used in non-standard ways." Thus the picture of the cube, the would-be expression of the rule for using the word 'cube', although it *suggests* a particular application to us, does not *force* one upon us. As in section 1.1.1 above, we now find ourselves on the brink of an infinite regress, because even if we imagine that not just the cube but also the correct method of projection comes before our mind—for example, a picture of two cubes connected by lines of projection—this projection schema itself can be interpreted in more than one way: "Can't I now imagine different applications of this schema too?" (§141).

Wittgenstein deliberately chose the example of a cube because it is easy to imagine how a cube can be projected onto another geometric object. But the moral applies generally, namely, even if we grant that following a particular rule can always be associated with a specific mental experience (and considerations outlined earlier seem to stymie even that claim), whatever this mental experience consists of—images, feelings, electrochemical activity, or whatnot—it can always be interpreted (applied) in more than one way. For example, to put things very crudely, if we could open up someone's head and pick out some network of neurons (or whatever) that was the physiological seat of some linguistic rule, it could always be shown that the form of the network had no unique "read off." Thus, how the network could be said to *embody* a rule would always remain mysterious. Mental mechanisms, although they may *accompany* rule-governed behavior, can only be "hypotheses, models designed to explain, to sum up, what you observe" (§156) and can never eliminate the underlying mystery.

1.1.2.4. Chomsky. In linguistics, one popular approach is to posit what Chomsky calls an I-language. An I-language is "a system represented in the mind/brain, ultimately in physical mechanisms that are now largely unknown" (Chomsky 1990:513)—'I' is supposed to suggest 'internalized'. This I-language Chomsky takes to embody our knowledge of language; it is what a grammar purports to describe. Our *use* of language is, in Chomsky's opinion, regulated by the form of the I-language. Let us consider the I-language in more detail.

Humans have, according to Chomsky, a language faculty, which can be considered a subsystem of the mind/brain. Prior to first-language acquisition, this subsystem is in a particular state, the 'initial state'. This initial state, which is a "true species property," is the subject matter of a universal grammar, understood as a scientist's theory (Chomsky 1990:513). A theory of universal grammar can be true or false in whatever sense any scientific theory can be true or false.

An I-language is the state that the language faculty attains "under certain external conditions" (1990:514), for example, if someone acquires what is informally called English. The true theory of English bears to this new state the same relation that a true theory of universal grammar bears to the initial state. Note that this new state is not attained through learning; rather, it develops in the mind/brain. Thus acquiring a language is something that happens, not something that one does; Chomsky compares language acquisition to a child's growing arms rather than wings (p. 514).

The initial state of the language faculty is regulated by a number of principles rather than by specific rules. These principles determine, for example, certain general features of the phrase structure of well-formed sentences. But they do not determine whether, for example, a grammatical head will come before or after its complements. In the acquisition of language, these choices are resolved in a determinate way: "The parameters are set." For example, if someone acquires Spanish or English, the 'head-initial' value will be chosen for the 'head parameter' (pp. 520-521).

A language is acquired, therefore, by selecting the values of the parameters of the initial state of the language faculty on the basis of external data, such as hearing people speak the language that you are acquiring. A "rich conceptual structure"—the basis for the lexicon—is already in place in the initial state. During the acquisition process, this is "awakened by experience" and labels are put to concepts (pp. 524-526). Once all this has occurred, "the system of knowledge is represented in the mind/brain," and it can now function, for example, through the assignment of a "status" to a sentence heard in conversation (p. 522).

For Chomsky, then, knowledge of language is represented in the structure or structures of the language faculty. (Note also that Chomsky would give a similar account of knowledge of arithmetic and logic, for they too are "systems of mentally represented knowledge" [p. 513].) Language and thought are, in Chomsky's words (p. 526), "awakened in the mind, and follow a largely predetermined course, much like other biological properties." Most significantly for our purposes, "I-languages are real entities, as real as chemical compounds" (p. 513).

This last quotation is important, for, as we have seen, the moment you try to represent or express a rule in a real entity, you come up against the problem of interpretation, namely, that there is no unique read-off. Consequently, although there *may* be something that is like an I-language, such an object could never be used to dissolve our fundamental problem of what it means to say that language use is rule governed. (Note that this has nothing to do with Chomsky's theory-specific distinction between rules, principles, and parameters [1990:519-523]. The term 'rule' is used here in a broad sense that would include both principles and parameter[-value]s, as well as any other like terms.) The reason for this is worth restating: Mental representations, like the examples of expressions for rules given earlier, can be interpreted in an infinite number of different ways (see Kripke 1982:85); hence, even if we could scientifically demonstrate that rules (principles, parameter-values, or whatever) were represented in the neurophysiology of the brain, we should still not have solved our fundamental problem. To take a concrete example, imagine that a neurosurgeon many years from now can point to some structure in the brain and say, "That represents rule *X*." Whatever the structure in the brain looks like, it is essentially in the same boat as Table 1.1 or our definition of the word 'Moses' in section 1.1.1 above: There is nothing, indeed there *cannot* be anything, about it that determines that it should be interpreted in one way rather than another. If we are tempted to say that the mind or the brain *knows* how to interpret such a structure correctly, we simply shift the problem to another level. For, to explain *that* knowledge, we should have to postulate some *other* structure in the brain: The regress is infinite.

Our problem is, in fact, not an empirical one that could be argued one way or the other in the light of physical evidence. Rather, it is a logical matter, a question of the *role* in our own language of turns of phrase such as 'this word means . . .' or 'Smith is using that word correctly' or 'that series obeys the following rule', and so on.

1.1.3. The Solution to the Paradox

The above considerations lead to what is perhaps the central problem of *Philosophical Investigations,* which can be summarized thusly: Any action can be made out to accord with (the representation of) a rule; thus any action can be made out to conflict with it; and so, in Wittgenstein's words (I, §201), "There would be neither accord nor conflict here." As Kripke (1982:22) puts it, "It seems that the entire idea of meaning vanishes into thin air."

How, then, do we account for our intuition that when we do math, speak a language, or make inferences in logic, we obey rules (tacitly or otherwise)? Wittgenstein's answer to this is summarized below. Note that Wittgenstein's formulation of his paradox about rules stands as an achievement on its own, and that we can recognize the paradox without thereby having to accept the proposed solution. Such a course of action would, of course, leave us in a sort of skeptical limbo, convinced of the irrelevance of psychophysiological explanations of rule following but unsatisfied by the proposed solution. Nevertheless, skeptical disquiet would seem to be preferable to misplaced certainty.

So, to Wittgenstein's solution. As we have seen, a causal account could never dissolve the paradox; thus formulations of the type,

(3)   Smith has a proper understanding of the word 'table';
      therefore he will use the word for that and similar objects,

are wrongly drafted. Rather, what we ought to say is this:

(4)   Smith has a proper understanding of the word 'table'
      because he uses the word for that and similar objects.

Formulation (4) certainly seems more appropriate than (3), but still it fails to dissolve our paradox, for what determines which objects are such that if Smith uses the word 'table' for them, he has a proper understanding of this word's meaning? Wittgenstein's answer to this is quite simple: agreement among human beings. As he puts it (*Philosophical Investigations*, I, §224), "The word 'agreement' and the word 'rule' are *related* to one another, they are cousins." What Wittgenstein has in mind here is not the everyday sort of agreement that might be characterized as *agreement of opinions,* but a more fundamental and possibly species-specific property, an agreement in what Wittgenstein calls *"form of life"* (I, §241). The form of life is the ultimate bedrock on which all rule following, all concept formation, rests: It is "the given" (*Philosophical Investigations*, II, p. 226), a primitive and unreasoned uniformity in human nature. Paradoxically, and as Kripke (1982:97) points out, it is here that Chomsky's and Wittgenstein's views actually coincide, for, as we saw, Chomsky too attributed the faculty of using language to a species-specific property, although, of course, the role this plays in his theory is quite different from the one it plays in Wittgenstein's thought.

To recapitulate, the expression of a rule can be interpreted in an infinite number of different ways. Thus the reasons we could give for using a word—applying an algebraic formula or whatever—in a certain way will never exclude all *possible* doubt, although, of course, they may well suffice in terms of "getting the penny to drop." In the final analysis, according to Wittgenstein, we simply act (I, §211), and it is conformity with a regularity across society that gives substance to the notion of an individual's grasping a rule or concept, rather than vice versa. For example, if we see a sign pointing in a certain direction, there is no logical barrier to our interpreting it as meaning we should go in the opposite direction. If we go in the correct direction, or, rather, if we *can be said* to go in the correct direction, it is because there is "a regular use of sign-posts" (I, §198). Rules, therefore, cannot inhere in individuals but only in society as a whole. Obeying a rule is a custom or an institution; so, according to the Wittgenstein view, it makes no sense to talk of a rule's being obeyed on a single occasion (I, §199) or in private (I, §202).

Note that Wittgenstein's solution to his paradox does not entail that general agreement is the final arbiter concerning whether a rule has been followed. It might be that everyone *thought,* for example, that two plus two was five; however, two plus two would still *be* four (*Philosophical Investigations,* II, pp. 226-227). Wittgenstein's view is, rather, that the question whether a rule has been followed can be given a determinate answer only *within the context of* a community, because only in the context of what he calls a form of life can we escape from the infinite regress of differing interpretations.

1.2. Does the Structure of Language Reflect the Structure of the World?

1.2.1. Introduction

A popular theory, and one famously elaborated by Wittgenstein himself as a young man, is the thesis that there is some fundamental isomorphism or commonality of structure cutting across language and the world. According to that view, all languages, natural or otherwise, that can be used meaningfully are cut from essentially the same pattern and that pattern or structure (or form) is identified with logic. The idea is essentially this: "One and the same fact may be expressed in a thousand different languages, and the thousand different propositions will all have the same structure, and the fact which they express will have the same structure too" (Schlick 1938:156, translation from Waismann 1965:315). Note that what is meant by the "structure of a proposition" is not the superficial grammatical form but the putative underlying or "real" logical form (see Wittgenstein, *Tractatus Logico-Philosophicus*, 4.0031). An idea of what is meant by the "structure of a fact" can be gotten from this remark of Russell's:

> Two facts are said to have the same form when they differ only as regards their constituents. In this case we may suppose the one to result from the other by *substitution* of different constituents. We can represent the form of a fact by the use of variables: thus "*xRy* " may be used to represent the form of the fact "that Socrates loves Plato". (Russell 1919b:2)

Logical structure is thus seen as being somehow projected through language and reality and also, although this is not apparent from the above quotations, through thought. In the later Wittgenstein's words, "These concepts: proposition, language, thought, world [seem to] stand in line, one behind the other, each equivalent to each" (*Philosophical Investigations*, I, §96). If the idea of logical structure seems to be a little abstract, it might help to think in these terms: The laws of physics determine what *is* the case, whereas (according to the view discussed here) the laws of logic determine what *can* be the case.

Let us now consider the theory put forward in Wittgenstein's *Tractatus Logico-Philosophicus* (first published 1921), which can be viewed as one of the most uncompromising expositions ever written of what might be called the theory of the common structure. Note that the Wittgenstein of the *Tractatus,* the early Wittgenstein, held rather different views than the Wittgenstein of *Philosophical Investigations* (first published 1953)—the later Wittgenstein. Note also that, as Kripke (1982:71) points out, versions of the common-structure theory underlie a good deal of modern work in the theory of meaning. In particular, the innocuous-sounding assertion that a proposition is true if and only if it *corresponds* to some state of affairs (compare Cann 1993:15) is, in reality, very close in spirit to the *Tractatus,* for in what does this correspondence consist, if not in commonality of structure?

1.2.2. Mathematical Multiplicity

The young Wittgenstein called a sign that represented a fact a *Satzzeichen.* By the same token, a *Satzzeichen* was the formal expression of a proposition. A declarative sentence from a natural language, for example, would be a type of *Satzzeichen,* although its real structure was not to be identified with its superficial grammatical form (*Tractatus,* 4.002) (see 1.2.3 below). A *Satzzeichen* was taken to be a fact in itself (*Tractatus,* 3.14), an arrangement of simple signs, considered nonlinguistic objects. Now, Wittgenstein's whole conception of language in the *Tractatus* depended on the idea that when two facts shared the same structure, one fact could be used to represent the other. Wittgenstein was impressed to learn how model cars were used in Paris courtrooms to depict traffic accidents. In such a reconstruction, the fact that particular models—acting as proxies for the vehicles in an accident— were in a particular spatial relationship had, he thought, a common structure with the fact in which the accident itself consisted. The reconstruction was, as it were, a direct *projection* of the accident, and vice versa. He took this to be the way in which *Satzzeichen* represented facts, although in the case of actual sentences, the proxies would be linguistic expressions and not model vehicles.

Wittgenstein thought that certain features of a *Satzzeichen,* indeed of any fact, were not relevant to its ability to represent other facts (*Tractatus,* 3.34-3.341). We can see roughly what he meant by considering a simple example. In English, it is significant whether a name follows the verb or precedes it: 'Jane likes John' and 'John likes Jane' describe different facts. But word order, although significant according to English grammar, is not *essential* to the ability of a sentence, considered as a *Satzzeichen,* to represent another fact. This is shown by the circumstance that the fact described by the English sentence 'Jane likes John' can be described by a sentence in another language in which the order of the words is different, for example, in Latin. Thus the spatial relation of objects in a fact—in this case, the words in a sentence—is not essential to its representational form. But certain abstract relations *are* essential, or so thought the Wittgenstein of the *Tractatus*. In particular, for a *Satzzeichen* to stand as a representation of another fact, it had to have the same "mathematical multiplicity," that is, the same number of constituents, as the fact it represented (*Tractatus*, 4.04). For Wittgenstein, it was the essential features of facts that determined their logical structure.

1.2.3. The *Gegenstände*

Wittgenstein drew a sharp distinction between simple and complex symbols in language. The simple symbols he called names (*Namen*) (*Tractatus*, 3.26). The names stood for what Wittgenstein called the *Gegenstände* (literally: 'objects'), the supposedly ultimate and indestructible building blocks of reality (*Tractatus*, 3.203-3.22). Note that while the *Gegenstände* were thought to exist as a matter of logical necessity, the name-*Gegenstand* correlation was envisaged as being entirely a matter of arbitrary convention. Wittgenstein was never explicit about what counted as a *Gegenstand*, but in the *Notebooks* (p. 69) he mentions the "material points of physics," and in the critique of the *Tractatus* contained in the earlier parts of *Philosophical Investigations*, he mentions colors (I, §§48-49, §58, §73), bits of wood (I, §47), and atoms (I, §47). Also, he talks (I, §39) of how one is tempted to feel that an ordinary proper name such as 'Excalibur' could be analyzed into component genuine names, each naming an atomic or irreducibly simple piece of the sword.

Now, in natural languages, colors are typically encoded as predicates, such as '(is) red', whereas material points, bits of wood, and atoms might well appear as subject expressions, such as 'that piece of wood'. Clearly then, Wittgenstein's conception of the *Gegenstände* is independent of the superficial grammatical distinction between subject and predicate; in particular, his use of the term 'name' is very different than the use that is nowadays made of the term 'proper name'. A revealing remark comes in the *Notebooks* (p. 69), where Wittgenstein is talking of how an expression for a complex thing can *appear* to be a name (although, of course, given Wittgenstein's view that names stood only for simple objects, this could not *actually* be so). He says that both the individual Socrates (strictly speaking, not a simple object) *and* the universal property mortality can function as *Gegenstände*. The moral of all this is that, when trying to understand Wittgenstein, a linguist needs to escape from the subject-predicate mind-set.

The *Gegenstände* combined together to create simple or atomic states of affairs (*Sachverhalte*) (*Tractatus*, 2.01). Every *Sachverhalt* was logically independent of all other *Sachverhalte;* in other words, the circumstance that a given *Sachverhalt* obtained was compatible with any other possible *Sachverhalt*'s obtaining. Sachverhalte combined with one another to form complex states of affairs or 'facts' (*Tatsachen*). Wittgenstein also applied the term *Tatsache* generally, to any state of affairs, regardless of whether it was simple or not. Thus, although a *Sachverhalt* was also a *Tatsache,* the converse was not true. Henceforth, the term 'fact' will be used in the general sense of foatsache; for facts that are specifically *Sachverhalte,* the term 'atomic fact' will be used. The sign for a fact (Satzzeichen) was complex in form and was built up from simple signs: "The configuration of objects [*Gegenstände*] in a situation corresponds to the configuration of simple signs in the propositional sign [*Satzzeichen*]" (*Tractatus*, 3.21). As we have seen, an example of a *Satzzeichen* is a sentence in a language.

Now, not every combination of *Gegenstände* was logically possible, for each *Gegenstand* was of a specific type, which determined how it could enter into an atomic fact. The notion of there being restrictions on how particular simple objects (*Gegenstände*) could enter into atomic facts is difficult to grasp at the very abstract level at which Wittgenstein was thinking when he wrote the *Tractatus*. However, a good analogy can be drawn with the ability of a physical object of a certain shape to be inserted into one type of space (for example, a square-shaped hole) rather than another. As Wittgenstein put it, "Each thing is, as it were, in a space of possible states of affairs (*Sachverhalte*)" (*Tractatus*, 2.013). By way of a supporting explanation, Wittgenstein points out that, for example, every patch in the visual field must have some color; it is, so to speak, "surrounded by colour-space" (2.0131). By this he means that it would be senseless to talk of a colorless patch in the visual field; thus there could never be a state of affairs in which a patch in the visual field was supposed to be colorless. Wittgenstein called the particular capability that an object had to enter into atomic facts the "form of an object" (*die Form des Gegenstandes*) (2.0141). Paralleling the form of an object was what Wittgenstein called the "logico-syntactical employment"

(3.327) of the name that stood for it. Thus the structural constraints on possible atomic facts, embodied as we have said in the so-called form of objects, were mirrored in the logical syntax of language; that is, they were mirrored in the fundamental structure of language, its *underlying* syntax as opposed to its misleading superficial grammatical form. Note that the paradigm for logical syntax was something like Frege's concept-script (*Begriffsschrift*) or the symbolic notation employed by Bertrand Russell (see, for example, Russell 1919a) and not anything like the D(eep)-structure or the L(ogical) F(orm) of Chomsky-inspired Generative Grammar—although, of course, both schools of thought share the assumption that naturally occurring language can be seen as a projection from some fundamental system of rules.

To anyone steeped in common sense, it might seem odd that Wittgenstein should have ever posited the *Gegenstände*. However, if we consider an example sentence, say,

(5)   The European Union is in the northern hemisphere,

it can be demonstrated that both *Gegenstände* and their linguistic counterparts—that is, names—are in fact *required* if it is supposed that the structure of language mirrors the structure of reality. Let us suppose for a moment that the structure of language does mirror the structure of reality, that sentence (5) is a representation of some possible fact in the world. From the outset, we see that the subject expression 'the European Union' cannot be said to designate a genuine constituent of the possible fact in question, for, if the sentence were uttered in 50 years' time, there might not even be a European Union, but the sentence would still be meaningful, it would still—by hypothesis—share its structure with a possible fact. Therefore, at the level of logical structure (logical syntax), the definite description 'the European Union' is not a genuine constituent of the sentence (or of the proposition that it expresses), although, of course, it is a constituent at the superficial grammatical level. We might try saying that the real constituents of the possible fact are the member states of the Union, namely, France, Britain, Germany, and so on. However, these too might disappear. For example, Britain could be broken up into England, Scotland, and Wales, with Northern Ireland going to the Republic of Ireland. But the sentence 'The European Union is in the northern hemisphere' would still be meaningful, hence have the structure of a possible fact. We might then try as candidates for the constituents of the fact the various regions of the countries in the European Union. But this would not work either, for they too are destructible. To prevent this regress becoming an infinite one, we have to make the bold assumption, as Wittgenstein did, that at some point in the process of decomposition, you reach a kind of linguistic and metaphysical bedrock beyond which it is impossible to proceed. At this point we would have uncovered our names (on the linguistic side) and our *Gegenstände* (on the metaphysical side). Thus we see that it is only by invoking the notions of names (in his sense) and *Gegenstände* that Wittgenstein can give content to the thesis that sentences/propositions are representations of facts.

1.2.4. Truth Functions and Complex Facts

We have seen that the structure of possible *Sachverhalte* was taken to be regulated by the fundamental laws of the universe—laws that, unlike the laws of physics, we simply could not imagine to be otherwise. But where did this leave the structure of the complex facts? The answer to this question is more easily given in terms of signs (including words and sentences) than facts. Before the answer can be stated, the concept of a *truth-functional compound* needs to grasped. Note that, in what follows, truth and falsity will be ascribed to sentences rather than to propositions. This is done to avoid cluttering up the text with repetitions of the formula 'the proposition expressed by . . .'.

A truth-functional compound is a complex sentence whose truth-value (true or false) is determined systematically by the truth-values of its component sentences (i.e., its clauses). The closed set of expressions that connect the component clauses of a truth-functional compound are called the *truth-functional connectives* or, sometimes, the *logical connectives*. The truth-functional connectives, together with their ordinary-language counterparts, are given in Table 1.3.

Each of the connectives can be defined in terms of a *truth table*. The truth tables for the connectives in Table 1.3 appear as Tables 1.4 through 1.8. Each truth table specifies a truth-value for each overall sentence for every possible permutation of truth-values of the component sentences. In each case, the overall truth-value appears below the symbol for the

Table 1.3 Truth-Functional Connectives

Symbol	Connective	Example	Read as
&	conjunction	p & q	p and q
∽	negation	∽p	Not-p
→	conditional	$p \rightarrow q$	If p, then q
∨	disjunction	$p \vee q$	p or q
↔	biconditional	$p \leftrightarrow q$	p if and only if q

NOTE: 'p' and 'q' stand for arbitrary sentences or propositions.

Table 1.4 Truth Table for '&'

p	&	q
T	T	T
F	F	F
T	F	F
F	F	T

Table 1.5 Truth Table for '∽'

∽	p
F	T
T	F

Table 1.6 Truth Table for '→'

p	→	q
T	T	T
F	T	F
T	F	F
F	T	T

Table 1.7 Truth Table for '∨'

p	∨	q
T	T	T
F	F	F
T	T	F
F	T	T

Table 1.8 Truth Table for '↔'

p	↔	q
T	T	T
F	T	F
T	F	F
F	F	T

connective, while truth-values for the component sentences occur below the letters 'p' and 'q'.

Each table, by showing how the truth-value of the overall sentence is a function of the truth-values of the component sentences, defines the role of the relevant connective. If the meaning of each table is not clear, consider the following examples. Table 1.4 shows that a compound sentence derived from conjoining two sentences using 'and'/'&', say,

(6)   Smith is happy and Jones is sad,

is true if the component sentences, namely, 'Smith is happy' and 'Jones is sad', are both true, and that it is false otherwise. Similarly, Table 1.6 indicates that, for example, the overall sentence,

(7)   If Smith is happy, then Jones is sad,

is false if the antecedent clause 'Smith is happy' is true while the consequent clause 'Jones is sad' is false, and that it is true otherwise. Many people find this definition of 'If . . . then' to be slightly surprising. This is because we are tempted to think that 'If . . . then' implies some

Table 1.9 Truth Table for '$\backsim$ (... & $\backsim$ ...)'

p	q	$\backsim q$	p & $\backsim q$	$\backsim(p$ & $\backsim q)$
T	T	F	F	T
F	F	T	F	T
T	F	T	T	F
F	T	F	F	T

sort of causal relationship between the antecedent and consequent clauses. But this is not so. Consider the above example (7). If we think about it carefully, we see that what it asserts is simply this: It cannot be the case that, on the one hand, Smith is happy, and, on the other, Jones is *not* sad. Similarly, if we have

(8)   If Clinton is president, then he won the election,

what we are saying is that the following is *not* the case: Clinton is president and yet did not win the election. So we see that the form 'If p, then q' is really an abbreviation for 'Not (p and not-q)'; that is, '$\backsim$ (p & $\backsim q$)'. Now, by deleting the 'p' and 'q' from '$\backsim(p$ & $\backsim q)$', we obtain a composite connective, namely, '$\backsim(\ldots$ & $\backsim\ldots)$'. The truth table for this is given in Table 1.9.

If we consider only the first two and the final columns of Table 1.9, we see that '$\backsim(p$ & $\backsim q)$' is false if p is true but q false, and that it is true otherwise. Now, as has just been observed, '$p \to q$' is really an abbreviation for '$\backsim(p$ & $\backsim q)$'. Thus Table 1.9 shows us that compound sentences having the form '$p \to q$' will be false if p is true but q false, and that they will be true otherwise. In this way, we arrive at Table 1.6 for 'If ... then'.

To return to the *Tractatus*, we can summarize Wittgenstein's theory of complex facts as saying that the sign for a complex fact had to be a truth-functional compound of signs for simple facts (*Sachverhalte*). Obviously, this is not the case in ordinary language. For example,

(9)   Smith believes that Jones is the culprit

is not a truth-functional compound. But what Wittgenstein had in mind was the underlying logical structure or syntax to which he supposed ordinary language could be reduced, were we able to eliminate the "enormously complicated" tacit conventions (*Abmachungen*) on which its understanding depended (see *Tractatus*, 4.002).

To understand the general conception, consider the following example, which is based on *Philosophical Investigations* (I, §60). The Wittgenstein of the *Tractatus* would not have thought of a broom as a simple object (*Gegenstand*); rather, he would have regarded the word 'broom' as describing a complex of simple objects. Thus any sentence about a broom would necessarily express a complex proposition: "Every statement about complexes can be resolved into a statement about their constituents and into the propositions that describe the complexes completely" (*Tractatus*, 2.0201). For instance, a sentence such as

(10) My broom is in the corner,

although superficially simple, actually would be complex at the logical level (would express a complex proposition). Now, as has just been observed, the only complex sentences/propositions Wittgenstein recognized, at least at the level of logical syntax, were truth-functional compounds. So, to reveal the logical structure of (10), we would need to analyze the sentence into a truth-functional compound that only contained, apart from logical connectives, names for *Gegenstände*. Let us assume for the sake of simplicity that the *Gegenstände* of which a broom is composed are the broomstick and the brush (an implausible but useful assumption). Then, according to the view put forward in the *Tractatus* (10), when fully analyzed, would have a structure that would look like this:

(11) My brush is in the corner & my broomstick is in the corner & my broomstick is attached to my brush,

which is a truth-functional compound of sentences about the would-be *Gegenstände*—we leave aside the question of whether the predicative expression 'in the corner' and the relational expression 'attached to' would also be eliminated in favor of names for *Gegenstände*; they would have to be analyzed into something, but exactly what Wittgenstein never made clear (see 1.2.3, end of second paragraph).

1.2.5. Why the Theory Fails

The theory developed by the earlier Wittgenstein implies that logic is some mysterious substructure setting limits to the empirical content of the world—a "scaffolding" in the *Tractatus* (3.42) and, ironically, "the *hardest* thing there is" in *Philosophical Investigations* (I, §97). Logical structure thus conceived is what enables a sentence to represent a nonlinguistic fact for, according to the theory, it is only insofar as it duplicates logical structure that language can mirror the world. Furthermore, as we saw earlier, the theory presupposes a naked correlating of simple signs with irreducible extralinguistic *Gegenstände* (objects).

Both assumptions, although their necessity is normally not recognized, seem ultimately to be unavoidable in any representational conception of language. To see this, consider this example from Waismann (1965:315):

(12)   *A* is north of *B,* and *B* is north of *C.*

According to the representational view, (12) has the same structure as some piece of reality: If commonality of structure is not claimed, the assertion that (12) represents some state of affairs has no content. To bring out its structure, we can replace the words of (12) with letters and symbols (semantically empty words, such as 'of' and 'is', are simply eliminated). If we do that, we have

(13) $N(a, b)$ & $N(b, c)$.

Is there any content to the assertion that (12) has the same structure as the piece of reality it supposedly represents? It seems that there cannot be, for we could represent exactly the same piece of reality using this sentence:

(14)   *A* is north of *C,* and *B* is between *A* and *C,*

which, when stripped down to its basic structure, becomes something like this:

(15) $N(a, c)$ & $B(b, a, c)$.

Examples (13) and (15) have quite different forms. Now which of the two structures represents reality?

What Waismann's example illustrates is that, at the superficial level at least, there really is no *objective* correspondence between the structure of language and the structure of the world. Thus, to sustain the claim that language somehow mirrors reality, we have to assume that the alleged structural convergence occurs *below the surface*. But, as we saw in connection with sentence (5), when we try to get beneath the surface, we find that there is no natural end point to the process of analysis. To avoid going into analytical free fall, we have to follow Wittgenstein and assume, in an act of faith, (a) that the decomposition of linguistic expressions and of facts eventually reaches a terminus, a point at which we uncover the simple building blocks of language and the ultimate furniture of the world, and (b) that, despite appearances, there in fact *does* exist some immanent, although hidden, logical structure that simultaneously determines the underlying syntax of language and the possible shape of reality.

In fact, neither assumption is tenable. The first assumption fails because there is no absolute simplicity, a circumstance that Wittgenstein recognized in *Philosophical Investigations* (I, §§47-50). What counts as simple or composite is always relative to the purpose at hand. For example, a chessboard is composite, but is it to be analyzed into 32 white squares and 32 black squares? Or should it instead be broken down into the colors black and white plus the schema of squares (I, §47)? Similarly, what are the simple components of a chair? Are they the bits of wood, the molecules, or the atoms? Asking whether something is composite or simple outside the framework of a particular purpose is like wondering whether a particular verb is active or passive per se, outside of a particular sentence (I, §47).

The second assumption has to be rejected for the same reason that psychophysiological considerations fail to dissolve the later Wittgenstein's paradox about rules. For to argue that logical structure is founded in the nature of reality is to suppose that there is a unique set of logical laws. But laws are rules, and rules, as we have seen, can be interpreted in an infinite number of different ways. Thus no content is left to the assertion that the structure of language is ultimately determined by the laws of logic. In the *Tractatus,* Wittgenstein was in a sense insulated from the need to recognize this, because he took the view that "logic must look after itself" (5.473). Why he took this view can be explained as follows:

Sentences, he thought, could represent the whole of reality, but they could not represent what they shared with it, namely, logical structure. To use a sentence *depicting,* rather than *exhibiting,* logical structure, we should have to station ourselves outside logic, hence outside the world, which was inconceivable (*Tractatus,* 4.12). A corollary of this thesis was the idea that what was *shown* by language could not be *said* in language (*Tractatus,* 4.121). Wittgenstein's notion of 'saying' needs to be understood as meaning 'saying informatively'. To see why what was shown could not be said, consider this sentence:

(16)   Jones is happy.

Sentence (16) is about the individual Jones and, through its form, it shows this; but it does not *say* this. Nor, according to the Wittgenstein of the *Tractatus,* could this be stated informatively in another sentence. Superficially, Wittgenstein's view seems to be just wrong, for have I not just written that (16) is about Jones? But, in fact, my statement to that effect was expressed in English, so anyone understanding it must already understand English and so would already know that (16) was about Jones; hence my statement would be uninformative. What if I had expressed myself in French to a French person who knew no English? Surely, in that case, my statement would have been informative. It would not if it is supposed, as the early Wittgenstein supposed, that all meaningful languages are just superficially distinct forms of the same system, namely, logic. According to the Wittgenstein of the *Tractatus,* once we know any language (indeed, once we can think at all), we have a tacit awareness of logical syntax; therefore, all that stands between us and the understanding of any other language is ignorance of superficial conventions. So once we have a language in which, as Wittgenstein put it, "everything is all right," we have already a "correct logical point of view" (*Tractatus,* 4.1213): Logic takes care of itself.

1.3. Summary

In this chapter we have considered two fundamental questions: What is meaning? And does the structure of language mirror the structure of reality?

Concerning the first question, we have seen that rules, including rules of meaning, cannot be identified with concrete facts. Thus any theory of the meaningful use of language that appeals to concrete facts—psychological, physiological, or whatever—although not necessarily false in terms of what it says, must be irrelevant in terms of our objective. The Wittgenstein of *Philosophical Investigations* expressed these matters in the form of a paradox. His solution was essentially this: It is not that we use 'X' in such and such a way *because* we mean Y, but, instead, by 'X' we can be said to mean Y because we use 'X' in such and such a way. In other words, Wittgenstein's strategy is to reverse the normal way of looking at the problem of meaning (and rule following in general) and to make the *regularity of use* the primary concept, with the idea of an underlying rule or meaning being relegated to a status of derived importance.

Concerning the second question, we have seen that there is no objective correspondence between the structure of reality and that of language. To sustain the thesis that there is, it becomes necessary to make two highly implausible suppositions. The Wittgenstein of the *Tractatus* opted for that course of action, but the very assumptions that he made to enable the theory to get off the ground turned out to be untenable. As we have seen, he was forced to retrace many of his steps in *Philosophical Investigations*.

2

The Semantic
Conception of Truth

<hr />

2.1. No Absolute Truth

The importance of truth to semantics and the study of language cannot be overestimated. The role of truth can be stated simply: *Understanding the meaning of a declarative sentence consists in knowing when it (or the proposition it expresses) would be true and when false.*

Now, we can ask ourselves what it is that makes a sentence true or false. One popular view is this:

(1)   *The truth of a sentence consists in its agreement with (or correspondence to) reality.* (Tarski 1949:54)

Note that the above formulation, although cited by Tarski, does not necessarily reflect his own view, as we shall see.

There seem to be two quite distinct ways in which (1) can be understood. First, we can see it as affirming the truism that if a proposition is true, it is so in virtue of extralinguistic facts. From this perspective, the truth or falsity (the truth-value) of, for example,

(2)   There is life on Mars

can be gauged only through empirical investigation. Presumably no one would wish to question this anodyne claim. It is our second possible reading of formulation (1) that is problematic. According to the second reading, (1) implies that a sentence—or at least the proposition it expresses—in some way has the *same form* as the piece of reality to which it corresponds. The reason (1) might be interpreted in this second way is that, if a sentence corresponds to a possible piece of reality (a possible fact), it can seem that there must (ambiguities apart) be some unique way in which we read this fact off from the sentence. Otherwise, how would we know what fact must be the case for the proposition that the sentence expresses to be true? The idea of a unique read-off seems to presuppose that sentence and fact have the same structure.

Now, this idea is problematic. The reason for this is discussed in the previous chapter (section 1.2.5). Essentially, the problem is that the sort of structure a sentence has, involving connections between nouns, verbs, prepositions, and so on, seems entirely different from any features of the nonlinguistic world—witness sentence (2) above.

Many, following loosely in the footsteps of the early Russell (e.g., Russell 1919a) and Wittgenstein (*Tractatus*), argue that although the sentences of natural languages may not converge with reality *in the form in which they occur in everyday use,* they do converge at some underlying level. To get an idea of what is meant by underlying structure—in this sense, as opposed to the sense the term has in Generative Linguistics—consider this example from Kenny (1973, pp. 39, 79):

(3)   Austria-Hungary is allied to Russia.

Thinkers who adopt a Wittgenstein type of approach might say that the empire Austria-Hungary is (or rather was) a complex object, and that to uncover the "real" structure of (3) we should have to make reference only to genuinely simple objects. Thus if, for convenience, we make the false assumption that 'Austria' and 'Hungary' are names for irreducibly simple objects (things, entities), the underlying or logical structure of (3) would be something like this:

(4)   Austria is allied to Russia and Hungary is allied to Russia and Austria is united to Hungary.

The analytical assumption behind our expansion of (3) to (4) can be represented symbolically as follows:

(5) ϕa & ϕb & aRb =Def $\phi[aRb]$. (See Wittgenstein, *Notebooks*, p. 4.)

The symbol '=Def' indicates that the flanking expressions are to be regarded as being synonymous with each other. (5) can be taken to mean that the compound statement—that (i) a has the property ϕ, (ii) b has the property ϕ, and (iii) a is in the relation R to b—can be abbreviated to the statement that the thing consisting in a's being in the relation R to b has the property ϕ.

The problem with this type of approach should be immediately obvious to the reader, and indeed it was already apparent in the falsity of our assumption that 'Austria' and 'Hungary' are names for irreducibly simple objects. Austria and Hungary are not simple, in an absolute sense, any more than Austria-Hungary is. So what *are* the simple components of Austria-Hungary? The cities in the empire? The citizens? The biological cells of these people? When we attempt to analyze the sentences of natural languages into supposedly simpler components, what we discover is that there is *no* natural terminus to the process of decomposition. Consequently, appealing to the idea of underlying structure, so as to salvage the theory that language and reality have a common form, gets us nowhere.

We are thus led to the view that there is no objective structural convergence between language and reality, that the objects with which our language furnishes the world are posits. True, certain middle-size objects—human beings, for example—are extremely useful in the conduct of our daily affairs and as such acquire a degree of fixity in what the American philosopher Quine calls our "conceptual scheme" (see Quine 1960, pp. 3, 92, 123, 161). Nevertheless, even these are posits of our language. Although they impinge upon our senses much more directly than, say, the theoretical entities of physics, the difference is one of degree rather than kind. As Quine puts it (1960:22), "Though for the archaic and unconscious hypothesis of ordinary physical objects we can no more speak of a motive than of motives for being human or mammalian, yet in point of function and survival value it and the hypothesis of molecules are alike."

A corollary of the thesis that sentences (at some level of analysis) have structural affinities with reality is the idea that the proposition expressed by a declarative sentence in some sense *fits* the truth, as one cogwheel fits another. Wittgenstein takes this idea to task in *Philosophical Investigations* (I, §136). There he points out that although it is correct to say that a proposition/sentence (*Satz*) can be defined as whatever can be true or false, all this means is that we call something a proposition whenever we are prepared to apply the word 'true' (or 'false') to it. Thus it is not the case that there are two independent things, a proposition and truth, the one a mirror image of the other. Rather, the concepts of truth and proposition are mutually supportive, like the stones in an arch. Take away one, and the whole structure collapses. This idea is further brought out by an analogy with chess. The possibility of being checked belongs to the concept of the king, but this connection is just part of the game and is not conditioned by any overarching fact, such as a general human dislike for games in which a king is not a piece that can be checked. Similarly, the fact that only propositions can be true is part of the game (activity) of making assertions, and is not determined by the nature of the universe or anything like that.

2.2. The Semantic Conception of Truth

2.2.1. Introduction

One way of avoiding the whole question of the relation between language and reality is to say, simply, that a sentence 'p' is true if p, and false otherwise. In other words, if our sentence is, for example,

(6)   Humility is a rare virtue,

we have

(7)   'Humility is a rare virtue' is true if humility is a rare virtue, and it is false otherwise.

Trivial though this strategy might appear at first sight, it at least prevents us from having to think about what facts must obtain in the world for (6) to be true. This is because the specification given in (7) of the condition for the truth of (6) is couched in exactly the same terms as (6). Thus we don't have to worry about the conceptual scheme implicit in (6). Sentence (7), to adapt a remark of Quine's (1960:24), is "made from the point of view of the same surrounding body of theory" as (6) and is "in the same boat."

Note that if we follow the proposed strategy, we are more or less obliged to dispense with the 'proposition expressed by' phraseology, because the particular advantage of the current maneuver consists in relativizing our statement of (6)'s truth condition to the language from which (6) issues. Such a relativization is lost if we talk in terms of propositions, which are deemed to be language-neutral.

The conception of truth embodied in (7) is known as the *semantic conception of truth,* and it was first formulated explicitly by Tarski in a paper called "The Concept of Truth in Formalized Languages" (first published in Polish 1933, which appears here as Tarski 1983). The following discussion is based partly on that paper but mainly on another, "The Semantic Conception of Truth" (which appears here as Tarski 1949). According to Tarski, a definition of truth (under the semantic conception) will be a form of words from which, for any possible sentence in a given language, a corresponding sentence of the sort exemplified by (7) can be derived (compare Tarski 1949:55). Let us see how such a definition can be achieved.

2.2.2. A Tarski-Inspired Definition of Truth

2.2.2.1. Material adequacy. Sentence (7) can be rewritten as

(8)   'Humility is a rare virtue' is true if humility is a rare virtue and false if humility is not a rare virtue.

Now it is readily seen that sentence (6), namely, 'Humility is a rare virtue', occurs three times in (8). If we replace each of the occurrences of sentence (6) in sentence (8) with the arbitrary letter 'p', we have

(9)   'p' is true if p and false if not-p.

Note that (9) is not itself a sentence but a general schema that represents the structure of a certain type of sentence. Schema (9) can be rewritten as

(10)   'p' is true if and only if p.

That schema (10) represents the same structure as (9) may not be immediately obvious. The explanation is as follows. The connecting expression 'if and only if' is normally defined by semanticists and logicians as indicating that the clauses (subsentences) that it joins together are either both true or both false. In the case of (10), the expression 'if and only if' joins the schemata

(11)   'p' is true

and

(12) p.

Thus a sentence having the form represented by (10) says of its two subsentences, one exhibiting the structure shown in (11) and the other the structure shown in (12), that either both are true or both are false; that is, that both have the same *truth-value*. Now isn't this what a sentence exhibiting the structure represented by (9) says? (See also 1.2.4, especially Table 1.8. Note that the logical symbol for 'if and only if' is '↔'.)

So we see that schema (9) can be rewritten as (10). And, indeed, that is the standard practice. Now, if we write a value for p into (10), say, 'Snow is white' (to borrow Tarski's famous example), we have

(13)   'Snow is white' is true if and only if snow is white.
       (Compare Tarski 1949:54.)

One way of looking at (13) involves seeing

> (14) 'Snow is white'

as a *quotation name* for the sentence

> (15) Snow is white.

(Note the use of quotation marks in (14).) Quotation names are not the only conceivable names for sentences. For example, we might decide to use the letter '*A*' as a name for sentence (15). In that case, we have

> (16) *A* is true if and only if snow is white.

(Note that '*A*' in (16) is the name of a particular sentence and is not a variable like '*p*' in (9) to (12).) What we see, then, is that the general schema instantiated in (13) is best regarded as being not (10) but

> (17) *X* is true if and only if *p*,

in which '*p*' is replaceable by a sentence and '*X*' by *any* name (quotational or otherwise) for that sentence. The form represented by (17) is called *form* (*T*) (Tarski 1949:55).

The stipulation that the definition of truth should entail for any sentence a corresponding sentence exhibiting form (T) determines a criterion for what Tarski called the *material adequacy* of the definition (Tarski 1949:54-56). The concept of the definition's material adequacy is contrasted with its *formal correctness* (pp. 66-68). To be formally correct, the definition should, in particular, be noncircular; that is, the use of the term being defined (i.e., 'true') should be avoided.

2.2.2.2. Metalanguage and object language. As we have seen, under the semantic conception, truth is relativized to a particular language. Now, there is a technical problem with this approach. In particular, it leads to a version of what is known as Epimenides' Liar Paradox. Consider the following sentence:

> (18) Sentence (18) is not true.

What (18) asserts is that (18) is not true. So if (18) is true, then (18) is false, and if (18) is false, then (18) is true. This is an evident paradox, the source of which is the possibility of self-reference in the ascription of truth. Specifically, the problem arises from the possibility, in one and the same language *L,* of naming (referring to) a sentence from *L* and ascribing truth to it.

Sentence (18) has a slightly phoney air about it, for it seems to offend against some unspoken convention. Declarative sentences are designed for us to make assertions but (18), by denying its own truth, forestalls that objective. It seems not to be playing by the rules. This, of course, is just an intuition and (18) is certainly grammatically correct. Tarski's strategy was, in a sense, to formalize this intuition. He began by drawing a distinction between, on the one hand, the language in which a sentence '*p*' can be named and asserted to be true and, on the other, the language to which '*p*' belongs in the first place. The first he called the *metalanguage* and the second the *object language* (Tarski 1949:60-61). According to this way of viewing matters, the letter '*A*' in (16), for example, names a sentence belonging to the object language, and (16) itself is a sentence belonging to the corresponding metalanguage. Notice that the metalanguage and the object language are both versions of English. This does not matter, because the distinction between object language and metalanguage is fundamentally theoretical rather than practical. Now, the advantage of drawing this distinction is that it enables us to prohibit, by fiat, the occurrence in an object language *L* of names for any of the sentences of *L* and, also, to ban the use in *L* of semantic terms such as 'true' and 'false'. By making this stipulation, we ensure that forms such as (18) do not count as legitimate sentences, or, at least, we ensure that they don't count as sentences that we are prepared to bring within the scope of the semantic method.

Readers might feel that this is an arbitrary exclusion because, as has just been observed, (18) is not actually grammatically incorrect. Strictly speaking, they would be quite right in thinking that. All that can be said in reply is this: If we don't ink in a distinction between the language *for* which truth is being defined and the language *in* which it is being defined, then paradoxes such as that exhibited in (18) will necessarily arise when we try to do semantics. In addition, as was suggested at the beginning of the previous paragraph, we do at least have a vague intuition that there is something not quite right about (18), and this may be viewed as justification, albeit of a rather flimsy sort, for a maneuver that is in any case forced upon us by the nature of the semantic enterprise.

Thus in semantics (in the technical sense) we introduce a difference of linguistic level, with an object language being the subject of a metalanguage. The definition of truth for the object language is given in the metalanguage. Now, as we saw in 2.2.2.1, to be materially adequate in Tarski's sense, the truth definition must be such that we can derive from it (in the metalanguage) sentences having the form represented by schema (17). This general condition imposes two constraints on the structure of the metalanguage.

First, the metalanguage has to be rich enough to enable names to be constructed of all the sentences of the object language (Tarski 1949:60-61). As we have seen, one way of naming a sentence is by enclosing it between quotation marks. Another way is by specifying the structure of the sentence named, that is, by giving a *structural-descriptive* name of the sentence (see Tarski 1983:156-157). For example, we could name the sentence,

(19)   Snow is white,

by using this form of words:

(20)   An expression consisting of three words, of which the first
       is composed of the letters S, N, O, and W (in that order),
       the second of the letters I and S (in that order), and the
       third of the letters W, H, I, T, and E (in that order).

The second constraint concerns form (T), shown in schema (17). In that schema, the letter p is replaceable by any sentence from the object language, and so, strictly speaking, we must be capable of creating in the metalanguage all the sentences that can be created in the object language; that is, *the metalanguage must contain the object language.* In fact, we can relax this constraint slightly, and it will suffice that p be replaceable by a *translation,* in the metalanguage, of any sentence from the object language.

Notice that the terms 'metalanguage' and 'object language' have a purely relative meaning. For example, if we became interested in the question of what it was for a sentence in the metalanguage to be true, the metalanguage itself would become the object language and we would have to go to a metalanguage of higher level (Tarski 1949:60). Thus we have the possibility of an endless regress of ever richer metalanguages. This confirms the point that was made in 2.1, namely, that there is no absolute truth.

2.2.2.3. The actual definition. To avoid circularity, Tarski framed his definition of truth in terms of the notion of *satisfaction.* Satisfaction is a relation that holds between objects or sequences of objects and what are called *sentential functions* (in Chapter 6, the term 'propositional function' is used). A sentential function is a sentence minus one or more object-designating expressions. For example, consider the sentence,

(21)   Chicago is a port in northeast Illinois.

We can make (21) into a sentential function by deleting the proper name 'Chicago' (which designates the object Chicago) and inserting in its place an arbitrary letter, thus

(22) x is a port in northeast Illinois.

We can then say that the object Chicago *satisfies* sentential function (22).

Now, defining truth in terms of satisfaction turns out to be rather complicated (see Tarski 1983:189-193). For simplicity, we employ an equivalent method introduced by the great German logician Carnap (1956, 1958). Let us consider Carnap's method in more detail.

To keep the explanation relatively straightforward, we shall assume that truth is being defined for a very simple language S_1 that contains only three types of expression. S_1 is a symbolic language, whose vocabulary consists of letters and symbols rather than words.

The first kinds of expressions that S_1 contains are *individual constants* 'a', 'b', 'c', and so on. An individual constant can be thought of as a kind of proper name, in that its function is simply to stand for an object. Note that an individual constant designates a specific object, and is not a mere placeholder like, for example, the 'X' and 'p' of (17).

Second, S_1 contains predicates 'F', 'G', 'H', and so on. A predicate is an expression—in natural languages, normally a noun, verb, or adjective—that combines with an object-designating expression to form a complete sentence. Examples of predicates in English are the intransitive verb 'swims', the noun 'cook', and the adjective 'French'. Each of these words can be combined with a proper name, for instance, to form a complete sentence:

(23) Jones swims/is a cook/is French.

Note that, in this case at least, the words 'is' and 'a' are of no importance. They are treated as empty grammatical markers. From a logical point of view, we might just as well write

(24) Jones cook

as

(25) Jones is a cook.

As was mentioned earlier, S_1's vocabulary consists only of letters and symbols. However, as we shall see in a moment, the predicates and proper names of English can be translated into S_1, using capital and lowercase letters, respectively. For example, the English sentence (25) can be translated into S_1 as

(26) Cj

in which 'C' is the translation of 'cook' and 'j' is the translation of 'Jones'.

The third type of expression contained in our imaginary language S_1 comprises the logical or *truth-functional* connective expressions '~', '&', '∨', '→', and '↔', which correspond to the English expressions 'not', 'and', 'or', 'if . . . then', and 'if and only if', respectively. These expressions are defined and explained in 1.2.4. If the reader is unsure what the truth-functional connectives are, he or she should consult that section now.

It is assumed that S_1 contains only the three types of expressions mentioned above.

At this point, a distinction needs to be drawn between the simple or *atomic* sentences of S_1 and that language's *complex* sentences. Simple sentences involve only expressions of the first two types mentioned above. Complex sentences involve expressions of all three types. For example, sentence (26) is atomic, as is

(27) *Hj* (i.e., a symbolic translation of 'Jones is human').

On the other hand,

(28) *Cj → Hj*

and

(29) *⌐Cj*

are complex. (The latter is composed of the simple sentence '*Cj*' plus the truth-functional connective '⌐'.) Note that the distinction, *as it is drawn here,* between atomic and complex sentences is purely a linguistic one; that is, it is made without any ancillary supposition that there is a corresponding language-external distinction between simple and complex facts (compare 1.2.3).

Carnap's version of the semantic definition of truth is recursive; that is, truth is defined in the first instance for atomic sentences and then, derivatively, for complex sentences. Thus the starting point is the definition of what it is for an atomic sentence to be true. Truth is defined via what Carnap calls *rules of truth* (Carnap 1956:5).

Now, truth, as was pointed out earlier, is defined in a metalanguage *M.* We take, as *M,* a suitable part of the English language. Our object language in the present case is S_1. In accordance with the remarks made in 2.2.2.2 above, we assume that every expression that occurs in S_1 also occurs in *M,* or at least that it can be correlated with an expression in *M* of which it is a translation. Carnap gives such translations in what he calls *rules of designation* (Carnap 1956:4). Examples of such rules are as follows:

(30) '*j*' is a symbolic translation of 'Jones'.

(31) 's' is a symbolic translation of 'Walter Scott'.

(32) 'H' is a symbolic translation of 'human'.

(33) 'B' is a symbolic translation of 'biped'.

Expressions of individual type, such as 'j' and 's' in S_1 and 'Jones' and 'Walter Scott' in M, can be envisaged as designating (standing for) the objects Jones and Walter Scott, respectively. On the other hand, it is by no means clear what the expressions 'human' and 'biped' (together with their counterparts in S_1) designate. Indeed, in ordinary language it is not customary to say that predicates *designate* things at all. Nevertheless, for convenience we can say that 'human' and 'biped' designate *classes of objects,* namely, the classes of things that are human and bipeds, respectively. More generally, we can say that a predicate designates (has as its *extension*) the class of objects of which it is true; for example, the expression 'human' can be said to be *true of* the individual Bill Clinton (see Carnap 1956, §4).

We assume that there is a rule of designation for every individual constant and every predicate that occurs in S_1.

We can now proceed to the rule of truth for atomic sentences:

(34) *Rule of truth* for atomic sentences: An atomic sentence in S_1 consisting of a predicate followed by an individual constant is true if and only if the object designated by the individual constant is a member of the class designated by the predicate. (Compare Carnap 1956:5; also §4, §§33-38.)

(34) gives us a definition of what it is for an atomic sentence in S_1 to be true. From the point of view of what was referred to earlier as the formal correctness of the definition, the important thing to note is that, although the word 'true' occurs to the left of the expression 'if and only if', it does not occur to the right, which is where the notion of truth is actually explained. In this way, circularity is avoided.

Given the rules of designation (31) and (33), the rule of truth (34) enables us to derive, for example, the following sentence in M:

(35)   The sentence '*Bs*' is true if and only if Scott is a biped.
(Carnap 1956:5)

Now that we have a rule of truth for atomic sentences, we can give rules of truth for complex sentences. These correspond to the truth-tables 1.4 to 1.8 in Chapter 1. Here, only two rules of truth are given for complex sentences. The others can be easily constructed by the reader, on the basis of the truth-tables given in Chapter 1. Below, the letters p and q are used to stand for arbitrary atomic sentences of S_1:

(36)   *Rule of truth* for '$\vee$': A sentence of the form $p \vee q$ in S_1 is true if and only if at least one of the components is true.

(37)   *Rule of truth* for '$\leftrightarrow$': A sentence of the form $p \leftrightarrow q$ in S_1 is true if and only if either both components are true or both are not true. (Compare Carnap 1956:5.)

Rule (37), for example, together with the truth-rule for atomic sentences (rule (34)) and the rules of designation (31) to (33), enables us to derive the following sentence in *M:*

(38)   The sentence '*Bs $\leftrightarrow$ Hs*' is true if and only if *either* Scott is a biped and Scott is Human *or* Scott is not a biped and Scott is not human.

All the rules of truth, taken together, constitute a recursive definition of the expression 'true in S_1'. This definition meets Tarski's condition for material adequacy because, for every possible sentence in S_1 (atomic or complex), we can derive from the definition a sentence that conforms to schema (17)—at least, that is, if we allow the letter p in (17) to be replaceable by the translation of a sentence from S_1 rather than the sentence itself. It might be thought that our Carnap-style recursive definition did not meet Tarski's criterion for formal correctness, because the word 'true' occurs to the right of the expression 'if and only if' in the rules of truth relating to complex sentences. In fact, this circumstance does not render the definition formally incorrect, because the term 'true' as it occurs, for example, in (36) and (37) is really an abbreviation for an appropriate form of words based on (34).

That is to say, we could in principle express what (36) and (37) express in such a way that the term 'true' did not occur to the right of the expression 'if and only if'. However, so as not to clutter up our rules of truth for complex sentences, we choose not to do that and, instead, rely on (34) as an ancillary definition. Thus the important point, in terms of avoiding circularity, turns out to be the avoidance of the word 'true' in the definition of truth for *atomic* sentences. Because the word 'true' does not occur to the right of the expression 'if and only if' in (34), our Carnap-style definition of truth can be said to be formally correct, at least insofar as it avoids circularity.

2.2.3. Extensions of the Tarski-Carnap Definition of Truth

The language S_1 for which truth was defined above is very simple. In principle, however, the same technique can be applied to much more complex languages (including natural languages). At the current moment, we do not have a complete truth definition (i.e., a complete semantic theory) for any natural language, but more and more linguistic phenomena are being brought within the scope of the Tarskian paradigm. Below are some of the ways in which the theory can be expanded.

2.2.3.1. Predicates of higher degree. One obvious oversimplification in S_1 consists in the fact that S_1's sentences are all of the form ϕx, where ϕ is replaceable by a predicate and x by a single individual constant. In other words, the only predicates that occur in S_1 are of *degree* one (see Carnap 1958, vol. 1, p. 17). In natural languages, on the other hand, there are sentences involving predicates of a degree greater than one, such as

(39)   Jones talks to Walter Scott

and

(40)   Tom denounced Walter Scott to Jones.

The above sentences contain predicates of degree two and degree three, respectively.

So consider a new symbolic language S_2 that contains, in addition to all the sentences of S_1, sentences containing predicates of degree $n >$ 1, that is, predicates of degree two or greater. The metalanguage M contains appropriate rules of designation, such as the following:

(41) 'T' is a symbolic translation of 'talks to'.

(42) 'D' is a symbolic translation of 'denounces . . . to'.

Given (41) and (42), the translations of (39) and (40) into S_2 (ignoring tense) are

(43) *Tjs*

and

(44) *Dtsj*,

respectively.

Sentences such as (43) and (44) are atomic sentences, and so they would fall within the purview of an expanded version of rule (34), the truth rule for atomic sentences. Before seeing how such a rule can be drafted, the concept of a *sequence of objects* needs to explained. As we have seen, a predicate of degree one, such as the English noun 'doctor' or the adjective 'happy', can be said to be *true of* a specific object, say, the person Jones. Thus if Jones is a doctor, the predicate 'doctor' is true of Jones, or if Jones is happy, the predicate 'happy' is true of him. Analogously, we say of a predicate of degree $n > 1$ that it is true of a *sequence* with $n > 1$ terms, that is, of a certain number of objects taken in a particular order (see Carnap 1958, vol. 1, pp. 18-19). For example, if the English sentence (39) is true, the predicate (of degree two) 'talks to' is true of a sequence of objects that we can represent as

(45) <Jones, Walter Scott>.

Likewise, if (40) is true, the predicate (of degree three) 'denounced' can be said to be true of the following sequence:

(46)   <Tom, Walter Scott, Jones>.

Note that in a sequence, one and the same object may occur at different places. Consider, for example, the English sentence

(47)   Tom denounced himself to Jones.

In (47), the positions of denouncer and denounced are occupied by expressions for one and the same object, namely, Tom. Thus if (47) is true, the sequence of objects of which the predicate 'denounced' can be said to be true is as follows:

(48)   <Tom, Tom, Jones>

with Tom appearing twice over. (48) represents a sequence with *three terms* but only *two members*.

It was remarked earlier that what we are now calling predicates of degree one could be taken to designate classes of single objects. Analogously, we can say that a predicate of degree n designates a class of sequences, each with n terms. For example, we can say that 'denounces' (or, instead, 'denounces . . . to') designates the class of all those sequences (with three terms) whose members stand in the denouncer-denounced-denouncee relation.

Now, we can also have sequences with a *single* term. Thus, instead of saying that predicates of degree one designate classes of single objects, we can say that they too designate classes of sequences (with a single term). This circumstance simplifies our task of framing a truth rule that is applicable to atomic sentences containing predicates of degree $n > 1$:

(49)   *Rule of truth* for atomic sentences: An atomic sentence in S_2 consisting of a predicate (of degree n) followed by n individual constant(s) is true if and only if the sequence represented by the individual constant(s), taken in the order in which they occur in the sentence, is a member of the class designated by the predicate. (See also Carnap 1958, vol. 1, pp. 18-19.)

The above rule of truth, together with the rules of designation, enables us to derive, for example, the following sentence in the metalanguage *M* (we ignore the question of tense):

(50)   The sentence *'Dtsj'* is true if and only if Tom denounced Walter Scott to Jones.

2.2.3.2. Deixis, noun phrases, subordination. Tarski's method for defining truth was devised with a particular formalized language in mind (the so-called calculus of classes; see Tarski 1983:168). In such a language, there are no deictic features, such as tenses, demonstratives, and personal pronouns. Now, the problem with deictic features is that they adjust their reference from one circumstance to another. For example,

(51)   I am happy

may be true when spoken by *X* but not when spoken by *Y*, or it may be true when spoken at time *t* but not at time *u*. Similarly,

(52)   That is a human

will be true when what is being pointed at is a human being but not when it is a rhinoceros. The American philosopher Donald Davidson famously addressed this point in "Truth and Meaning" (published 1967). He pointed out that a definition of truth for a natural language needed to be such that we could derive from it metalinguistic sentences like the following:

'I am tired' is true as (potentially) spoken by *p* at *t* if and only if *p* is tired at *t*.

'That book was stolen' is true as (potentially) spoken by *p* at *t* if and only if the book demonstrated by *p* at *t* is stolen prior to *t*. (Davidson 1967:319-320)

For our definition of truth to be capable of including sentences such as the above, we need to regard truth not as a *property of sentences* (as we took it to be earlier) but as a *relation between a sentence, a person, and a time* (see Davidson 1967:319). This perspective is not in any way at variance with the spirit of Tarski's original method of defining truth. It simply reflects one major difference between natural and formalized languages.

The above maneuver still leaves untamed a great many other phenomena that occur in natural languages—a "staggering list of difficulties and conundrums," as Davidson put it (1967:321). Two features that have received an enormous amount of attention are noun phrases (as opposed to the individual constants of our languages S_1 and S_2) and subordinate clauses. *Definite* noun phrases are discussed in Part III of this book, while *indefinite* noun phrases are discussed in Part V. Subordinate clauses controlled by psychological verbs such as 'believe that' are discussed in Chapter 10.

2.3. Summary

We have seen that there is no absolute truth and that, consequently, the attempt to explain the notion of the truth of a sentence in terms of extralinguistic circumstances is doomed to failure. The semantic definition of truth implies nothing regarding the extralinguistic conditions under which sentences are true or false. To paraphrase Tarski (1949:71), it implies only that, whenever we assert or reject a sentence '*p*', we must be ready to assert or reject the correlated sentence '*the sentence "p" is true*'. Many readers might regard this language-relative conception of truth as rather disappointing. So it may be worth recalling the following remarks of Tarski's (1949:56):

> Semantics as it is conceived in this paper (and in former papers of the author) is a sober and modest discipline which has no pretensions of being a universal patent-medicine for all the ills and diseases of mankind, whether imaginary or real. You will not find in semantics any remedy for decayed teeth or illusions of grandeur or class conflicts. Nor is semantics a device for establishing that everyone except the speaker and his friends is speaking nonsense.

3

Logical Truth
and Analyticity

3.1. Unconditional and Contingent Truths

Philosophers have long since distinguished between two types of true propositions, namely, propositions that are true unconditionally and propositions that are true only contingently. Examples of the first kind are as follows:

(1)   It is not raining or it is raining.

(2)   If Smith is a bachelor, he is not married.

To ascertain that (1) and (2) are true, there is no need to consider extralinguistic facts, for (1) and (2)'s truth is guaranteed by their meaning alone. In this respect, they are unlike

(3)   The current U.S. president is from Arkansas,

which is only true if corroborated by the facts. However, there is an important difference between (1) and (2). To determine whether (1) is true, we need only consider the logical words 'not' and 'or' (for an explanation of 'not', 'or', and the other *truth-functional connectives,* see 1.2.4), the remainder of the sentence not being a factor in its overall truth. Thus we could replace the subsentence

(4)   It is raining

(at *both* its places of occurrence in (1)) with any other sentence and this would not produce a change in truth-value overall. If we try the same maneuver on sentence (2), we get a different result. In this case, we have two distinct subsentences, namely, 'Smith is a bachelor' and 'Smith is married' (note that the pronoun 'he' is supplanted by its antecedent when the subsentence in which it occurs is cited in isolation), and each must be replaced by a *different* sentence. Let us insert, say, 'Smith is in London' and 'Smith is happy', in that order, into the positions occupied by 'Smith is a bachelor' and 'Smith is married'. This move yields:

(5)   If Smith is in London, he is not happy,

which, if true, is true only contingently—for example, Smith may like London; in which case, (5) would most likely be false.

Thus we see that in (2), unlike in (1), the content of the subsentences *is* a factor in the overall truth. More specifically, the truth of (2) is conditioned by an incompatibility between the predicates 'married' and 'bachelor'.

Propositions such as that expressed by (3) are said to be *factual* or *synthetic.* Propositions such as that expressed by (1) are said to be *analytic* and, moreover, *logically true.* Propositions such as that expressed by (2) are said to be analytic but not logically true (see Carnap 1956:222; Quine 1951:23).

3.2. Logical Truth

3.2.1. Validity

One way of looking at logical truth is to see it as being embodied in the structure of certain sentences rather than in their content. Note that 'structure' in this sense refers not to grammatical structure but to what is taken to be *logical structure*. What counts as logical structure is, as we shall see, determined by the logical theory within which one is working. Let us assume, for the moment, that we are working within the theory of truth functions. (If the reader is unfamiliar with the concept of a truth function, he or she should consult 1.2.4 now.)

Consider the following true sentence:

(6)   Clinton is not a Democrat or Clinton is a Democrat.

As with (1), we can view (6) as being composed of a subsentence—here, 'Clinton is a Democrat', which occurs twice—and the truth-functional expressions 'not' and 'or'. As in the case of (1), we can replace the subsentence with any sentence that we choose and, as long as we substitute uniformly, there will be no overall change in truth-value. Thus, as was the case with (1), the actual content of the subsentence is irrelevant to the question of whether the overall sentence is true or false. To reflect this fact, we can replace 'Clinton is a Democrat' with the schematic or dummy letter '*p*', a move that produces:

(7)   Not-*p* or *p*.

Using symbols instead of words, we can rewrite (7) as

(8) $\backsim p \lor p$.

Notice that (8) is not an actual sentence (as (6) is) but a *schema* (plural: *schemata*). Schemata are logical diagrams of sentences, the dummy letters serving to obliterate all content that is not relevant to the logical theory with which we are concerned. Here, we are concerned with truth-functional logic and schema (8) represents the *truth-functional structure* of sentence (6), stripped, as it were, of all extraneous material. Conversely, sentence (6) is an *instance* of truth-functional schema (8). Any actual sentence, for example, 'Clinton is a Democrat', that is imagined as being substituted for a dummy letter in a schema may be called an *interpretation* of that letter (see Quine 1950:22). The important point about schema (8) is that, as we have seen, it comes out true under every interpretation of its letters. Thus it is a *valid schema*. A logical truth can be regarded as a truth expressed by a sentence that is an instance of a valid schema; hence the logical truth of (6) can be regarded as residing in the circumstance that (6) *is an instance of a valid schema*.

Note that 'validity' is not a term of praise. Indeed, a sentence conforming to a valid schema is by nature uninformative—witness (1) and (6) above. What factual content is expressed in the sentences that serve as the interpretation of a valid schema's dummy letters is, as it were, canceled out by the way the logical words 'or', 'not', 'if', and so on, or their symbolic counterparts, are arranged in the schema itself.

3.2.2. Ways of Determining Validity

3.2.2.1. Truth tables. Whether (8) is valid or not is very obvious, but it is easy to construct more complex schemata whose validity or invalidity is not so easily discovered. In truth-function theory, we are fortunate in having the device of truth tables. Introduced by Wittgenstein (*Tractatus Logico-Philosophicus*, 4.31-4.45, 5.101), this technique provides us with a mechanical *decision procedure* for determining whether a particular schema is valid with respect to truth-functional logic. The truth table method is best explained by means of an example. Consider the schema:

(9) $\smallfrown(p \vee q) \vee (p \,\&\, q)$.

To determine whether (9) is valid or not, we construct a truth table for it, which is presented as Table 3.1.

For every combination of 'T's and 'F's that can be assigned to the schematic letters '*p*' and '*q*' in (9), Table 3.1 records the outcome of the successive application of Tables 1.7, 1.4, 1.5, and 1.7 (again) from Chapter 1. (The reader not familiar with the truth tables for '∨', '&',

Table 3.1   Truth-Table for $\smallfrown(p \vee q) \vee (p \,\&\, q)$

p	q	$p \vee q$	$p \,\&\, q$	$\smallfrown(p \vee q)$	$\smallfrown(p \vee q) \vee (p \,\&\, q)$
T	T	T	T	F	T
F	F	F	F	T	T
T	F	T	F	F	F
F	T	T	F	F	F

and '$\smallfrown$' should consult 1.2.4.) To better understand the meaning of Table 3.1, the reader can think of the 'T's and 'F's as standing for 'True' and 'False', respectively. However, it should be remembered that the 'T's and 'F's are assigned to schemata, which are not capable of being true or false.

We see from the final column in Table 3.1 that schema (9) *overall* is assigned a 'T' twice and an 'F' twice. This shows that (9) is *not* valid, for, to be valid, a truth-functional schema must have only 'T's in the final column of its truth table. On the other hand, (9) is not actually a *contradiction,* because it is not the case that only 'F's appear in the final column.

We saw earlier that sentence (2) consisted of two distinct subsentences plus the logical words 'if' and 'not'. Replacing logical words with symbols, we can represent (2)'s truth-functional structure as follows: '$p \rightarrow \smallfrown q$'. Using Tables 1.5 and 1.6 from Chapter 1, the reader can construct a truth table for this schema. Such a truth table shows that the schema is invalid. This result confirms what was pointed out earlier, namely, that although (2) is analytic, it is not logically true.

3.2.2.2. Proof. Prior to the introduction of the truth-table method, whether a truth-functional schema was valid or not had to be determined by seeing whether it could be *proved,* that is, by seeing whether it could be derived syntactically from what are called the *axioms* of truth-functional logic. Axioms are *initial* schemata that are simply taken for granted, and sometimes they are thought of as representing fundamental logical laws. In stating axioms, we need to generalize about schemata and, to do so, we can use Greek letters 'ϕ', 'μ', 'ψ', and so on. These are to be understood as standing in place of arbitrary schemata. The choice of axioms is, to a certain extent, arbitrary. Here, we assume that a schema conforming to any of the following is an axiom of truth-functional logic (compare Carnap 1958, vol. 1, p. 165):

(10) $\smallfrown(\phi \vee \phi) \vee \phi$

(11) $\smallfrown\phi \vee (\phi \vee \mu)$

(12) $\smallfrown[\smallfrown\phi \vee \mu] \vee [\smallfrown(\psi \vee \phi) \vee (\psi \vee \mu)]$.

(The brackets and parentheses merely indicate how each formula is to be read.)

To derive one schema from another, we employ what are called *transformation rules*. Let us assume that we have the following transformation rule:

(13) From '$\smallfrown\phi \vee \mu$' and 'ϕ', derive 'μ'.

As in the case of the axioms, we simply have to accept (13), without further question, as embodying a fundamental law of reasoning. If the reader is unconvinced that (13) does embody such a law, he or she should consider the following two sentences:

(14) Smith was not in Tijuana or Jones is lying.

(15) Smith was in Tijuana.

From (14) and (15), taken in conjunction with each other, it seems perfectly natural to infer or derive the sentence 'Jones is lying'. If we replace 'Smith was in Tijuana' with the schematic letter 'p' and 'Jones is lying' with 'q', we can represent the above inference or derivation thus:

(16) From '$\smallfrown p \vee q$' and 'p', derive 'q'.

Now, (16) is a rule that generalizes about sentences, whereas a transformation rule for truth-functional logic must generalize about schemata. To give (16) the required degree of generality, we need to replace the schematic letters '*p*' and '*q*' with the Greek letters 'φ' and 'μ', which, we have decided, are to stand in place of schemata. Thus we have

(17)   From '⌐φ ∨ μ' and 'φ', derive 'μ',

which is the same as (13).

Let us now return to our axioms, which, it will be recalled, are any schemata conforming to (10), (11), or (12). Given those, let us see if we can prove schema (8).

If we replace 'φ', 'μ', and 'ψ' in (12) with '*p* ∨ *p*', '*p*', and '⌐*p*', respectively, we see that the following schema is an axiom of truth-functional logic:

(18)   ⌐{⌐(*p* ∨ *p*) ∨ *p*} ∨ {⌐[⌐*p* ∨ (*p* ∨ *p*)] ∨ [⌐*p* ∨ *p*]}.

(Note that the curly brackets, '{' and '}', are used simply to delimit high-level constituents. They are preferred to parentheses or square brackets solely because they are visually distinct.) Now, it is readily seen that the string '⌐(*p* ∨ *p*) ∨ *p*' in (18) conforms to (10) and is thus an axiom itself. So we could rewrite (18) as

(19)   ⌐ axiom ∨ {⌐[⌐*p* ∨ (*p* ∨ *p*)] ∨ [⌐*p* ∨ *p*]}.

If we replace 'axiom' in (19) with 'φ' and everything between the curly brackets with 'μ', we see that, at one level, (19) has the following structure:

(20)   ⌐φ ∨ μ.

The schema in place of which 'φ' in (20) stands is, as we have just seen, an axiom, and axioms, it will be recalled, are simply taken for granted. Thus, in addition to (20), we have

(21)   φ.

From (20) and (21) we can, in accordance with rule (13), derive

(22)   μ;

that is, in this particular case,

(23) $\smallfrown[\smallfrown p \vee (p \vee p)] \vee [\smallfrown p \vee p]$.

Now, it is readily seen that the string '$\smallfrown p \vee (p \vee p)$' in (23) conforms to (11); different Greek letters 'φ', 'μ', 'ψ', and so on, *may*, but *need not*, be understood as standing in place of different schemata. So (23) can be rewritten as

(24) $\smallfrown$ axiom $\vee$ [$\smallfrown p \vee p$],

which, after substitution using Greek letters, gives us

(25) $\smallfrown\varphi \vee \mu$,

with 'φ' standing in place of an axiom. Thus we have '$\smallfrown\varphi \vee \mu$' and 'φ', from which, in accordance with (13), we derive 'μ'; that is, in this case,

(26) $\smallfrown p \vee p$.

Schema (26) reproduces (8), and so we see that schema (8) is indeed provable in truth-function theory.

3.2.3. Validity in Quantification Theory

Syntactic proofs of the above sort are not needed to establish the validity of truth-functional schemata because the truth-table technique provides us with a decision procedure. However, quantification theory, the branch of logic that deals with sentences such as the following,

(27) Jones didn't bet on any horses or he bet on at least one horse,

is not so fortunate. In that theory, as Quine puts it (1950:190), "No mechanical routine can be generally adequate to decide validity." (This circumstance was famously shown by Alonzo Church; see Church 1936.) Thus we generally have to grope around for a proof to establish the validity of a given quantificational schema (the definition of validity for quantificational schemata is analogous to the definition of validity for truth-functional schemata). Moreover, failure to hit upon a proof is no guarantee that a given schema is not actually valid, for such failure may simply indicate a lack of ingenuity on our part or plain bad luck.

Quantification is not discussed in this volume until 6.1.3.1, so it would be pointless to give examples here either of quantificational schemata or of proofs in quantification theory. Interested readers should consult Quine 1950 (especially §§27 and 32).

3.2.4. Possible States of Affairs

3.2.4.1. State descriptions. We see from the foregoing that logical truth can be construed as conformity to a valid schema of, say, the theory of truth functions or the theory of quantification.

Now, it is also possible to construe logical truth as *truth in all possible states of affairs.* Consider, for example, our earlier sentence (6), reproduced below as (28):

(28)   Clinton is not a Democrat or Clinton is a Democrat.

From one point of view, we impute the logical truth of (28) to either of the circumstances (i) that the truth table for the schema '$\sim p \vee p$' contains only 'T's in its final column and (ii) that the schema '$\sim p \vee p$' is provable in the theory of truth functions. Under the semantic conception, on the other hand, the logical truth of (28) resides in the circumstance that (28), or the proposition that it expresses, is true *however we imagine the world to be.* The difference between the two perspectives is that, from the former, we see (28) in terms solely of its logical structure, whereas, from the latter, we see (28) in its relation to the extralinguistic world, that is, in its relation to possible states of affairs.

Carnap (1956:9) devised a technique for reconstructing possible states of affairs that has been highly influential in formal linguistic semantics. He called such a reconstruction a *state description,* although it should be noted that nowadays most linguists and philosophers prefer the more picturesque idiom of *possible worlds.* The latter term has its roots in the work of the seventeenth-century German mathematician and philosopher Leibniz.

Before seeing how a state description can be defined, the concept of an *atomic* sentence needs to be introduced (see also 2.2.2.3). In essence, an atomic sentence is one that contains no logical expressions. For example, of the following,

(29)   Smith is happy,

(30)   All Spaniards like football,

only (29) is atomic, for the word 'all' counts as a logical expression in quantification theory, the branch of logic that deals with *general sentences* (see 6.1.3.1).

Given the concept of an atomic sentence, a state description in a given language *L* can be defined as a class of sentences that contains, for every atomic sentence that can be created in *L*, either that sentence or its negation, but not both, and no other sentences (compare Carnap 1956:9; see also Lyons 1977:162). To understand the idea of a state description, consider the following imaginary language, which we shall call *S*.

The nonlogical vocabulary of *S*, a much impoverished version of English, consists of the proper names 'Tom', 'Smith', and 'Jones' and the predicates 'is eating' and 'is singing'. Thus the atomic sentences that can be created in *S* are as follows:

(31)   Tom is eating, Smith is eating, Jones is eating, Tom is
         singing, Smith is singing, Jones is singing.

Because state descriptions can include negative sentences, we can form 64 different state descriptions from the sentences listed in (31), of which one would be

(32)   {Tom is eating, Smith is not eating, Jones is eating, Tom is
         singing, Smith is not singing, Jones is singing}.

(The curly brackets indicate that, together, the sentences constitute a class or set.)

3.2.4.2. Rules of ranges. It is possible to lay down semantic rules that, taken together, determine the *range* of any sentence; that is, they determine in what state descriptions the sentence *holds* (see Carnap 1956:9). In nontechnical terms, to say of a sentence *p*, which may or may not be atomic, that it *holds* in a state description implies that *p* would be true if that state description corresponded to the *actual* state of affairs. Carnap called the semantic rules that determine a sentence's range *rules of ranges*. A few informal examples will illustrate the general idea:

(33) An atomic sentence holds in a state description if and only if it belongs to it.

(34) A sentence of the form 'not-*p*' holds in a state description if and only if '*p*' does not hold in it.

(35) A sentence of the form '*p* or *q*' holds in a state description if and only if '*p*' holds in it or '*q*' holds in it.

(36) A sentence of the form 'If *p*, then *q*' holds in a state description if and only if 'not-*p*' holds in it or '*q*' holds in it.

(It is readily seen that the rules of ranges concerning truth-functional compounds are based on the standard truth tables for the truth-functional connectives, which are given in Tables 1.4-1.8 in Chapter 1.) We can see, for example, from rules (33), (34), and (36) that the sentence

(37) If Clinton is president, then he won the election

will *hold* in a given state description as long as the atomic sentence

(38) Clinton is president

does not *belong* to that state description or the atomic sentence

(39) Clinton won the election

does.

What rules of ranges we decide to lay down depends upon what sort of logical structure is being considered. So far, apart from rule (33) concerning atomic sentences, we have referred only to rules of ranges that relate to truth-functional compounds. One obvious extension would be to include rules of ranges for *general* sentences, that is, for sentences containing words such as 'all', 'each', 'some', and 'no' or their counterparts in logical notation. (For *generality,* see 6.1.3.1 and also Chapter 10.) We could also lay down a rule for identity sentences, according to which any sentence of the form '*a* is identical to *a*' would hold in all state descriptions. (The expression 'is identical to', together with its symbolic counterpart '=', is thus treated as a logical expression.)

3.2.4.3. L-truth. Using the apparatus of state descriptions and rules of ranges, we can define logical truth (or L-truth, as Carnap calls it) in the following way:

(40)   An L-true sentence is one that holds in every state description. (Compare Carnap 1956:10.)

On the basis of (40), we can define an *L-false* sentence or *logical contradiction* as a sentence whose negation is L-true. An *L-determinate* sentence can then be defined as one that is either L-true or L-false.

From the foregoing remarks, it is readily seen that whether a sentence is L-true or not will depend solely on the rules of ranges. For example, rules (33) to (35) determine that the compound sentence

(41)   Bill Clinton is American or he is not American

holds in every state description; hence they determine that it is L-true. In this way, a reconstruction is achieved of logical truth as truth in all possible states of affairs.

3.3. Analyticity

3.3.1. Meaning Postulates

As we saw in connection with examples (1) and (2), the class of analytic truths includes the class of logical truths, but not vice versa. Now it is readily seen that Carnap's device of state descriptions is, as Quine (1951:24) puts it, "A reconstruction at best of logical truth."

Consider, for example, our earlier sentence (2), reproduced below as (42):

(42)   If Smith is a bachelor, he is not married.

As we have seen, the words 'bachelor' and 'married' do not count as logical expressions. Thus the two subsentences

(43)   Smith is a bachelor

and

(44)   Smith is married

have to be regarded as atomic. This means that in a language containing sentences (43) and (44), there would be at least one Carnap-style state description to which both belonged and one to which neither belonged. Therefore, given rules (33), (34), and (36), there would be at least one state description in which (42) did not hold and at least one in which it did hold. Thus (42) would come out as L-indeterminate (i.e., factual or synthetic), whereas most people would regard it as being analytic.

To ensure that sentences such as (42) do not come out as factual, we need to introduce what Carnap (1956:222-229) called *meaning postulates,* that is, *universal sentences* such as the following:

(45)   No bachelors are married.

The examples of rules of ranges (33) to (36) that we gave earlier are not sufficient in themselves to determine which state descriptions sentence (45) holds in. Specifying the additional rule that is required would, in fact, presuppose that the reader was already familiar with quantification theory (see 6.1.3.1 and Chapter 10). Let us, however, simply *assume* that appropriate rules of ranges have been laid down and that, on the basis of them, we can determine the range of sentence (45). (For the reader already familiar with quantification theory, the additional rule needed would be this: A universal sentence holds in a state description if and only if all the substitution instances of its scope hold in it. In the case of (45), the scope is 'If x is a bachelor, then x is not married'. Thus

(45) would hold in all those state descriptions in which 'If Smith is a bachelor, then he is not married', 'If Jones is a bachelor, then he is not married', and so on held. See Carnap 1956:9.)

Given postulates such as (45), we can characterize analyticity in an analogous way to logical truth. First, we consider the class α of all and only those state descriptions in which all of the meaning postulates that we have decided to lay down hold. Analyticity can then be defined as follows:

> (46) An analytic sentence is one that holds in every state description in α. (Compare Carnap 1956:226.)

Sentence (42), for instance, will hold in every state description in which the meaning postulates, of which (45) is an example, hold; hence it will hold in every state description in α and therefore will come out as analytic. On the other hand, as we have seen, sentence (42) will not come out as L-true, for there will be state descriptions (not belonging to α) in which it does not hold. Note that, because L-true sentences are those that hold in *every* state description, all L-true sentences will hold in all the state descriptions in α. However, not every sentence that holds in all the state descriptions in α will hold in *every* state description that can be constructed. Thus Carnap's device of meaning postulates is fashioned in such a way as to ensure that, although all L-true sentences count as analytic, the converse is not the case. This, of course, is the desired result.

3.3.2. Different Kinds of Terms

If we feel that (42) is analytic, this is because we are struck by an apparent meaning connection between the predicates 'bachelor' and 'married'. Now, not all predicates lend themselves equally to such intuitions. For example, the sentence

> (47) All whales are mammals,

although true unconditionally (nonfactually), is not such an obvious candidate for an analytic sentence as (42) (compare Kripke 1980:138). Similarly, nonfactually true sentences about theoretical entities, such as

(48) A body's momentum is the product of its mass and its
velocity (compare Quine 1960:57),

are not readily thought of as being analytic.

The point is that, in the recent literature at least, analyticity is ascribed primarily to sentences such as (42) rather than to sentences about natural kinds (47) or to sentences about theoretical entities (48). Two conclusions can be drawn from this circumstance.

First, we might say that for a sentence to be analytic, it must be true not only unconditionally but, also, a priori; that is, its truth must be capable of being known independently of experience. Sentence (42) satisfies both these criteria, in that it is true unconditionally and, also, anyone with an adequate command of English knows it to be true regardless of any experience they may have had. On the other hand, (47) and (48) express truths that are not mere by-products of the English language. They express truths that need to be learned to be known, and so they would not count as analytic. From this perspective, 'analytic' is redefined as meaning 'necessarily true (true unconditionally) *and* true a priori'. This, in essence, is the maneuver favored by Kripke (1980:39). Note that Carnap's device of meaning postulates is independent of the question of whether analyticity involves a prioricity, because he envisages the postulates to be entirely stipulative (1956:225); that is, it is a matter of free choice which postulates we lay down, although we may well allow ourselves to be guided by intuitions of one sort or another.

A more radical move, one favored by Quine (1951, 1960:65-67), is to regard analyticity as a pseudoconcept. Quine (1960:56-57) distinguishes between three types of predicates. First, there are what he calls *observational terms* (which include terms for natural kinds). Essentially, we learn these through exposure to samples rather than through verbal definition, although, of course, exposure to a sample may well be supplemented with a verbal explanation. Observational expressions have strong affinities for what Quine (1960:42) calls *observation sentences*. Observation sentences are sentences whose truth-value can, in practice if not in principle, be reckoned without appealing to 'collateral information'. For example, whether

(49) That is a rabbit

expressed a truth or not would normally be ascertainable simply by looking at the object indicated; hence (49) is very much an observation sentence. On the other hand,

(50)   That is a bachelor

is in a rather different boat, for however much we study the object indicated, we need to know something of its personal history to decide whether (50) is true.

The word 'bachelor', in fact, is a paradigm instance of Quine's second category of expression. The acquisition of this and comparable terms, such as 'brother' and 'sister', is mediated by their connection with other words that are closer to sensory experience. For example, learning 'bachelor' presupposes knowing the word 'man', which is more like the observational terms just mentioned. Words like 'bachelor' have little or no affinity for observation sentences and, generally speaking, the weaker that affinity is, the less securely a term's meaning is anchored in direct experience. Thus, in the case of a word like 'bachelor', it is the *intralinguistic* connection with other, more firmly anchored terms that guarantees its utility in communication. Cut that link and you leave it "no very evident social determination" (Quine 1960:56).

As Quine points out, the difference between the above two ways of learning terms corresponds to Russell's distinction between acquaintance and description (see 6.1.1), the latter lending itself more readily than the former to perceived meaning connections. Thus we have a strong intuition that all bachelors *must* be unmarried precisely because mastering 'unmarried' or 'not married' is an essential step in mastering 'bachelor'. On the other hand, we can go through life successfully using the word 'whale' without ever encountering the word 'mammal'. Quine's point is that the difference between the two types of terms is *a matter of degree,* and that therefore there is no *fundamental cleavage* between truths arising through the use of terms of the first kind (factual truths) and those arising through use of terms of the second (analytic truths).

The theoretical terms of science form a third class of expression. For, as a rule, they play no role in observation sentences, yet they rarely give rise to analyticity intuitions (witness (48) above). The reason for this, according to Quine, is that theoretical terms like 'momentum' are linked to the rest of language in a more complex way than words like 'bachelor'. The result is that no single link or group of links is salient, and therefore we are less inclined to impute the truth of sentences such as (48) to meaning relations. Thus, if physicists revised mechanics so that (48) was no longer true, the change would most probably be seen as a change in theory rather than in the meaning of the word 'momentum' (see Quine 1960:57).

It is perhaps worth expanding on Quine's views. For, in contrast to those who believe in a sweeping dichotomy between the analytic and the synthetic, Quine famously portrayed the whole of our knowledge and beliefs—concerning, for example, historical matters, scientific theories, and logical relations—as forming a unified whole, a single inclusive theory, a vast network of interrelated sentences. In the interior of the theory, there were the laws of logic, mathematics, science, and so on; but, on the periphery, there were sentences that were more or less directly conditioned by experience. The overall network was seen as a man-made fabric whose edges, and sometimes parts closer to the center, were continually being rewoven. Conflicts with sensory evidence necessitated a redistribution of truth-values over certain sentences, and the reevaluation of these sentences might in turn trigger the reevaluation of others to which they were logically connected. Any readjustments occasioned by the evaluation of a sentence that was "germane to sense experience" (1951:40) would probably be confined to the outer edge of the theory, whereas a revision of a scientific law or an ontological assumption would have fairly profound repercussions in many sectors within the system.

3.4. Summary

In this chapter, we have seen that a distinction is often drawn between analytic and synthetic or factual truths. A logical truth is a particular type of analytic truth, namely, one that arises from a particular combination of logical expressions. A logically true sentence can be characterized as one having the structure of a valid schema. Alternatively, from the semantic point of view, a logically true sentence can be regarded as one that is true in all possible states of affairs. If possible states of affairs are reconstructed as state descriptions (i.e., as classes of atomic or negated atomic sentences), we can say that a logical truth is a truth expressed by a sentence that holds in every state description. To extend the semantic treatment to the broader category of analytic sentences, meaning postulates need to be introduced. An analytic sentence can then be construed as one that holds in every state description in which the meaning postulates hold.

It turns out that analyticity is more readily ascribed to sentences containing words like 'bachelor' than to observational or theoretical sentences. Kripke sees this as indicating that analyticity is in part an epistemological concept. Quine, on the other hand, sees this as evidence that the distinction between analytic and synthetic sentences is essentially a harmless myth.

Part I: Further Reading

For Wittgenstein's paradox, see *Philosophical Investigations*, I, §§136-202. This is quite a difficult read. However, Hallett 1977 and Baker and Hacker 1985 provide good running commentaries. Kenny 1973 (esp. pp. 175-176) is very useful and Kripke 1982 is indispensable.

Chomsky 1990 is an extremely useful summary of Chomsky's views on the nature of language. Readers who want more detail should consult Chomsky 1986.

Wittgenstein's exposition of the picture theory in the *Tractatus* is compressed, to put it mildly. Russell's introduction, which appears in the Pears and McGuinness translation, is a good starting point. Black (1964) provides a superb running commentary and Kenny (1973:54-101), as ever, is concise and highly readable.

For a critique of the picture theory, see *Philosophical Investigations*, I, §§39-136. See also Waismann 1965:304-322, which is much easier to understand.

The view that truth is always relative to a given linguistic framework is eloquently expressed by Quine (1960, chapter 1, esp. §6). See also Carnap 1956:205-221.

Tarski's semantic definition of truth is best approached by reading Tarski 1949 first. Tarski 1983 is very technical but persistence is well rewarded. Carnap (1958, vol. 1, §§7-12) defines truth in a slightly different way. The whole concept of semantics, as opposed to syntax, is discussed perspicuously and authoritatively in Carnap 1958, vol. 1, §§1-6. The method exhibited in Carnap 1956 forms the basis for much contemporary work in linguistic semantics.

For arguments *against* analyticity, see Quine 1951 and Quine 1960, §14. For a defense of analyticity, see Grice and Strawson 1956. The ancestry of most formal techniques for capturing analytic connections can be traced to Carnap 1956:222-229. For a linguist's point of view, see Chierchia and McConnell-Ginet 1990:360-377.

PART II

NAMING

4

Names, Sense, and Nominatum

4.1. The Name Relation

It is customary in philosophy of language and semantics to adopt some form of what Carnap (1956:96-144) called the *method of the name relation*. The name relation is normally thought to hold between an expression in a language and a concrete or abstract object, of which the expression is said to be a name. Various terms are used to express this relation, for example: '*x* is a name for *y*,' '*x* designates *y*', '*x* stands for *y*', '*x* refers to *y*', '*x* denotes *y*' (although the last has a rather different sense in the work of Russell). Conversely, the object named by a given expression may be called the *nominatum* (plural: *nominata*) of that expression (other terms are 'reference' and 'denotation').

Carnap characterized the method of the name relation as having three principles:

(1)   'Every name has exactly one nominatum'.

(2)   'Any sentence speaks about the nominata of the names occurring in it'.

(3)   'If a name occurring in a true sentence is ₋₋placed by another name with the same nominatum, the sentence remains true'. (Carnap 1956:96)

Carnap (1956:98) called the above three principles *the principle of univocality, the principle of subject matter,* and *the principle of interchangeability,* respectively. Note that, here, 'interchangeability' means 'interchangeability *salva veritate,*' that is, interchangeability *with truth preserved.*

The principle of univocality applies only to unambiguous artificially constructed languages or to natural languages that have been modified in some way to eliminate ambiguities. Because the main concern of this book is language in general—that is, both ambiguous and unambiguous languages fall within its purview—we shall ignore the principle of univocality.

The second of the principles identified by Carnap, the principle of subject matter, might be considered to be rather vague. For what does it mean to say that a sentence 'speaks about' the nominata of its names? To understand the answer to this question, consider the sentence

(4)   Jones is wise.

We would use sentence (4) to state something about the world, namely, that Jones is wise. In some way or other, then, (4) has to 'hook onto' the world, for if there were no point of convergence between language and the world, it would be impossible to use language to describe the world. Intuitively, the proper name 'Jones' is what gives (4) its purchase on the extralinguistic and, to that extent, (4) *speaks about* or *is about* Jones. Thus the proper name 'Jones' is a name in the technical sense described above and its nominatum is the individual Jones. (Some thinkers also treat predicates such as '[is] wise' as names, either of properties or of classes of individuals having a particular property. If the concept of being a name is extended to that type of expression, then sentence (4) is about—in the favored sense—both Jones *and* either the property wise or the class of wise individuals.)

The point about the principle of subject matter is that it is what makes the third principle, the principle of interchangeability, plausible (compare Carnap 1956:98). For, as has often been pointed out (see, for example, Aristotle, *Topics,* Bk. 7, chapter 1, 15), two things are identical when what is said of the one should also be said of the other; thus if sentences are taken to speak *about* the nominata of their names, it seems that when a sentence '*p*' is true, so must any other sentence be that can be constructed from '*p*' by replacing its names with other names designating the same nominata.

As we shall see, there are contexts in which the principle of interchangeability does not hold. Nevertheless, the concept of the name relation implies that interchangeability is to be expected, that it is the default case.

4.2. The Paradox of the Name Relation

As Carnap points out, the method of the name relation leads to a well-known paradox, which was famously discussed by the twentieth-century English philosopher Bertrand Russell in "On Denoting" (1905). Russell accepted the principle of interchangeability: "If *a* is identical with *b,* whatever is true of one is true of the other, and either may be substituted for the other in any proposition without altering the truth or falsehood of that proposition" (Russell 1905:485).

Now, Scott and the author of *Waverley* were one and the same individual. Thus, in accordance with the principle of interchangeability, the expressions 'Scott' and 'the author of *Waverley*' ought to be interchangeable. Russell applied this reasoning to the sentence

(5)   George IV wished to know whether Scott was the author of *Waverley.*

Although (5) is reportedly true, it is almost certainly false that George IV wished to know whether Scott was Scott. As Russell put it, "An interest in the law of identity can hardly be attributed to the first gentleman of Europe" (Russell 1905:485). Thus we see that the principle of interchangeability, although it appears to be inherent in the concept of a name, fails in the sort of case exemplified by (5).

The American philosopher Quine (1943) constructed the same paradox for modal sentences, that is, for sentences in which any of the words 'necessarily', 'possibly', and the like occur (see also Chapter 8 of this book). Consider the following example:

(6)   9 is necessarily greater than 7. (Quine 1943:121)

If any truths can be said to be necessary, the truths of arithmetic are such. Thus sentence (6) may be considered to be true. Now, the number 9 is identical to the number of planets. So, according to the principle of interchangeability, we ought to be able to substitute the expression 'the number of planets' for the numeral '9' in sentence (6):

(7)   The number of planets is necessarily greater than 7.

However, that there are more than seven planets is a historical accident and not a necessary truth. Thus (7) is false, according to Quine at any rate.

Contexts in which the principle of interchangeability seems to fail are called *nonextensional.* Thus sentence (5), for example, exhibits a nonextensional context.

4.3. Solution to the Paradox of the Name Relation

4.3.1. Frege

4.3.1.1. Sense and nominatum. In "Ueber Sinn und Bedeutung" (which appears here as Frege 1949), Frege drew a fundamental distinction between the nominatum (Bedeutung) of a name and its sense (Sinn). (Note that Frege sometimes uses the term 'proper name' in place of just 'name', hence *not* to indicate what *we* refer to as 'ordinary proper names' such as 'Smith' and 'Jones'.) We have already seen in what a name's nominatum consists. The concept of a name's sense is explained in the following way: "[In the sense] is contained the manner and context of presentation" of the nominatum (Frege 1949:86).

The distinction between sense and nominatum can be illustrated by the case of the expressions 'morning star' and 'evening star'. According to Frege, these have the same nominatum (i.e., the planet Venus) but different senses (p. 86). On account of this circumstance, the identity sentence

(8)   The morning star is the evening star

expresses what Frege (p. 86) called a 'genuine cognition'; that is, it is informative. The reason (8) expresses a cognition is that the expressions 'morning star' and 'evening star' present their common nominatum in different ways, namely, as the star seen in the morning and the star seen in the evening, respectively; so it is possible not to know that the morning star is the evening star.

As Frege stressed (pp. 85-86), a difference of sense, that is, a difference in the mode of presentation of the nominatum, was more than just a difference in the form of the signs or linguistic expressions used:

> If the sign 'a' differs from the sign 'b' only as an object (here by its shape) but not by its rôle as a sign, that is to say, not in the manner in which it designates anything, then the cognitive significance of "a = a" would be essentially the same as that of "a = b", if "a = b" is true. (Frege 1949:86)

According to Frege, the sense of a name was grasped by everyone who knew the language to which the name belonged (p. 86). However, the nominatum was not fully determined by the sense but only illuminated in a very one-sided way (*einseitig beleuchtet*). Thus, to ascertain the nominatum of a name, more was required than a grasp of the sense, namely, knowledge of the facts. For example, to know that the definite noun phrase

(9)   the first Italian to reach the New World

designates Columbus, we need to have some appreciation of the historical facts. Conversely, we might not know enough about a given nominatum to determine whether a given sense corresponds to it. As Frege put it, "Complete knowledge of the nominatum" would mean that "we could tell immediately in the case of any given sense whether it belongs to the nominatum. This we shall never be able to do" (p. 86).

Frege thought that in the case of ordinary proper names, "opinions as regards their sense may diverge" (p. 86, note 2). Thus, for some people, the sense of the proper name 'Aristotle' might be Plato's disciple and the teacher of Alexander the Great, whereas, for others, it might be the Stagirite teacher of Alexander the Great. Many thinkers would now dispute the claim that ordinary proper names have senses at all (see 5.1.3).

4.3.1.2. The Fregean solution. Frege did not explicitly introduce the above sense-nominatum distinction to solve the antinomy or paradox of the name relation. His reasoning in "Ueber Sinn und Bedeutung" gives the impression that the distinction appeared to him to be natural in itself. However, as Carnap (1956:136) put it, "The strongest argument in favor of Frege's method [lies] in the fact that it is a way of solving the antinomy." The reason Frege's method provides a solution to the paradox of the name relation is explained below. To understand the explanation, it needs to be realized that Frege regarded whole sentences as a species of name. Thus he thought that sentences had both a nominatum and a sense. (Although the idea of a sentence's having a sense seems quite plausible, many people might be baffled by the claim that a sentence has a nominatum.) The explanation given below of the Fregean solution to the paradox has the following structure: First, an account is given of what Frege took to be the nominatum and what he took to be the sense of a sentence and also of the reasoning by which he was guided. Then Frege's distinction between a sentence's customary nominatum and its indirect nominatum is introduced. The customary-indirect distinction is then applied to types of expression other than sentences. It is then shown that this distinction can be used to solve the paradox of the name relation.

In "Ueber Sinn und Bedeutung," Frege tacitly assumed the following principles:

(10) The nominatum of a complex name is a function of the nominata of the names occurring in it.

(11) The sense of a complex name is a function of the senses of the names occurring in it.

(Frege nowhere states these principles explicitly, but they are clear from some of the remarks he makes.) Now, what (10) and (11) mean is that if we take a complex expression, say,

(12) the number that immediately follows 9,

then (i) the overall nominatum will be unchanged if we replace any name within it with another that has the same nominatum and (ii) the overall sense will be unchanged if we replace any name within it with another that has the same sense. The reader can confirm that principle (10) holds by replacing the numeral '9' in (12) with, for example, the description 'the number that is identical to the number of planets', which has an identical nominatum.

Principle (11) is not so easily confirmed, because Frege supplies no criterion for identity of sense. Later thinkers, following Carnap (1956:125-126), have assumed that two expressions that have the same *intension* have the same Fregean sense. Identity of intension can be characterized as follows:

(13) Two expressions ϕ and μ whose identity sentence '$\phi = \mu$' is necessarily true have the same intension. (Compare Carnap 1956, pp. 10, 14, 23.)

However, it is questionable whether identity of intension is a sufficiently strong criterion for identity in the Fregean sense. In an earlier paper, "Funktion und Begriff" (which appears here as Frege 1960:21-41), Frege had said that the expressions '2^4' and '4^2' had different senses (although, of course, they designate the same thing, namely, the number 16). On the other hand, the identity sentence

(14) $2^4 = 4^2$

expresses a necessary truth; hence the expressions '2^4' and '4^2' have the same intension, in Carnap's sense. So it seems that a Fregean sense and a Carnap-style intension are not quite the same thing.

Now, as we have seen, Frege thought that two names (standing for the same nominatum) that differed in form but not in mode of presentation expressed the same sense. Presumably, then, the numerals 'IX' and '9' have the same Fregean sense. So if Frege's tacit principle (11) is correct, the sense of (12) should remain constant if we replace the expression '9' with 'IX', a move that yields

(15)   the number that immediately follows IX.

We saw earlier that identity sentences in which the expressions flanking the identity sign had the same sense did not express what Frege called a genuine cognition; that is, they were uninformative. Thus, to test whether (15) and (12) have the same sense, we can construct an identity sentence and see whether it expresses a genuine cognition:

(16)   The number that immediately follows 9 = the number that immediately follows IX.

Clearly, the difference between the two expressions flanking the identity sign does not in any way correspond to a difference in the way in which the designated object, namely, the number 10, is presented. Thus (16) does not express a genuine cognition. Therefore, (15) and (12) express the same Fregean sense.

Now, using principles (10) and (11), Frege considered the question of what was the nominatum of a sentence and what was its sense. He considered two sentences that were identical except for the occurrence of the expressions 'the morning star' in one and 'the evening star' in the other (p. 90):

(17)   The morning star is a body illuminated by the sun.

(18)   The evening star is a body illuminated by the sun.

As we have seen, the expressions 'the morning star' and 'the evening star' have the same nominatum and so, in accordance with principle

(10), the two containing sentences (17) and (18) must also have a common nominatum. But what is this common element? The *proposition* expressed, Frege thought, could not be this shared element, for one could believe what (17) says while denying what (18) says (p. 90). Therefore, a proposition had to be a sentence's *sense*—Frege assumed, again tacitly, that a proposition was *either* the nominatum *or* the sense of a sentence (p. 89).

Now, one thing that (17) and (18) do have in common is the truth-value True. Furthermore, it is readily seen that, when we attribute no nominatum to a sentence component, the containing sentence has no truth-value. Thus, Frege pointed out, if the name 'Odysseus' has no nominatum but only a sense, the proposition expressed by the sentence 'Odysseus deeply asleep was disembarked at Ithaca' loses some of its interest for us (p. 90). Therefore, Frege concluded, "we find ourselves persuaded to accept the *truth-value* of a sentence as its nominatum" (p. 91).

By the above reasoning, Frege arrived at the following two results (pp. 90-91):

(19) The sense of a sentence is the proposition it expresses.

(20) The nominatum of a sentence is its truth-value.

Frege's tacit principles (10) and (11) applied to names in general (of which sentences were one particular syntactic category). Frege's stated results (19) and (20) enable us to state the following special forms of (10) and (11):

(21) The truth-value of a sentence is a function of the nominata of the names occurring in it.

(22) The proposition expressed by a sentence is a function of the senses of the names occurring in it.

In other words:

(23) The truth-value of a sentence is unchanged if any name within it is replaced by another that has the same nominatum.

(24)   The proposition expressed by a sentence is unchanged if
       any name within it is replaced by another that has the same
       sense.

(The reader will notice that (3), the principle of interchangeability, is
implied by (23).)

Now, Frege was compelled to consider certain cases as exceptions
to (23) and (24); indeed, much of "Ueber Sinn und Bedeutung" is given
over to a consideration of such cases. For our purposes, the most
important of these is when a sentence has what Frege called an *oblique*
(or *indirect*) occurrence. Sentences or clauses have an oblique occurrence (i) in indirect discourse (p. 93); (ii) when governed by a psychological verb such as 'believe', 'regret', and 'infer' (pp. 93-94); (iii) when
governed by purposive conjunctions such as 'so that' (p. 94); (iv) when
governed by verbs such as 'command' and 'request' (p. 94); and (v) in
indirect questions (p. 94). (This list is intended to give the reader an
idea of what an oblique context is, rather than be exhaustive.) It is
readily seen that Frege's oblique contexts are a subclass of what we
referred to earlier as nonextensional contexts. Indeed, Frege's remarks
concerning oblique contexts can be seen as applying, mutatis mutandis,
to other types of nonextensional context.

As an example of Frege's treatment of oblique contexts, we can
consider the following sentence (p. 93):

(25)   Copernicus believed that the planetary orbits are circles.

According to principle (21), the truth-value of sentence (25) should be
a function of the nominata of the names that occur in it. Now, the
subordinate clause

(26)   the planetary orbits are circles

is also a sentence and therefore must be considered as one of the names
that occur in (25). However, (26)'s nominatum, that is, the truth-value
False, does not in any way affect the truth-value of the containing
sentence (25). This Frege demonstrated by observing that we can replace
(26) with the true sentence

(27) The appearance of the sun's motion is produced by the real motion of the earth

without affecting the truth-value of the containing sentence (25); both (25) and the sentence derived from it by substituting (27) for (26) are true.

In this way, it is shown that principle (21) does not hold for sentences such as (25). In other words, principle (23) does not hold for such sentences.

Frege's response to the failure of principle (23) in oblique contexts was to say that, in such a context, a name had a different nominatum than the one it had normally (and also a different sense). He thus distinguished the *oblique* or *indirect nominatum* of a name from its *customary nominatum* (pp. 87, 93, 102). Concerning the oblique nominatum, he stated what amounts to the following:

(28) A name's oblique nominatum is the same as its customary sense. (Compare pp. 87, 93.)

In the specific case in which the name in question is a sentence, the analogue of (28) is

(29) A sentence's oblique nominatum is the proposition that is its customary sense. (Compare p. 92.)

For example, the customary nominatum of (26) would be the *truth-value* False, whereas its nominatum in the oblique context of (25) would be the *proposition* that the planetary orbits are circles.

The reason Frege takes the oblique nominatum of a name to be its sense is apparent from a remark he makes at the beginning of "Ueber Sinn und Bedeutung":

In indirect (oblique) discourse we speak of the sense, e.g., of the words of someone else. From this it becomes clear that also in indirect discourse words do not have their customary nominata; they here name what customarily would be their sense. (p. 87)

Notice that, as Carnap points out (1956:123), Frege's reasoning seems to presuppose tacitly the principle of subject matter, which was stated earlier as (2). We can see this more clearly if we consider a concrete example, such as sentence (25). This is taken to speak *about* something. However, as we have seen, Frege recognized that such a sentence did not speak about the truth-value of its subordinate clause, in this case: 'the planetary orbits are circles'. It is clear also that (25) does not—in the Fregean analysis—speak about the actual words employed, for it was only in direct quotations that words referred to words (pp. 87, 92). So Frege's method, by a process of elimination, leads us to the view that (25) speaks about the proposition expressed by the subordinate clause (26).

Now, Frege's principle (28), of which (29) is a special case, provides a solution to the paradox of the name relation, at least insofar as it affects his oblique contexts. The paradox consists in the circumstance that, although it seems to be implicit in the very concept of a name, the principle of interchangeability appears to fail in a certain type of context, namely, nonextensional contexts. The principle of interchangeability states that a true sentence remains true if its names are swapped for others with the same nominata. Frege took sentences to be names, and the failure of interchangeability affects them also. Thus, although (25) may be true, the following sentence derived from it by replacing the subordinate clause (26) with another designating the same nominatum (i.e., truth-value)

(30)   Copernicus believed that the sun rises in the west

is not (presumably). Now Frege argued that, in what amounts to a large subclass of nonextensional contexts, namely, his oblique contexts, the nominatum of a name is its customary sense. This means that the Fregean nominatum of (26) as it occurs in (25) is not its truth-value but its customary sense, namely, the proposition that the planetary orbits are circles; hence the subordinate clause in (30) and the subordinate clause in (25), namely, (26), *do not have the same nominatum* (although they *do* have the same nominatum when they occur as isolated sentences). Thus, in the Fregean method, the substitution by which we derived (30) from (25) represents an improper application of the principle of interchangeability. A *legitimate* application of that principle would involve replacing (26) in (25) with another sentence expressing the proposition that the planetary orbits are circles. As Frege put it, "Such replacement may be made only by expressions of the same indirect nominatum, i.e., of the same customary sense" (p. 93).

So far, we have considered Frege's solution only with regard to names that are complete sentences or clauses. Our initial problem, however, concerned ordinary proper names and definite descriptions (see examples (5) and (6) above). Although much of Frege's paper "Ueber Sinn und Bedeutung" concerns names that are sentences or clauses, it is clear that the apparatus of indirect and customary nominata is intended to apply also to names that are definite descriptions or ordinary proper names.

Let us consider Russell's construction of the paradox with regard to the indirect question '. . . whether Scott was the author of *Waverley*' (see example (5) above). Frege explicitly states that in contexts such as this one, words have their indirect nominata, and that therefore "a . . . name cannot generally be replaced by another of the same object" (p. 94). Thus the premise on which Russell constructed the paradox, namely, that the interchange of 'Scott' and 'the author of *Waverley*' is in accordance with the principle of interchangeability, turns out, under Fregean assumptions, to be false. The same applies, mutatis mutandis, to Quine's version of the paradox. For although Frege did not consider modal contexts, we can extend the Fregean method to that type of case. Thus, given that the numeral '9' and the description 'the number of planets' do not have the same sense—the sentence 'The number of planets = 9' expresses a genuine cognition—their exchange in a modal sentence is not a legitimate application of the principle of interchangeability.

So we see that Frege's treatment of oblique contexts rests on the assumption that names are always referentially ambiguous. In some contexts, they designate one thing, their customary nominata, while in others, they designate something else, their customary sense. Thus in Frege's theory, as Kaplan put it (1968-69:184), "obliquity indicates ambiguity."

4.3.2. Other Solutions

4.3.2.1. *Quine.* Quine subscribes to a version of the name relation. He writes:

I call an occurrence of a singular term in a statement *purely referential* (Frege: *gerade* [i.e., direct or customary]), if, roughly speaking, the term serves in that particular context simply to refer to its object. (Quine 1953:66)

Quine seems to recognize the principle of subject matter. For example, he writes (1953:67) of the sentence

(31)   Cicero has a six-letter name

that it "[says] something about the man Cicero." He also recognizes the principle of interchangeability (he calls it *substitutivity of identity*) as a criterion for referential occurrence. For example, he points out (1953: 67) that the above sentence (31) remains true if we replace the name 'Cicero' with 'Tully', Cicero and Tully being one and the same individual (see also Quine 1960:142).

When an expression does not have a purely referential occurrence, it is said by Quine to occur in a *referentially opaque context*. He regards direct quotation as "the referentially opaque context *par excellence*" (1953:67). Indeed, he regards all other referentially opaque contexts as being like contexts of direct quotation. Now, he views occurrences inside direct quotations as being in some sense sealed off from the rest of the sentence in which the quotation is embedded. For example, he would consider the occurrence of '9' in

(32)   '9 > 7' is a truth of arithmetic

to be like the occurrence of 'cat' in the word 'cattle': In both cases, the form in question does not occur as an independent expression (see Quine 1953:67). Thus the quotation ' "9 > 7" ' in sentence (32) is to be viewed as a single unstructured unit.

From the foregoing, we see that Quine's treatment of the oblique occurrence of names is like Frege's to the extent that neither thinker ascribes the customary nominatum to such an occurrence. However, while Frege, as we have seen, ascribes a different nominatum, namely, the customary sense, Quine ascribes no nominatum at all. This aspect of Quine's thinking is discussed in Chapters 8 and 9 of this book. In anticipation of the remarks made in those chapters, it can be pointed out that Quine would regard, for example,

(33)   Tom believes Jones is in Tijuana

as meaning (on one reading at least) something like:

(34)   Tom believes-to-be-true 'Jones is in Tijuana',

which is to be understood as asserting a relation between Tom and the quoted sentence "'Jones is in Tijuana'". Given that direct quotations are to be understood as single unstructured units, the occurrence of 'Jones' in (34) would be like the occurrence of the form 'cat' in 'cattle'; that is, it would be a notational accident and not an actual occurrence of the *name* 'Jones'. Thus the question of a nominatum would not even arise.

Quine's method solves the paradox of the name relation, but it does so by restricting the name relation to contexts in which names do not occur obliquely. So, where Frege sees referential ambiguity, Quine sees no reference at all.

4.3.2.2. Russell. As we have seen, Russell constructs the paradox of the name relation with regard to definite descriptions and proper names. Thus the true sentence (5)

(5)   George IV wished to know whether Scott was the author of *Waverley*

does not remain true if we replace the description 'the author of *Waverley*' with the proper name 'Scott', despite the fact that these two expressions have the same nominatum. In Frege's theory, the puzzle would be solved by the fact that (5) exhibits an oblique context and so 'the author of *Waverley*' would be interchangeable only with another expression that had the same sense; and the proper name 'Scott' does not, or at least it *need* not and for most people probably *would* not, have the same Fregean sense as 'the author of *Waverley*'. In Quine's theory, the embedded sentence in (5), namely, 'Scott was the author of *Waverley*', is to be regarded as being on a par with a direct quotation; hence the principle of interchangeability is not even *supposed* to apply to 'the author of *Waverley*'. Thus Quine avoids the paradox altogether.

Russell (1905, 1919a) proposed a solution to the paradox that is equally ingenious. This is considered in detail in 6.3. Here we give a rough outline only. In the first place, Russell argued that genuine names *were* interchangeable salva veritate in *all* contexts, although ordinary proper names such as 'Scott' would not meet the rather stringent criteria that Russell laid down for genuine names. Expressions such as 'Scott' would, in Russell's theory, count as disguised definite descriptions; thus 'Scott' might simply be an abbreviation for 'the person named "Scott"' (Russell 1919a:174). Regarding definite descriptions, either of the overt kind (e.g., 'the author of *Waverley*') or of the disguised kind (e.g., 'Scott'), Russell proposed *analyzing them out of existence*. Consider the following sentence:

(35)   The author of *Waverley* was Scotch. (Russell 1919a:177)

According to Russell, this is actually an abbreviation for the following:

(36)   At least one person wrote *Waverley;* and at most one person wrote *Waverley;* and whoever wrote *Waverley* was Scotch.

It is readily seen that, in expanding (35) to (36), Russell thereby eliminates the description 'the author of *Waverley*', which occurs in (35) but not in (36).

If we apply the same technique to sentence (5), we discover that the subordinate sentence 'Scott was the author of *Waverley*' does not, in Russell's words, "contain any constituent 'the author of *Waverley*' for which we could substitute 'Scott'" (Russell 1905:489). Thus, in Russell's theory, we see that, when their containing sentences are fully analyzed, definite descriptions cease to exist; hence the question of their interchangeability does not arise and the paradox of the name relation is eliminated.

4.4. Summary

In this chapter, we have seen that certain linguistic expressions, which for convenience can be called *names,* are often regarded as naming or

standing for extralinguistic objects. Given that if two things are identical, what is true of the one is true of the other, it seems that names standing for the same object must be interchangeable salva veritate. However, as we have seen, in nonextensional contexts this principle of interchangeability fails.

The Fregean solution to this puzzle consisted in treating names as systematically ambiguous. Thus, in what he called oblique contexts, a name stood not for its customary nominatum but for its customary sense, and so could only be exchanged for another name that had the same sense. In this way, it is shown that the principle of interchangeability does in fact hold in oblique contexts, but that it is names with the same *sense,* and not names with the same *nominatum,* that can be exchanged in such contexts.

Quine's solution consisted in regarding the forms that appear in nonextensional contexts as not names at all. Thus he restricts the principle of interchangeability to extensional contexts.

Russell argued that genuine names *were* always interchangeable salva veritate, but that definite descriptions and ordinary proper names did not count as genuine names. He thought that, when the real logical structure of a sentence was revealed through logical analysis, all descriptions and even ordinary proper names would turn out not to be genuine constituents; hence the question of their interchangeability did not, strictly speaking, arise.

5

The Causal Theory of Names

5.1. Ordinary Proper Names

5.1.1. Epistemic and Metaphysical Necessity

In recent years, the American philosopher Kripke has stressed a distinction between what he calls *epistemic necessity* (1979a:241) and *metaphysical necessity* (1979a, pp. 273, 281). The two concepts can be illustrated by the following example:

(1)   Beijing is Peking.

According to Kripke, an identity sentence involving two codesignative ordinary proper names—that is, two proper names standing for the same thing—cannot be false; hence the truth of (1) is not a matter of fact but of metaphysical necessity. On the other hand, the truth of (1) needs to be learned in order to be known, and therefore is *not* a matter of epistemic necessity. (The term 'epistemic' can be broadly paraphrased as 'concerning epistemology or knowledge'.) In what follows, the term 'necessary' is used of those truths that are matters of metaphysical necessity in Kripke's sense. Those truths that are a matter of epistemic necessity will be referred to as truths that are *known a priori;* that is, prior to experience.

5.1.2. Rigid Designation

Kripke espouses (1980:3) a view that can be expressed in the following way:

(2)   For any objects x and y: If $x = y$, then necessarily $x = y$.

He also espouses the view that ordinary proper names are what he calls *rigid designators* (1980, pp. 3-15, 48-49). A rigid designator is an expression that designates the same thing regardless of what state of affairs we entertain, assuming language is held constant. For example,

(3)   the 42nd U.S. president

is *not* a rigid designator, because we can entertain a possible (although nonactual) state of affairs in which Bill Clinton had never become president. If we wished to talk about that imaginary state of affairs, the expression 'the 42nd U.S. president' *as used by us* would not designate Clinton. On the other hand, the expression

(4)   nine

is a rigid designator, because it names the number 9 in whatever state of affairs we entertain. In other words, whatever we imagine, if we use the expression 'nine' in talking about some state of affairs, we must be talking about the number 9. To suppose that we are not is to suppose that we are using 'nine' in a new way that is at variance with the rules of English.

We saw earlier that Kripke regards true identity sentences between ordinary proper names—such as example (1)—as being necessarily true. The reason he takes that view can now be explained. The principle that we expressed as (2) implies the following principle:

(5)   For any two expressions ϕ and μ: '$\phi = \mu$', if true, is
        necessarily true if ϕ and μ are rigid designators.
        (Compare Kripke 1980:3-4.)

(Note that (2) is about objects, whereas (5) is about linguistic expressions.) Kripke regards ordinary proper names as a type of rigid designator; hence identity sentences between proper names must, given Kripke's assumptions, be true necessarily (see Kripke 1979a:243).

5.1.3. Transferring the Reference

In 4.3.1.1, we saw that in Frege's theory the referent or nominatum of an ordinary proper name was determined by the name's sense, that is, by the way in which the name presents the nominatum. For example, the proper name 'Aristotle' might have this sense: Plato's disciple and the teacher of Alexander the Great. The nominatum would then be the individual who fitted the sense. Of course, such a view is incompatible with the idea that ordinary proper names are rigid designators, for a state of affairs can well be imagined in which not Aristotle but somebody else had been Alexander the Great's teacher. Thus, in Kripke's theory, the reference of an ordinary proper name cannot be secured by a sense. Indeed, Kripke thinks that proper names do not have Frege-style senses at all.

Kripke argues that the link between a name and its referent is determined by a historical chain of communication (1980:91-97). For example, a baby is born; his or her parents call it 'X'; they talk about X to their friends; their friends meet other people, and gradually the name is spread. Anyone who uses the name 'X' to talk about X will thus be part of a historical chain of reference-transference leading back ultimately to the referent itself. Anyone on this chain can use the name 'X' to refer to X without having any qualitative knowledge concerning X. Normally, of course, when one comes across a new name, one likes to know some sort of fact about the bearer—one likes to get qualitative purchase on the referent—but this is not essential for the transfer of reference to have taken place. All that is essential is that the receiver of the name should intend to use the name with the same reference as the person from whom he or she has received the name (1980:96)—Kripke takes the "notion of intending to use the same reference" (p. 97) as a given; thus his explanation is not designed to *eliminate* the notion of reference.

The above account, which is sometimes referred to as the 'causal theory' of names, does not rule out the possibility that the initial 'baptism' (1980:96) of the referent can be achieved through a description. For example, the nineteenth-century French astronomer Leverrier reportedly fixed the reference of the name 'Neptune' as the planet responsible for such and such perturbations in the orbits of certain other planets (Kripke 1980:79) before the planet Neptune was actually observed. Having a description at the beginning of the chain is by no means essential, however, because the reference could be fixed by other means, for example, by pointing at the object in question (1980:96).

5.2. Modal Sentences

A modal sentence is one in which any of the words 'necessarily', 'possibly', and the like occurs as a grammatical sentence adjunct (see also Chapter 8). Now, just as—according to Kripke—sentences such as (1) express necessary truths, so their modal counterparts express plain truths:

(6)   Necessarily Beijing is Peking.

Obviously, modal identity sentences between *identical* proper names express truths also:

(7)   Necessarily Beijing is Beijing.

Therefore, according to Kripke's assumptions, codesignative ordinary proper names in modal identity sentences can be considered to be interchangeable *salva veritate;* that is, with truth preserved (for the principle of interchangeability, see 4.1). Indeed, Kripke goes further and argues that codesignative proper names are interchangeable, not just in modal identity sentences such as (6) but "in *all* contexts of (metaphysical) necessity and possibility" (1979a:243, my italics).

5.3. Epistemic Sentences

Quine thinks that epistemic sentences involving proper names only, for example,

(8)   Tom believes that Cicero denounced Catiline,

can be understood in such a way that, if any of the names following the 'believes that' construction are swapped for others standing for the same individuals, the containing sentence, if it is true, will not necessarily remain so. In short, Quine believes that the principle of interchangeability fails for *ordinary proper names* in epistemic contexts, on one type of reading at least (see Quine 1960, §30). Of course, Frege ("*Ueber Sinn und Bedeutung*") and Russell (1905) had already shown that other types of *names,* in a broad sense, could not be exchanged in such contexts (see 4.2 and 4.3).

The Quinean view, which is still prevalent, is based on what Kripke (1979a:248-249) calls the *disquotational principle,* according to which, if someone sincerely assents to a sentence '*p*', he or she believes *that p*—assuming he or she is not subject to any linguistic confusions or failures of rationality. To see how use of the disquotational principle leads to an apparent failure of the principle of interchangeability, consider the following sentences:

(9)   Beijing is not the capital of China.

(10)   Peking is the capital of China.

Let us assume that Smith assents, sincerely, to both of the above. Using the disquotational principle, we can infer the truth of (11) below from Smith's assent to (9) and (10):

(11)   Smith believes that Beijing is not the capital of China and he believes that Peking is the capital of China.

Now, despite Smith's ignorance in this respect, it is well known that the proper names 'Beijing' and 'Peking' stand for the same thing, namely, the city that is the present capital of China. However, swapping 'Peking' for 'Beijing' in (11) results in the following sentence:

(12) Smith believes that Peking is not the capital of China and he believes that Peking is the capital of China.

There are two ways of reading (12). First, it can be seen as describing a situation in which Smith believes *of a specific object,* namely, the city now called Beijing, that it is and is not the capital of China (compare Kripke 1979a, note 24, first paragraph). On this reading, (12) does not ascribe contradictory beliefs to Smith, for believing ϕ and not-ϕ of a specific object does not necessarily involve a suspension of logic. For example, Jones, a student of French literature, might fail to realize that Stendhal and Henri Beyle are in fact one and the same individual. Jones might therefore think of Stendhal as a great novelist, but of Henri Beyle as an obscure Frenchman of no literary distinction. In those circumstances, Jones would believe *of* Stendhal that he was a great writer and that he was not.

According to its second possible reading, (12) does attribute contradictory beliefs to Smith. On this reading, Smith simply believes two propositions that are mutually contradictory, namely, (i) that Peking is not the capital of China and (ii) that Peking is the capital of China. It is under this second reading that the principle of interchangeability appears to fail; for, if we assume that Smith is a rational human being, it seems that we ought not to be able to derive (12) from (11).

Kripke argues (1979a:268) that the sort of problem that surfaces in (12) is due not to the attempted application of the principle of interchangeability but to the (normally tacit) use of the disquotational principle. Using the disquotational principle, according to Kripke, we can end up attributing contradictory beliefs to someone even when we do not attempt to exchange one codesignative proper name for another (as long as we assume that correct translation preserves truth; 1979a:250). Kripke supports this claim by referring to the following imaginary situation (1979a:254-267). Pierre, a monolingual French speaker living in France, assents (sincerely) to

(13) Londres est jolie,

although in fact he has never been to London; perhaps he has read travel brochures or seen films set in London. Pierre later moves to London—although it never occurs to him that Londres and London are one and the same—and learns English, not through translation but by being in contact with English-speaking people. He lives in an unattractive district and, as a consequence, is inclined to assent to

(14) London is not pretty.

Because he cannot translate between French and English and is quite set in his ways, he has no inclination to withdraw his assent from (13). Using the disquotational principle (which, if it holds at all, presumably holds in all languages), the following sentences can be inferred from (13) and (14):

(15) Pierre croit que Londres est jolie.

(16) Pierre believes that London is not pretty.

Given that we are assuming correct translation to preserve truth, from (15) we can infer

(17) Pierre believes that London is pretty,

which, when conjoined to (16), ascribes contradictory beliefs to Pierre (Kripke 1979a:254-256).

We can obtain a similar result even if we dispense with the assumption of truth-preserving translation (Kripke 1979a:265). One appropriate scenario is as follows. Peter first comes across the name 'Paderewski' in circumstances that lead him to be inclined to assent to the following:

(18) Paderewski had musical talent.

Later, he hears of what he takes to be another Paderewski (in fact, it is the same man), whose profession is politics. Believing that politicians are never gifted musicians, Peter now assents to this:

(19) Paderewski had no musical talent.

Despite Peter's misconception, he can in both cases be said to be using the expression 'Paderewski' as a name for the same individual, namely, Paderewski; for it is not as if there were two Paderewskis, one a musician and one a politician. After applying the disquotational principle, we have the sentence

(20)   Peter believes that Paderewski had musical talent and he
         believes that Paderewski did not have musical talent,

which obviously ascribes contradictory beliefs to Peter.

Kripke's point is this: Quine and others have simultaneously applied the disquotational principle and the principle of interchangeability and in so doing have apparently demonstrated that, on the type of reading in question, the latter does not hold in belief contexts. However, the disquotational principle on its own (the Peter case), or together with the assumption of truth-preserving translation (the Pierre case), leads to exactly the same type of result as (12), despite the fact that there is no interchange of codesignative proper names. In other words, the paradoxical result exemplified by (12) cannot be blamed on the principle of interchangeability and, so, of itself, that result does not demonstrate that interchangeability fails for proper names in epistemic sentences. Nevertheless, Kripke (1979a:269) is reluctant to draw any firm conclusions; he has "no official doctrine" concerning such sentences (1980:21).

5.4. Names of Natural Kinds

5.4.1. Natural-Kind Terms Do Not Have Senses

The view of proper names outlined so far implies that such expressions do not have Fregean senses. Kripke (1980:127-134)—see also Putnam (1973)—has extended this view to terms for natural kinds, such as 'cow', and terms for natural phenomena, such as 'lightning'. (Frege himself, in his published writings, never made clear what the sense of a predicate such as 'cow' would be; see Kenny 1995, pp. 118, 152-153.) Thus Kripke writes (pp. 127-128), *"Perhaps* some 'general' names . . . express properties. In a significant sense, such general names as 'cow' and 'tiger' do not, unless *being a cow* counts trivially as a property." It might, for example, be thought that the word 'tiger' has some such sense as: 'large, tawny yellow, carnivorous, quadrupedal feline with black stripes.' However, we might very well encounter a three-legged tiger or one that did not eat meat or one that, as a result of some freak genetic mutation, was completely black. Thus, apart from felinity, none of the properties just mentioned are actually essential to tigerhood; that is, they cannot be thought of as constituting a putative sense of the word 'tiger'.

5.4.2. Essential Properties Are Not Senses

According to Kripke, certain properties are *essential* to given natural kinds and natural phenomena. For instance, if something is a cat, it follows necessarily that it is an animal; if something is gold, it must have the atomic number 79; if something is water, it necessarily has two atoms of hydrogen to every one of oxygen; and so on. However, such essential properties are to be distinguished from linguistic *senses*. For example, the discovery that whales belong in one category of the biological taxonomy, mammals, rather than another, fish, does not involve a change in the sense of the word 'fish' or a modification of some associated concept of fishhood (1980:138). Similarly, it is "present scientific theory," rather than a putative linguistic sense, that determines that gold is an element whose atomic number is 79 (1980:125).

5.4.3. Paradigms

5.4.3.1. Kripke. In Kripke's theory, just as an ordinary proper name is able to function as such because it is linked through a historical chain of communication to a particular individual, so a term for a natural kind or natural phenomenon is historically tied to an initial sample or *paradigm* (Kripke 1980:135-140). Thus, for a word like 'gold', some sort of initial baptism would take place that fixed the type of thing that counted as gold. This might consist simply in pointing to a sample of gold. For a phenomenal term such as 'heat' or 'electricity', the reference is fixed by establishing an identity between the phenomenon and what is sensed during a particular experience of sensation (as in the case of heat) or between the phenomenon and what is taken to be the cause of certain experimental effects (as in the case of electricity) (Kripke 1980:136-137).

With regard to words for natural kinds or substances, certain properties will help us to identify the original sample, and an analogous situation holds for natural phenomena. For instance, we may take gold to be a yellow metal with certain metallic properties such as ductility. None of these initial properties need be essential—thus the yellowness of gold may be an optical illusion—although some may be. Scientific investigation normally uncovers properties that are a far better guide than the characteristics of the original sample, and, moreover, the properties assigned to a natural kind or phenomenon by scientific theory *are* essential (Kripke 1980:138). For example, anything that did not have an atomic weight of 196.97 or a valency of 1 or 3 would not be gold, and anything that was not an electrical discharge would not be lightning.

Kripke even hints (1980:99) that *all* scientific truths might be necessary truths: "Physical necessity *might* turn out to be necessity in the highest degree." This possibility is perhaps also raised implicitly when Kripke suggests (1980:125) that even such apparently contingent properties of gold as, say, its yellowness, will in fact be necessary properties if they follow necessarily from things like the atomic structure.

5.4.3.2. Wittgenstein. As we saw in 1.2, the Wittgenstein of *Philosophical Investigations* argued that the structure of language was not determined by the structure of the world but that it resided in regularities of usage. This does not mean that language is independent of reality, only that the interface between the two does not consist in a straightforward sign-object correlation, as Wittgenstein had thought when he wrote *Tractatus Logico-Philosophicus.*

Now this point is particularly relevant in connection with paradigms. Like Kripke, the Wittgenstein of *Philosophical Investigations* observed (I, §50) that the use of terms such as 'sepia' or 'meter' is determined by their correspondence with particular paradigms that can, to a certain extent, be referred to ostensively, that is, by pointing at them. (In the case of 'meter', there is—or used to be—an officially recognized standard meter in Paris.) However, unlike Kripke, Wittgenstein stresses that these paradigms should be viewed not as objectively given pieces of reality but as "instrument[s] of the language" (see also §16). For it is not as if, before human beings arrived, the length one meter and the color sepia were already 'out there', waiting for a name to be applied to them. On the contrary, such things acquire a place in our conceptual scheme only when a particular linguistic framework emerges. These remarks appear to apply more to some terms than others. For example, it seems odd to think of cows as not being 'out there' independently of language. However, as we saw in 2.1, some philosophers—most notably Quine—regard even ordinary physical objects as posits of our language. They think, for example, that the difference between ordinary things and the theoretical entities of physics is essentially a matter of degree, that in both cases the objects in question are by-products of particular conceptual frameworks (see Quine 1960, §6). The same would apply, mutatis mutandis, to the distinction between concrete natural kinds such as cows and more abstract objects such as colors and units of measurement.

Wittgenstein famously said that, on account of the circumstance that paradigms are instruments of language, it was senseless to say that the standard meter in Paris measures one meter (*Philosophical Investigations*, I, §50). Kripke (1980:54) suggests that Wittgenstein is mistaken when he says this, because the stick or rod that serves as the paradigm certainly has a length. However, it seems that Wittgenstein is not talking about the rod itself but the rod *qua paradigm*. Presumably, Wittgenstein would have agreed that the actual piece of platinum (or whatever metal is used) had a particular length.

5.4.4. Theoretical Identities

Theoretical terms such as 'meter', 'heat', and 'molecular motion', together with mass nouns for natural kinds such as 'gold', are regarded by Kripke as being rigid designators (1980, pp. 55, 136); that is, they name the same thing—in this case, a phenomenon or a natural substance—in all possible states of affairs. For example, assuming language is held constant, there can be no state of affairs in which the word 'meter' does not designate the unit of measurement that it designates in the actual state of affairs, namely, 100 centimeters.

One consequence of treating such terms as rigid designators is this: Given principle (5), identity sentences between mass nouns for natural kinds or between theoretical terms, if true, are *necessarily* true. Thus, on Kripke's assumptions, the sentence

(21)   Heat is molecular motion

expresses a necessary truth.

Now, although (21)'s truth is a matter of what Kripke calls metaphysical necessity, it needs to be discovered to be known; hence (21) does not express a truth that is known a priori (see 1980, pp. 132, 152-153). Thus we see that the distinction between metaphysical and epistemic necessity is as important in the case of theoretical identities as it was in the case of identity sentences involving proper names (see 5.1.1 above).

Kripke stresses that the converse case to (21) may also occur (1980:54-57). Thus imagine that we have decided to fix the reference of the term 'meter' as the length of a particular rod. X. Consider the following identity sentence:

(22)   One meter is the length of X.

Although the expression 'one meter' rigidly designates one meter, the reference of the description 'the length of X' depends on how long X is. This obviously varies across different states of affairs—for example, X's length will change if it is heated sufficiently. Therefore, (22) is not an identity between two rigid designators and so does not express a necessary truth. Nevertheless, that the metal rod in question, namely, X, measures one meter is something that is known by us *a priori;* this must be the case, for it is we who have selected X to fix the reference of the expression 'one meter'. Thus, while (21) expresses a necessary non-a priori truth, (22) expresses a nonnecessary a priori truth. Kripke uses the term *necessary a posteriori truth* for the former and the term *contingent a priori truth* for the latter.

5.4.5. The Sociolinguistic Hypothesis

Putnam (1973) puts forward some ideas that overlap with Kripke's, although he stresses the fact that such considerations tell against psychologistic theories of meaning, that is, theories in which linguistic meanings are thought to be somehow located in the human mind. Putnam argued, for example, that for someone who was unable to distinguish between a beech and an elm tree, there could be no difference in any mental concepts associated with the words 'elm' and 'beech', although these two expressions would not thereby cease to have different meanings. As Putnam put it (1973:704), "Cut the pie any way you like, 'meanings' just ain't in the *head!*"

Putnam (1973) posits what he calls a "sociolinguistic hypothesis" to account for the way in which the average person can use a word such as 'gold' without properly knowing how to identify gold. For example, while many people wear a gold wedding ring and while it is important for them that their ring should actually be gold, the knowledge necessary for telling whether something is genuine gold resides among a relatively small number of "expert" speakers. Thus, while a substance must satisfy certain criteria to count as gold (it must, as Kripke points out, have an atomic number of 79), there is no reason to suppose that such criteria are embodied in a generally available concept of goldness. Putnam suggests that there is a "division of labor" according to which, *taken as a whole,* the linguistic community will have highly specialized knowledge about the essential properties of natural kinds and substances but, generally speaking, only those whose role in society requires it will carry this knowledge about with them. In other words, the reference of a term of this sort is fixed not by a concept in the individual's mind but by the 'sociolinguistic state' of the community of speakers.

5.5. Summary

Kripke believes that ordinary proper names do not have Frege-style senses. In addition, he regards such expressions as rigid designators, that is, as expressions that stand for the same object in all possible states of affairs. On account of this view, he considers that ordinary proper names are interchangeable salva veritate in all modal contexts. The fact that the truth of modal identity sentences involving distinct proper names is not, generally speaking, of the a priori kind is accounted for in terms of a distinction that Kripke draws between metaphysical and epistemic necessity.

While Kripke does not say that codesignative proper names can be exchanged, salva veritate, in epistemic sentences, he seems to endorse the view that "the received platitude—that codesignative names are not interchangeable in belief contexts—may not be so clear as is generally supposed" (1979a:272). Specifically, he shows that paradoxical results of the sort exemplified by our sentence (12) occur even when we do not attempt to exchange one codesignative proper name for another but simply apply the disquotational principle.

Although ordinary proper names do not have senses, Kripke feels that the way in which their reference is secured can nevertheless be explained. He appeals to the concept of a causal or historical chain whereby the reference of a name is passed from person to person. In this account, the notion of reference is understood as a primitive.

Kripke also argues that names for natural kinds and theoretical terms have much stronger affinities with ordinary proper names than is commonly supposed. In particular, Frege-style senses cannot plausibly be attributed to such expressions. In addition, theoretical terms and mass nouns such as 'gold' can be regarded as rigid designators. Kripke thinks that the reference of natural-kind words is determined, in the first instance, through the association of the relevant term with a sample or paradigm. The reference is then passed from person to person in the same way as the reference of an ordinary proper name is transferred through links in a causal chain. The same applies to terms for natural phenomena, except that the reference is normally identified in the first instance as a particular sensation (the case of heat, for example) or as the cause of some concrete experimental effect (the case of lightning or electricity).

Finally, an important observation from Wittgenstein was briefly mentioned, namely, that paradigms or samples for natural kinds and the like do not have any objective status in their own right. Thus the color red, for example, is not a discrete object until rational observers have decided to segment the visible spectrum in such a way that red is one of the units identified.

Part II: Further Reading

The clearest and most perceptive account of the name relation is given in Carnap 1956, chapter III. See also Carnap 1958, vol. 1, §12. Quine 1949 is instructive also.

None of the English translations of "Ueber Sinn und Bedeutung" is free from error. For readers who know French, Claude Imbert's translation in Frege 1971 is excellent. Carnap's (1956, §§28-30) account of Frege's sense-nominatum distinction is concise and very illuminating. Kenny (1995:216-241) provides an excellent exegesis of "Ueber Sinn und Bedeutung." For the application of Fregean senses in linguistics, see Chierchia and McConnell-Ginet 1990 (pp. 210-212).

Kripke 1980 is a self-contained exposition of Kripke's views on names. Kripke 1979a is useful for Kripke's views on names in epistemic sentences. It is interesting to compare Kripke's views on natural kinds with Quine's (1960, §12) remarks about "observational terms." For natural kinds in linguistics, see Lyons 1995 (pp. 89-95).

PART III

DEFINITE DESCRIPTIONS

6

Description and Analysis

6.1. Russell's Theory of Descriptions

6.1.1. Acquaintance and Description

We saw in 4.1 that many philosophers have subscribed, often tacitly, to some form of what Carnap called the method of the name relation. In the work of the early Wittgenstein, this led to the view that the words of natural language were actually abbreviations for concatenations of genuine names, each of which was rigidly correlated with some ultimate constituent of reality (see 1.2.3). The twentieth-century English philosopher Bertrand Russell held similar views—during the earlier part of his career at least—and his famous theory of descriptions was the linchpin for much of the attendant analytical enterprise. Its importance can hardly be overstated.

Now, when linguists encounter the theory, they often get bogged down in the Strawson-Russell controversy concerning truth-value gaps; that is, in the question of whether a sentence such as

(1)   The marquis of Los Angeles is a keen cyclist

is simply false or is neither true nor false. But that is to miss the point somewhat, because the principal motivation for the theory appears to have been *epistemological*. In other words, the theory was designed to resolve a number of questions relating to how knowledge is acquired.

Russell drew a fundamental distinction between direct knowledge *of* things, which he called *acquaintance*, and knowledge *about* things. Acquaintance with a thing involved having direct perceptual contact with it, while knowledge about a thing involved only knowing certain facts about it.

We can illustrate this dichotomy with an example from *The Problems of Philosophy* (first published 1912, which appears here as Russell 1959). Thus imagine that we are in the presence of a table. Now although it might seem odd to someone steeped in common sense, Russell argued that we are never "directly aware of the table," that the table "is not, strictly speaking, known to us at all" (p. 26). Russell supported this view by observing that it would be possible, without absurdity, to doubt whether a table was actually present. There does seem to be some truth in this observation, because it might be possible that, although our sensory perception was accurate, what was really before us was not a table but something else, something so constructed that the sensations it produced in us were identical to those that a table might produce—circumstances of this sort are common enough in artificial illusions and conjuring tricks. According to this view, the reality of the table is in some sense a figment of our ability to project and construct on the basis of the sense impressions that it (or whatever is in fact before us) produces. In terms of the distinction between *acquaintance with* and *knowledge about,* we can say that we are acquainted only with the sense impressions produced by the table and that our knowledge of the table itself is of the *knowledge about* type.

But what exactly are these sense impressions? Russell gives the examples of the color of the table, together with its shape, texture, and hardness. These, he contends, are known to us directly. Moreover, they are known to us *completely.* For example, although we might learn some additional truth about the color of the table, such as that it is called dark brown, these truths do not make us know the color any better. In other words, once we have become aware of the color, "no further knowledge of it is even theoretically possible" (Russell 1912/1959:25).

6.1.2. Complex and Simple Symbols, Logical Form

Russell thought that the symbols or expressions of language could be divided into two kinds, the complex and the simple. Simple symbols were taken to designate the things with which we were directly acquainted, such as the simple sense impressions (also known as sense data) just mentioned. Complex symbols, on the other hand, were taken to designate constructed objects, such as the table in the above example. Russell thought that complex symbols were not directly connected with reality, and so their understanding presupposed their decomposition into simple symbols. This is clear from Russell's remark that "every proposition which we can understand must be composed wholly of constituents with which we are acquainted" (Russell 1912/1959:32) and also from the following:

> If we had a complete symbolic language, with a definition for everything definable, and an undefined symbol for everything indefinable, the undefined symbols in this language would represent symbolically what I mean by "the ultimate furniture of the world." (Russell 1919a:182)

By "the ultimate furniture of the world," Russell means the things with which we are directly acquainted.

Obviously, the words of ordinary language such as 'table' cannot themselves be decomposed or analyzed into simpler constituents. So Russell drew a distinction between the superficial grammatical structure of language and its 'real' logical form (see Russell 1919a:168). For example, an expression such as 'table' would in reality be more like this expression: 'object x such that x produces such-and-such sense-data' (see Russell 1912/1959:26), and the fact that in ordinary language this complex was reduced to a single word was put down to the misleading nature of superficial grammar.

Now, Russell (1919a:182) assigned the term 'name' to the simple expressions that stood for particular objects of acquaintance (such expressions would occur, of course, only in a logically perfect language), but what about expressions for objects with which we were not directly acquainted? These Russell called *descriptions* or *denoting phrases*. As its label suggests, a description *described* something, rather than naming it directly, as names did with sense data, for example. A description presented something to us, or purported to, via words for things with which we were directly acquainted; thus we could understand a description only as long as we could analyze it into epistemologically primitive components. This, of course, meant getting at its hidden logical form, for, as we have just seen, a word such as 'table' is not at first sight *capable* of being further analyzed.

As we shall see, Russell's analytical method was such that, at the level of logical form, descriptions had no independent existence. They were, in his words, 'incomplete symbols' (Russell 1919a:182). Thus it made no sense to talk of the logical structure of a description per se; rather, sentences *containing* descriptions had a logical form, to which the description contributed.

6.1.3. Russell's Technical Apparatus: The Generality Notation

6.1.3.1. The legacy of Frege. Russell's method for analyzing sentences containing descriptions consisted in treating them as a type of general sentence. A general sentence is one that is not about a specific thing but *all* things, *no*-thing or *some* thing(s)—normally, the idea of *some* thing(s) is taken to subsume that of *a* thing. In modern philosophy, logic, and linguistics, the analysis of general sentences is based on the special concept script (Begriffsschrift) that Frege introduced in his celebrated work of the same name (which appears here as Frege 1972). To understand Frege's method, we need to consider a few examples, although in what follows I adopt the modern practice and replace Frege's own notation with an equivalent but more perspicuous symbolism. (Frege's treatment of generality is discussed in detail in 10.3.)

Frege would have analyzed the following general sentence or proposition (a distinction is not important here),

(2)   Everything is red,

as what in the modern notation would be

(3)   (*x*) (*x* is red),

which is to be read as

(4)   For every object *x*: *x* is red.

The letter '*x*' that occurs in the second set of parentheses in (3) and after the colon in (4) is called a *variable,* meaning that it refers indefinitely to an object. On account of the variable, what is called the *scope* of (3) and (4), namely, the expression

(5)   *x* is red,

is not a determinate sentence but a *propositional function* (see Russell 1919a:155-166). To make (5) into a determinate sentence that would be capable of standing alone, and not merely as the scope of some larger construction, a subject expression has to be substituted for the variable.

The '(*x*)' part of (3) indicates that all substitution instances of (3)'s scope are true; that is to say, whatever subject expression we choose to substitute for the variable '*x*' in (5), the resulting sentence will turn out to express a true proposition. This is why (3) means the same as (2), which, as it happens, is false, although many of the substitution instances of (3)'s scope, for example,

(6)   Mars is red,

are true. Renderings of

(7)   Something is red

and

(8)   Nothing is red

can be obtained by inserting the negation symbol '⌐' at different points in (3). Thus

(9)   (*x*) (⌐*x* is red)

would mean 'Nothing is red', and

(10) $\backsim(x)$ ($\backsim x$ is red)

would mean 'Something is red'.

To achieve a formalization of more complex general sentences such as

(11) All swans are white,

the structure of what occurs in the second set of parentheses in the '. . . (x) (. . . x . . .)' notation has to be somewhat more complex than for simple general sentences. Thus, according to the Fregean analysis, (11) is to be represented as

(12) (x) (if x is a swan, then x is white),

which, using the symbolic notation introduced in 1.2.4, becomes

(13) (x) (x is a swan → x is white).

Similarly, 'Some swans are white' (or 'A swan is white') would be as follows:

(14) $\backsim(x)$ (x is a swan → $\backsim x$ is white).

Now, we saw in 1.2.4 that, if the letters 'p' and 'q' are understood as standing in place of arbitrary sentences, the schema

(15) $p \rightarrow q$

can be understood as being an abbreviation for

(16) $\backsim(p \; \& \; \backsim q)$.

We can see the validity of this claim by considering the sentence

(17) If Clinton is president, then he won the election.

This is composed of two subsentences

(18)   Clinton is president

and

(19)   Clinton won the election,

for which we can substitute the arbitrary letters 'p' and 'q', respectively (the fact that 'Clinton' in (19) gets supplanted by a pronoun in (17) can be ignored). Using the logical symbolism introduced in Chapter 1, we can now represent (17) schematically as

(20) $p \rightarrow q$,

which reproduces schema (15). Now, what we actually assert by uttering sentence (17) is this: that it cannot be the case that, on the one hand, Clinton *is* president and, on the other, he *did not* win the election; that is, in schematic form,

(21) $\sim(p \ \& \sim q)$,

which reproduces (16). Thus we see that schema (15) and schema (16) represent sentences that say the same thing; the one is an abbreviation for the other.

Given the equivalence between (15) and (16), and if we take

(22) x is a swan

to be p and

(23) $\sim x$ is white

to be q, we see that (14) can be transformed into

(24) $\sim(x) \sim(x$ is a swan $\& x$ is white).

This last formulation means:

(25)   It is not the case that all things are not both swans and white;

that is,

(26)   Some things are swans and white;

in other words:

(27)   Some swans are white.

In the modern notation, '⌐(x) ⌐' is normally replaced by the symbol
'(∃x)', which is called the *existential quantifier;* the symbol '(x)' is known
as the *universal quantifier.* Using the existential quantifier, (24) can be
rewritten as

(28)   (∃x) (x is a swan & x is white).

6.1.3.2. Russell's innovation. Russell's innovation was to treat
sentences of the form

(29)   The A is B

as being on a par with

(30)   An A is B;

that is,

(31)   Some As are B.

The difference between (29) and (30)/(31), according to Russell's theory, is that the former implies that there is only one thing that is A or is
an A, whereas this implication is not present in the case of the latter. So
Russell needed to build a uniqueness-securing clause into his definition
of 'the A'. To do this, he made use of the fact that if there is one and
only one thing x that has the property A (or is an A), then if any object
y is not identical to x, y cannot have the property A (or be an A). Put

another way, this means that if *y* has the property *A,* then *y* is identical to *x.* This can be represented in symbolic notation in the following way:

(32) (*y*) (*Ay* → *y* = *x*).

This last formulation can be read as

(33) For every object *y:* if *y* has the property *A,* then *y* is *x.*

Any object *x* satisfying (32) must be unique, for no object can be identical to every object that has the property *A* unless no more than one such object exists (for satisfaction, see 2.2.2.3).

Now, as Frege's work had shown, sentences of the form represented in (30) and (31) were to be analyzed as

(34) (∃*x*) (*Ax* & *Bx*).

If we combine (34) with (32), that is, with Russell's method for securing uniqueness, we have

(35) (∃*x*) [*Ax* & *Bx* & (*y*) (*Ay* → *y* = *x*)],

which can be read as

(36) For some object *x:* (*x* is *A* & *x* is *B* & for every object *y:* if *y* is *A, y* is identical to *x*).

(The parentheses in (36) are used to indicate that the whole of 'for every object *y:* if *y* is *A, y* is identical to *x*' is part of the scope of 'For some object *x:*'. Earlier, we talked about the scope of a sentence; now it can be seen that we were actually talking about the *scope of a quantifier.*) Formulation (35) gives us what Russell would have taken to be the true logical form of (29).

Let us apply the above apparatus to one of Russell's examples from "On Denoting," namely,

(37) The father of Charles II was executed. (Russell 1905:481)

First, we have

(38) ($\exists x$) (x begot Charles II & x was executed),

which expresses the fact that someone begot Charles II and was executed. If we now add Russell's uniqueness-securing clause, we have

(39) ($\exists x$) [x begot Charles II & x was executed & (y) (y begot Charles II → $y = x$)].

This gives us the correct Russellian logical form for

(40) The begetter of Charles II was executed,

which—extraneous details aside—reproduces (37).

6.1.3.3. Descriptions destitute of meaning. From the foregoing discussion we see that, at the level of logical form, there is no single identifiable unit that corresponds to a description from ordinary language. Instead, the content of the description is, as it were, dispersed throughout the formula that gives the logical form for the sentence as a whole, and Russell thereby achieves the "reduction of all propositions in which denoting phrases occur to forms in which no such phrases occur" (Russell 1905:482). This has the result that descriptions per se are exposed as "wholly destitute of meaning" (p. 481). Russell took this to be one of the great advantages of his theory, because it meant that although descriptions occurred as surface grammatical subjects (or objects), they could never occur as subject expressions in logical form—in Russell's symbolism, they simply had no logical integrity of their own.

6.1.3.4. Acquaintance with universals. Russell's two most famous examples of definite descriptions are 'the present king of France' and 'the author of *Waverley*' (see Russell 1905, 1919a). He analyzes these in terms of what are treated as primitive propositional functions: 'x is present-king-of-France' and 'x wrote-*Waverley*', respectively. Given Russell's pursuit of ultimate epistemological constituents, one would expect that, in a fuller analysis, these primitive functions would be expanded to compounds referring only to things with which we were directly acquainted, such as sense data. It might be thought that it would be difficult to carry through such an analysis, because the properties of being the author of *Waverley* and being the present king of France are quite abstract. However, Russell thought that, in addition to things like sense data, we were also acquainted with universals, that is, "general ideas, such as *whiteness, diversity* and *brotherhood*" (1959:28). Thus even such experientially remote properties as being a king or being an author can be reduced to things that Russell was prepared to regard as objects of acquaintance.

6.2. The Acquisition of the Referential Function

6.2.1. Introduction

Nowadays, few people would fully endorse the epistemological part of Russell's theory (although the technical apparatus still has a good deal of currency). Quine (1960:177-178) suggests that, to a certain extent, Russell's attempted reduction of descriptions to terms that are epistemologically primitive can be viewed as a kind of synchronic reconstruction—in reverse—of the process whereby the ability to use descriptions is *learned.* To see what he means by this, we need to consider Quine's account (1960:90-110) of the ontogenesis of reference (the acquisition of the referential function), which is important in its own right.

6.2.2. The First Phase

Following Quine (1960:90-95), we might suppose that the very first phase in the acquisition process consists in the learning of basic words given in immediate experience. These would be associated with recurrent and immediate sensory stimuli. For example, 'Mommy' might be associated with the face of the mother and 'water' with the sensation occurring at bath time. Quine introduces the idea of *divided reference,* and by this he means the circumstance that a word such as 'apple' or 'book' (normally called count nouns) refers to a class of individuals, each of the same type, rather than to a single object. He contends that, at the putative first stage in the ontogenesis of reference, the trick of divided reference has not yet been mastered by the learner, and so count words would initially be learned without the built-in criterion for reference division that characterizes their role in adult speech.

In fact, Quine assimilates all terms at this first stage to the model of mass nouns—'water', 'sugar', 'mud', and the like. These he takes to designate single "scattered" (p. 98) objects; for example, the word 'water' refers to the aqueous part of the world. (Notice that this way of looking at mass nouns finds expression in the tendency in Romance and other language groups to use mass nouns with the singular definite article, such as in French 'l'eau' and in Spanish 'el agua'.) Thus words as different in their mode of reference as 'Mommy', 'red', 'water', and 'apple' would all be learned initially as designating discontinuous yet essentially homogeneous portions of the space-time continuum. Just as, even in adult speech, the expression 'a water' presupposes reference division where there is none and hence is ungrammatical, so for the very young infant there would be no conception of *this* apple as opposed to *that* apple or of Mommy as a discrete individual. There would just be apple, Mommy, water, red, and so on.

6.2.3. The Second Phase

Now, it is only with the grasping of a quite sophisticated conceptual apparatus, involving the notions of mobility and duration in space-time and of sameness and differentiation, that the device of divided reference is mastered and, with it, the ability to employ words such as 'apple' as genuine count nouns. A contemporaneous development would be the recognition of single individuals as the referents of proper names such as 'Mommy': As such objects came more and more to be viewed as being self-integrated in space-time—rather than discontinuous like the referents of out-and-out mass terms such as 'water'—so proper names would part company with mass nouns, although both would retain their singular reference. It is in the transition to this second phase, according to Quine (1960:102), that demonstrative modifiers such as English 'this' and 'that' come into play, for understanding divided reference involves nothing more than being able to distinguish between *this* apple and *that* apple, *this* book and *that* book, and so on. The key linguistic development in the second phase, then, is the introduction of what Quine calls demonstrative singular terms, such as 'this book' or 'this tree' (compare Quine, pp. 100-105). The use of such expressions presupposes a grasp of divided reference but, at the same time, restricts the learner's referential scope to immediate experience.

According to Quine (1960:100), the great advantage of demonstrative singular terms is that they release us from the burden of having to remember individual names for everything. Moreover, such expressions facilitate the learning of new proper names. To use Quine's example, were it not for demonstrative singular terms, the teaching of the name 'Nile' would involve exposing the pupil to the relevant portion of the world, together with appropriate reinforcement and correction, until the reference of the name was finally recognized. However, as long as the pupil has mastered the count noun 'river', together with the associated criterion for reference division, the teacher can simply point to the Nile and say, "That river is the Nile." Just pointing at the river and saying, "Nile," or "That is the Nile," would not be as successful, because it would fail to rule out the possibility that the object being identified was a bend in the river or some stretch of it.

Historically, where languages have them, definite articles tend to have developed from demonstrative expressions, such as the French 'le' < Latin 'ille'. This diachronic fact obviously cannot be used to explain synchronic use, but it is noteworthy in that it provides a parallel with Quine's account of the ontogenesis of reference. He argues (p. 102) that definite descriptions are learned as "degenerate demonstrative singular terms." It is easy to imagine how the transition from demonstratives to the definite article might come about during the learning process. We are supposing that, during a given phase (phase 2 in Quine's account), the infant's referential apparatus is limited to noun phrases formed from one count noun plus a demonstrative modifier; thus reference would be largely, if not wholly, confined to the things with which the learner was directly acquainted. In these general circumstances, cases would arise in which attention could be directed toward an object without an explicit pointing gesture being necessary. In such cases, the contrast between demonstrative 'this/that' and degenerate 'the' would be suspended, thereby facilitating the infant's acquisition of the definite article. So, by the end of the second stage, we would already have rudimentary definite descriptions.

6.2.4. The Third Phase

At the third stage in the ontogenesis of reference (pp. 103-105), the attributive construction is introduced, whereby a noun is modified by an adjective. Generally speaking, a compound expression consisting in a count noun and an attributive adjective will be true only of those things of which the noun and the adjective are jointly true. For example, 'female executive' will be true only of those individuals that are both female and executives. However, not all combinations of attributive adjective plus count noun function in this way. Thus someone can be a financial wizard without having any magical powers, and a large spider is smaller than a small planet. In these and similar combinations, one or more of the terms has no independent meaning outside the collocation, which is best regarded as a single unstructured unit. Expressions of this sort are traditionally described as *syncategorematic*.

It is with the advent of compounding that the possibility of frequent failures of reference arises for the first time. Thus, given his or her mastery of the attributive construction, the young child can talk about such nonexistent entities as the round square. Failures of reference occur in compound descriptions because, although the component expressions (count nouns and attributive adjectives) are true of many things when taken severally, they are true of nothing when taken jointly.

6.2.5. The Fourth Phase

Although compounding yields an enormous number of new (compound) expressions, the nouns and adjectives of which they are composed will all, in principle, have been learned through acquaintance with samples of the objects of which they are true. It is the fourth phase, involving the acquisition of relational terms such as 'larger than' and 'brother of', that really broadens the learner's referential capability (Quine, 1960:105-108). The improvement in referential ability is greatly augmented through use of the relative clause construction, which enables propositional functions formed from relational terms to be converted into adjectival expressions. For example,

(41) x is smaller than that speck

becomes

(42)   which is smaller than that speck.

When combined with a grasp of generality or *quantification* (see 6.1.3.1. above), this new apparatus permits the learner to speculate about such remote matters as *the brightest star in the universe* (i.e., the star that is brighter than all other stars that are in the universe), *the most distant point from the earth,* or *the smallest part of this object* (i.e., the part that is smaller than all other parts).

6.2.6. Parallels With Russell's Theory of Descriptions

The foregoing sketch of how the ability to use definite descriptions might be acquired illustrates the way in which these expressions contribute to the enlargement of our conceptual horizons. Without them, we would be unable to refer, for example, to the last thing Caesar saw before he died, unless there was an official name for that particular object. However, what goes on during the ontogenesis of definite descriptions must not be confused with the synchronic functioning of such expressions in adult speech, and there is a case for saying that Russell, in his famous theory of descriptions, fell prey to something like that confusion.

What Russell appears to have done in his theory is something that amounts very roughly to the following. First, he has insisted that a term with singular reference can never be a simple symbol in logical form unless it is epistemologically basic. This we can gloss very roughly as meaning that the term has to have been learned through the primitive exposure to sense experience that Quine took to be characteristic of the very first phase in the ontogenesis of reference. Russell has then stipulated that all other terms with singular reference, whether or not in their surface form they consist in a single word, are to be rendered in logical form as compounds whose structure reflects the different ways in which they were learned; that is to say, they are to be rendered as compounds ultimately of the epistemologically basic expressions that figured at phase 1 in the acquisition process. Failures of reference are then guarded against by a mechanism that ensures that the 'official' referring expressions or names are never these now overtly compound terms, but the simple ones of which they are composed and whose own designata is epistemologically guaranteed (compare Quine 1960:177-178).

6.3. Three Additional Puzzles Solved by Russell

In analyzing sentences containing definite descriptions in the way set out in 6.1 above, Russell contrived simultaneously to solve three problems.

6.3.1. Truth-Value Gaps

First, he eliminated apparent truth-value gaps, which arise when a description has no referent. There is a logical principle (the law of the excluded middle) that says that any sentence (or proposition) is either true or false, and the concept of a truth-value gap is obviously at variance with this law. The problem of apparent truth-value gaps is solved in Russell's theory by the fact that one of the truth conditions for a formula such as

(43) $(\exists x)$ [x is king of France & (y) $(y$ is king of France $\to y = x)$ & x is bald]

is that at least one object (and only one object) must satisfy the propositional function

(44) x is king of France.

Thus, in the Russell theory, if there is no king of France (or if there is more than one), the sentence

(45) The king of France is bald

is simply false, rather than neither true nor false, as some might wish to claim. This may appear to be rather artificial, but Russell (like Frege and Wittgenstein) was trying to extract the logical substructure of language rather than exactly capture the 'feel' of everyday usage.

6.3.2. The Paradox of the Name Relation

6.3.2.1. Introduction. Russell produced a non-Fregean solution to the paradox of the name relation (see 4.2 and 4.3.2.2). Frege had already tried to solve the puzzle by drawing a distinction between *Sinn* or 'sense' and *Bedeutung* or 'nominatum' (see 4.3.1). In "On Denoting" (pp. 485-488), Russell rejected Frege's distinction as being wrongly conceived. Although Russell's solution to the paradox is ingenious, his objections against Frege's sense-nominatum distinction are, in Carnap's words (1956:140), "rather obscure." This appears to be because, at times, Russell confused the use of a linguistic expression with its mention. In the next three paragraphs, I try to beat a path through Russell's argument against Frege, but the reader may well find those paragraphs to be rather heavy going. Russell's solution to the paradox is given afterward.

6.3.2.2. Russell's objections against Frege. On the Fregean view, a definite description such as 'the world's highest mountain' is supposed to have a sense and a nominatum. (Russell used 'meaning' and 'denotation' for Frege's 'sense' and 'nominatum'. Also, he called definite descriptions 'denoting phrases' or 'denoting complexes'.) Intuitively, the nominatum is the thing designated by the description; in this case, it would be Mt. Everest. In Frege's "Ueber Sinn und Bedeutung," the sense of a description had been identified with the manner in which the description presented its nominatum, which leaves open the possibility that the sense can be identified with the words that actually constitute the description (see also Frege 1949:86, note 2). Russell, as we shall see, appears to have taken Fregean senses to be complexes of words.

Frege supposed that descriptions were a type of name, and he thought that when a name occurred in a sentence, the sentence was *about* the nominatum of the name. Thus the sentence

(46)   The world's highest mountain lies between Nepal and Tibet

would be about Mt. Everest and also Nepal and Tibet. By the same token, if we were to say,

(47)   The sense of the world's highest mountain is complex,

we would, if anything, be talking about the sense of Mt. Everest, that is, the sense of the nominatum (if such a thing were possible). To talk about the sense of the description 'the world's highest mountain', we put the description in quotation marks, as in

(48)   The sense of 'the world's highest mountain' is complex,

which Russell would have equated with the formulation

(49)   'The world's highest mountain' is complex,

presumably because, as has just been mentioned, Frege's characterization of the sense of a description in "Ueber Sinn und Bedeutung" implied that a sense *could* be a form of words—in the case of a description, this form of words would be the description itself. (Nowadays, of course, we would think that a description between inverted commas referred to the expression itself and not to its sense.)

Now, because Frege held that when a description occurred in a sentence, the sentence was *about* the nominatum of the description, Russell argued that for any description C the form 'C'—which is what he thought would occur in a sentence about the Fregean sense of the description—had to have a sense as its *nominatum;* that is to say, it had to designate a sense, which, as we have seen, Russell identified with the description C itself. But then what exactly was the relation of 'C' to its nominatum C? 'C' could not be equated with 'the sense of C', because, if anything, that denoted the sense of the *nominatum* of C (compare: 'The sense of the world's highest mountain'). However, neither could 'C' be explained as 'the sense of "C" ', because Russell, as we have just seen, assumed that this was the same as 'C' on its own, which was the very thing for which an explanation was being sought. The nub of the problem, as he saw it, was that

> the moment we put the complex [i.e., description] in a proposition, the proposition is about the denotation [i.e., nominatum]; and if we make a proposition in which the subject is "the meaning [i.e., sense] of C," then the subject is the meaning (if any) of the denotation, which was not intended. (Russell 1905:486-487)

Thus the relation between 'C', which gave the sense of C, and C itself was, in Russell's words, "wholly mysterious" (p. 487), and this fact he took to be one reason for rejecting Frege's concept of sense.

6.3.2.3. Russell's own solution. Russell's solution to the paradox of the name relation could not then be based on a sense-nominatum, or, as Russell expressed it, a meaning-denotation distinction.

The paradox, it will be recalled from Chapter 4, consists in the circumstance that, although it seems to be implicit in the very concept of a name or referring expression, the *principle of interchangeability* (see 4.1) appears to fail in a certain type of context, namely, nonextensional contexts such as this: 'George IV wished to know whether Scott was the author of *Waverley*'. While this sentence is reportedly true, it is almost certainly false that George IV wished to know whether Scott was Scott, despite the fact that 'Scott' and 'the author of *Waverley*' designate the same individual.

Now, as we have seen, in Russell's theory "every proposition which we can understand must be composed wholly of constituents with which we are acquainted" (Russell 1912/1959:32). But definite descriptions did not stand for things with which we were acquainted; hence they were not independent constituents at the level of logical form—they were "incomplete symbols" (Russell 1919a:182). By the same token, they did not *name* anything and so the principle of interchangeability was not even supposed to apply to such expressions. In this way, the paradox of the name relation was dissolved. (See also 6.1.3.3 above.)

It was true that, at the superficial level of ordinary grammar, descriptions denoting the same thing could be interchanged when they had what Russell called a primary occurrence (see 6.4 below). However, for Russell, this was interchangeability only in appearance, because at the level of Russellian logical form, there were no identifiable units that corresponded to the surface descriptions; hence, at that level, there could be no question of *genuine* intersubstitution (see Russell 1905:485).

6.3.3. Subjects That Referred to Nothing

The third puzzle addressed by Russell was this: If descriptions were treated as names rather than analyzed out of subject position (as Russell proposed), it seemed logically impossible to deny that anything was the case (Russell 1905, pp. 485, 490). Russell's reasoning here was as follows. The negation of a sentence expressing a relation between two objects, say, 'Venus revolves around Saturn', implies some corresponding sentence such as

(50) Venus's revolution around Saturn does not subsist.

Now, if descriptions such as 'Venus's revolution around Saturn' were taken to be names, they had to name something. But in a sentence such as (50), this appeared to be precisely what was being denied. Such a paradox occurred whenever one attempted to deny that something was the case, because an ancillary sentence of the form

(51) X's relation R to Y does not subsist

could always be generated.

This problem of apparent subjects such as 'Venus's revolution around Saturn' that named nothing dissolved when it was realized that, being denoting phrases rather than names, these would-be subjects were not to be brought within the scope of the name relation. Thus the reason it was perfectly possible to make assertions about such nonexistent objects as the revolution of the sun around the moon or the difference between a and b when a and b did not differ was that, at the level of logical form, the said objects were not constituents of the relevant propositions. The real constituents were the objects of acquaintance designated by the simple symbols into which the descriptions for the nonexistent objects could be analyzed.

Generally speaking, from any sentence expressing a relation between two or more objects, say,

(52) Stendhal admired Napoleon,

a description can be extracted such as

(53) Stendhal's admiration for Napoleon.

According to Russell, a description like (53) never *names* anything but, as long as the sentence from which it is extracted is true, it will *denote* something, where denotation is the relation between a description and its nominatum.

6.4. Scope

Russell's use of Frege's generality apparatus enabled him to capture in logical form certain ambiguities in the use of definite descriptions. For example (Russell 1905:489), the sentence

(54) I thought your yacht was larger than it is

could mean either

(55) The size that I thought your yacht was is greater than the size your yacht is

or, perversely,

(56) I thought the size of your yacht was greater than the size of your yacht.

The different readings of (54) can be systematically shown by varying the scope of the existential quantifier, that is, by varying what is included in the brackets following '($\exists x$)'. Thus, leaving out the uniqueness-securing clause, (55) can be represented as follows:

(57) ($\exists x$) (x = the size your yacht is & I thought your yacht is larger than x),

while (56) is

(58) I thought: ($\exists x$) (x = the size your yacht is & your yacht is larger than x).

Similarly, the sentence

(59) The duke of New York does not enjoy light opera

could express the statement that the duke does not like light opera or, less commonly, it could be used to deny the whole of the statement that the duke of New York enjoys light opera. The latter case might occur if someone wished to convey that there was no duke of New York to someone who had just asserted that the said personage enjoyed light opera. The difference between the two uses of (59) can be captured by whether or not the negation sign is included within the scope of the existential quantifier:

(60) $(\exists x)$ (x is the duke of New York & $\backsim x$ enjoys light opera)

versus

(61) $\backsim(\exists x)$ (x is the duke of New York & x enjoys light opera).

When the quantifier had the maximum possible scope, as in (57) and (60), the description was said by Russell to have a *primary occurrence;* when the quantifier had a narrower scope, the description had a *secondary occurrence.* Philosophers have often pointed out that the definite description in a sentence such as

(62) Jane believes that the writer of that unflattering article is from Newcastle

can be understood in two ways. Thus in (62) the expression 'the writer of that unflattering article' could designate either (a) *some specific person,* whom the speaker perhaps knows but does not want to mention by name (the so-called *de re* interpretation), or (b) *whoever* wrote the article (the *de dicto* interpretation). Many philosophers and logicians nowadays use Russell's distinction between primary and secondary occurrences of descriptions to disambiguate *de re* ('about the thing')-*de dicto* ('about the saying') ambiguities:

(63) $(\exists x)$ (x wrote that unflattering article & Jane believes x is from Newcastle).

(64) Jane believes (∃x) (x wrote that unflattering article & x is from Newcastle).

Formulation (63) represents the *de re* reading of (62), and (64), the *de dicto* reading (although see 9.3.2.1 for Quine's objections to formulations such as (63)).

6.5. Wittgenstein

6.5.1. Differences Between Wittgenstein and Russell

The Wittgenstein of *Tractatus Logico-Philosophicus* admired Russell for having shown that the "apparent logical form of a proposition" was not necessarily its real one (*Tractatus*, 4.0031), but there are differences between Wittgenstein's treatment of descriptions and Russell's. One difference is a fairly obvious technical one. Russell had used the identity sign in his notation to secure the uniqueness of the object denoted by the description. For example,

(65) (∃x) [x is king of France & (y) (y is king of France → y = x)]

is how Russell would have rendered

(66) There is one and only one king of France.

Wittgenstein outlawed the identity sign from ideal notation as superfluous. Thus, if he would have used the existential quantifier in his final analysis of sentences containing descriptions (and this is perhaps debatable), he would have rendered (66) as

(67) (∃x) [x is king of France & ⌐(∃x) (∃y) (x is king of France & y is king of France)],

which can be read as

(68)   There is a king of France, and it is not the case that there
are two different things that are king of France. (See
Tractatus, 5.5321.)

More important, from the philosophical point of view, Wittgenstein's conception of analysis was not inspired by epistemological
considerations, as Russell's was. Thus, while the guiding principle in
Russell's treatment of descriptions was the dictum, "Every proposition
which we can understand must be composed wholly of constituents with
which we are acquainted" (Russell 1912/1959:32), for Wittgenstein all
analysis was predicated on the more neutral assumption, "The configuration of objects in a situation corresponds to the configuration of
simple signs in the propositional sign" (*Tractatus*, 3.21).

As we have seen, Russell's fundamental contribution was to treat
definite descriptions, which Frege had regarded as a type of name, as
being on a par with indefinite noun phrases. Essentially, his method
consisted in using the quantifier-and-variable apparatus to disperse the
content of a description from subject (or object) position to predicative
position. Therefore, in Russell's theory, Frege's generality notation (or
an equivalent symbolism) was a sine qua non for the correct representation of sentences containing descriptions. As we shall see, where
Wittgenstein differed fundamentally from Russell in respect of descriptions was in his own attitude toward generality. (The theory of meaning
put forward in the *Tractatus* is discussed in detail in 1.2.1-1.2.5.)

6.5.2. Determinacy of Sense

Wittgenstein assumed that, at some level of analysis, every meaningful proposition had a *determinate* or completely explicit meaning
(*Tractatus*, 3.23). We saw in 1.2 that the Wittgenstein of *Tractatus
Logico-Philosophicus* viewed propositions as pictures of facts and supposed that there was a one-one correlation between each element of a
fact and each element of the proposition that described it. Combined
with this view of how language worked, the assumption that sense was
determinate led inexorably to the belief that the analysis of a sentence
would terminate only in the uncovering of irreducibly simple symbols
(names) standing for irreducibly simple objects (*Gegenstände*).

We can see why names and *Gegenstände* are required to secure determinacy of sense within the picture theory by considering the sentence

(69)   The European Union is in the northern hemisphere.
(See also 1.2.3.)

According to the picture theory, a meaningful sentence expresses a proposition that has an identical structure to the fact it describes. This means that we cannot say that the description 'the European Union' designates a constituent of the fact described by (69); for, if the sentence were uttered in 50 years' time, it would still be meaningful *but there might not be a European Union*. Thus, in Wittgenstein's picture theory, the description 'the European Union' would not count as a genuine constituent of the proposition expressed by (69), at least not when the proposition was fully analyzed. We might try saying that the real constituents of the fact are the member countries of the Union, namely, France, Britain, Germany, and so on. However, these too might disappear. For example, Britain could be broken up into England, Scotland, and Wales, with Northern Ireland going to the Republic of Ireland. But sentence (69) would still be meaningful. We might then try as candidates for the constituents of the fact the various regions of the countries in the European Union. But this would not work either, for they, too, are destructible.

To prevent this regress becoming an infinite one, we have to make the bold assumption, as Wittgenstein did, that at some point in the process of decomposition, you reach a kind of linguistic and metaphysical bedrock beyond which it is impossible to proceed. At this point, we would have uncovered our names (on the linguistic side) and our *Gegenstände* (on the metaphysical side). Thus we see that it is only by invoking the notions of names and *Gegenstände* that Wittgenstein can maintain that meaning is always determinate (definite, leaving nothing tacit) and, at the same time, hold to the view that propositions are pictures of facts.

6.5.3. The Concept of Description

The names and *Gegenstände* of the *Tractatus* are the building blocks in a conception of description (Beschreibung) that had an extremely general application, one that went well beyond the notion of definite descriptions. Nowhere is the significance of description made clearer than in section 5.4711 of the *Tractatus* (the theme is reprised in *Philosophical Investigations*, I, §§46, 49, but from a rather different perspective), where Wittgenstein equates "the essence of a proposition" with the "essence of all description." The model put forward by Wittgenstein in the *Tractatus* can be summed up as follows: Names stood for irreducibly simple objects in the world (*Gegenstände*), naming was a preparation for description, and description consisted in the compounding of names so as to describe the world (see *Tractatus*, 3.2-3.26); accordingly, the Gegenstände made up what Wittgenstein called the world's "substance" (2.021). When what was described was a fact, that is, something consisting in certain objects standing in a certain relation to each other, the term 'description' was synonymous with 'proposition'. When what was described was a complex object, such as my watch or your broom, the term 'description' was synonymous with 'definite description'.

This should not be taken to mean that for Wittgenstein the term 'description' had two distinct senses. The two ways in which description worked were two sides of the same coin, as appears to be confirmed by an entry to Wittgenstein's notebooks (*Notebooks 1914-1916*, p. 4). There, Wittgenstein jots down a symbolic representation of how a sentence containing a description might be analyzed:

(70) ϕa & ϕb & aRb =Def. $\phi[aRb]$.

(The symbol '=Def.' indicates that the flanking expressions are to be understood as synonyms for each other.) Now, Wittgenstein gives little explanation of (70), but it can plausibly be taken to mean that a statement that the thing consisting in a's being in the relation R to b is ϕ or is a ϕ is just an abbreviation for the conjunction of the statements (a) that a has the property ϕ, (b) that b has the property ϕ, and (c) that a is in the relation R to b. This rather abstract explanation is best understood in a concrete example. Take the sentence

(71) My broom is in the corner. (See *Philosophical Investigations*, I, §60.)

Here, the description 'my broom' would correspond to the '[aRb]' of (70), where 'a' stands in place of a name for the broomstick part of the broom, 'b' in place of a name for the brush, and 'R' in place of the relational expression 'is attached to'. In other words, 'my broom' is taken to be an abbreviation for something like

(72)   the thing consisting in my broomstick being attached to my brush.

The expression 'is in the corner' in (71) would correspond to the Greek letter 'φ' in (70). Given definition (70), sentence (71) would really mean something like

(73)   My broomstick is in the corner & my brush is in the corner & my broomstick is attached to my brush.

Now, if we assume that the broomstick and the brush are *Gegenstände* (they obviously are not), the expansion of (71) to (73) gives a rough idea of how the Wittgenstein of the *Tractatus* envisaged analyzing sentences containing descriptions (he never gave a worked example). It is important to note that (73) is a *truth-functional compound* (see 1.2.4) of what can be called *atomic propositions* (see 1.2.3 and 1.2.4), that is, simple propositions whose component expressions refer only to genuinely simple objects. Wittgenstein thought that every sentence in language must, in the final analysis, express a truth function of atomic propositions.

To return to (70), we can now see that there is an obvious similarity between the string '[aRb]', which gives the logical structure of a definite description, and the string 'aRb', which gives the form of an atomic proposition. The brackets '[. . .]' simply enable the string 'aRb' to be embedded in a superordinate proposition. What the similarity in question appears to indicate is that, for Wittgenstein, a definite description bore substantially the same relation to the names into which it could be resolved as a proposition did to the names of which it was composed.

6.5.4. General Sentences

6.5.4.1. Propositional prototypes. We see from the foregoing remarks that Wittgenstein's preoccupation with the determinacy of sense led him to suppose that all sentences/propositions could ultimately be expanded to truth functions of atomic propositions (see also 1.2.4). Given that supposition, general sentences presented a severe, and ultimately overwhelming, challenge.

General sentences differ from particular sentences, such as

(74)   Peter is next to Jane,

in that, in the former, something is asserted of *a* so and so, *some* so and so, *all* so and so's, or *no* so and so's. As we saw in 6.1.3.1 above (see also Chapter 10), the analysis of general sentences is based on the notion of a propositional function or propositional prototype. In the *Tractatus,* Wittgenstein sometimes uses the term *Urbild,* which translates into English as something like 'proto-picture'. The reason a propositional function can be seen as a prototype is that we can use such an expression as a kind of blueprint for forming determinate propositions or sentences by inserting different names into the gap provisionally filled by the variable 'x', 'y', and so on.

Thus we can say that

(75)   All things are extended in space,

for example, can be analyzed as saying that the function

(76) x is extended in space

produces a true sentence whatever we substitute for x. In other words, if (75) is true, we could go through the entire range of substitution instances for (76), inserting in turn every object expression we can think of—'your dog', 'this stone', 'Smith's bike', 'Humphrey Bogart', and so on—and none of the resulting sentences would be false.

It is because general sentences are based on an *Urbild*—to use Wittgenstein's term—that they are necessarily indeterminate; for the whole point of an *Urbild* is that it contains variables instead of names.

6.5.4.2. All ordinary sentences express general propositions. Now, the Wittgenstein of the *Tractatus* thought that in ordinary language, *all* our sentences expressed general propositions. We can see why Wittgenstein thought this by considering one of his favorite examples:

(77)   The watch is lying on the table. (*Notebooks,* pp. 69-70)

The expression 'the watch' in (77) is a definite description and so the whole sentence can be expanded to something with a structure comparable to 'ϕa & ϕb & aRb' (with many more names than just a and b).To effect such an expansion, however, we would have to decompose the description 'the watch' into simple symbols that were each individually correlated with the *Gegenstände* that went into the composition of the watch—the spring, the hands, the metal plate, and so on. But it is quite implausible to suppose that whenever someone uses a sentence such as (77), he or she is saying something about the individual components of the watch.

Wittgenstein avoided this unpalatable supposition by saying that the understanding of everyday language was based on "tacit conventions" (*Abmachungen*) that were "enormously complicated" (*Tractatus,* 4.002). In an entry to the *Notebooks* (p. 70), Wittgenstein makes clear what these *Abmachungen* were: They were "definitions with *a certain generality of form*" (*Allgemeinheit der Form*). In other words, when we used ordinary language, we were always using expressions that could be analyzed using the generality notation (*Allgemeinheitsbezeichnung*). Wittgenstein reiterates this point in section 3.24 of the *Tractatus,* where he says, first of all, that when a description occurs in a sentence or proposition, this can be seen from a certain indeterminacy in the proposition, and then he immediately adds: "In fact the notation for generality *contains* a prototype (*Urbild*)." If we apply this thesis to (77), it seems that in uttering such a sentence we are expressing something that, in very broad outline, amounts to this:

(78)   ($\exists x$) ($\exists y$) etc. ($\exists \phi$) (ϕxy etc. & x is lying on the table & y is lying on the table etc.).

(The Greek letter 'ϕ' in (78) is a variable like 'x' and 'y', but it refers to relations and not to things.) In other words, (77) is really a disguised general sentence. In this respect, the Wittgenstein of the *Tractatus* and Russell coincide.

6.5.4.3. Alignment of general propositions and truth functions. But if we employed only sentences that expressed general propositions, Wittgenstein's entire logico-philosophical apparatus would be inapplicable to ordinary language. For, as we have seen, Wittgenstein thought that all sentences expressed truth functions of atomic propositions. In the *Tractatus,* he sought to resolve this problem by aligning general propositions with truth-functional compounds of atomic propositions. To see how he went about this, we have to consider some of the special symbolism he employed.

In section 5.501 of the *Tractatus,* Wittgenstein introduced the symbol '$(\bar{\xi})$'. This stood for a class of propositions. The letter 'N', when prefixed to '$(\bar{\xi})$', expressed the joint negation of all the propositions in the class designated by '$(\bar{\xi})$'. So if '$(\bar{\xi})$' stood for the propositions p, q, and r, the expression 'N$(\bar{\xi})$' would stand for the joint negation of p, q, and r; that is,

(79) $N(\bar{\xi}) = \sim p \ \& \sim q \ \& \sim r.$

Where Wittgenstein shows his inclination to explain generality in terms of atomic propositions is in section 5.52. There, he considers the case where $(\bar{\xi})$ is the class of all propositions that can be formed from a given function fx. In other words, he considers the case in which, if a, b, c, and so on are all the objects in the world:

(80) $N(\bar{\xi}) = \sim fa \ \& \sim fb \ \& \sim fc$ etc.

Now Wittgenstein argues (5.52) that, when $N(\bar{\xi})$ is determined as in (80), then

(81) $N(\bar{\xi}) = \sim (\exists x) \ (fx).$

That is to say,

(82) $\sim (\exists x) \ (fx) = \sim fa \ \& \sim fb \ \& \sim fc$ etc.

In other words, a general sentence such as

(83)   Nothing is extended in space

would be equivalent to

(84)   *a* is not extended in space & *b* is not extended in space & *c* is not extended in space etc.,

where *a*, *b*, *c*, and so on are all the objects in the world.
Now, from (82), we can derive definitions of

(85) $(\exists x)\,(fx)$

(86) $(x)\,(fx)$

by invoking some simple logical laws. Let us start with (85), that is, with *existential quantification*. (85) is the negation of

(87) $\sim(\exists x)\,(fx)$.

Therefore, given identity (81), we have

(88) $\sim N(\bar{\xi}) = (\exists x)\,(fx)$.

The expression '$N(\bar{\xi})$', it will be recalled, stood for

(89) $\sim fa$ & $\sim fb$ & $\sim fc$ etc.

Now there is a logical law that says that the negation of a joint negation, that is,

(90) $\sim(\sim p\ \&\ \sim q)$

is equivalent to a plain disjunction:

(91) $p \vee q$.

((91) can be read as '*p* or *q*'. [For truth-functional symbols, see 1.2.4.])
Thus the negation of (89) is

(92) $fa \lor fb \lor fc$ etc.

Therefore, given (88),

(93) $(\exists x) (fx) = fa \lor fb \lor fc$ etc.

In other words,

(94) Something is extended in space

would be equivalent to

(95) *a* is extended in space or *b* is extended in space or *c* is
extended in space etc.

We can now consider (86), that is, *universal quantification.* Obviously enough, (86) is equivalent to

(96) $\smallsmile(\exists x) (\smallsmile fx)$.

(96) is just like (87), except that we have '$\smallsmile fx$' instead of 'fx'. Therefore, given (82), we have

(97) $\smallsmile(\exists x) (\smallsmile fx) = \smallsmile\smallsmile fa \ \& \ \smallsmile\smallsmile fb \ \& \ \smallsmile\smallsmile fc$ etc;

that is,

(98) $\smallsmile(\exists x) (\smallsmile fx) = fa \ \& \ fb \ \& \ fc$ etc.

In other words, given that (86) and (96) are equivalent, a universal sentence such as

(99) Everything is extended in space

would be analyzable as

(100) *a* is extended in space and *b* is extended in space and *c* is extended in space etc.

6.5.4.4. The problem unresolved. So, in the sections of the *Tractatus* to which we have just referred, Wittgenstein appears to be saying that general propositions or sentences are actually enormously long truth functions of atomic propositions. A further indication of Wittgenstein's attitude toward generality is given by section 5.522, according to which the generality notation "gives prominence to constants." Constants, in contrast to variables, are permanently correlated with objects in the world. Thus the constants Wittgenstein has in mind here might well be the names that can be inserted into propositional functions to produce atomic propositions. In other words, generality is again to be looked at in terms of the atomic propositions that result when names are inserted in place of a variable.

The view that general propositions can be replaced by truth functions of atomic propositions resolves the problem of how general sentences can have a determinate sense but, on other hand, if general propositions *are* simply truth functions of atomic propositions, there is no way of escaping the conclusion that a sentence such as (77) expresses a proposition in which every single component of the watch is a constituent.

Thus Wittgenstein faced an irreconcilable dilemma. The existence of general propositions, as explained in the classical Fregean manner, was at variance with his view that determinacy of sense could be guaranteed only if all propositions could be expanded to truth functions of atomic propositions. However, if general propositions too were reduced to long truth functions of atomic propositions, they could no longer be used to capture the indeterminacy inherent in human language.

To a certain extent, Wittgenstein tried to finesse the problem. This is noticeable when he introduces the symbol '($\bar{\xi}$)' in section 5.501. There, he explains that the set of propositions for which '($\bar{\xi}$)' stands can be determined in any one of three ways. First, by direct enumeration: *p* & *q* & *r* etc.; second, using a propositional prototype such as *fx*; and, third, using what Wittgenstein calls a "formal law." The third method need not concern us here but the difference between the other two is crucial, in that effectively it *is* the distinction between the two views of generality with which Wittgenstein wrestled. If every general proposition can be replaced by some operation such as joint negation on a class of atomic propositions (ξ̄) that is given by enumeration, there is no place for indeterminacy in language. On the other hand, if (ξ) is based upon some protoproposition or function *fx*, generality is not reducible to truth functions of atomic propositions; hence there will be a way of expressing indeterminacy. Wittgenstein says that which method is chosen for defining (ξ̄) is unimportant (5.501). As has just been observed, however, it is of the utmost importance. Indeed, the whole problem concerning the reduction of generality to truth functions of atomic propositions given by enumeration is that it is wholly implausible, at least as an account of how natural language works. By dismissing the distinction between defining (ξ̄) by enumeration and defining it as all the propositions that can be obtained from a given propositional function, Wittgenstein appears to be abstaining from saying explicitly whether or not general propositions *actually* can be replaced by long truth functions of atomic propositions.

6.6. Summary

Like Frege, the linguist is naturally tempted to regard descriptions as a subclass of proper names, owing to apparently obvious similarities between the two types of expressions: Names and definite noun phrases have identical distributional ranges in syntax, and it frequently appears to be the case that a description is being used, as names are, to refer to an individual. On the other hand, epistemologically speaking, descriptions appear to be designed for a very different purpose than names. Thus, as Russell pointed out in "On Denoting," a definite description enables us to talk about things with which we are not directly acquainted, such as the center of mass of the solar system at a particular moment or the sensation of heat experienced by another person on a particular occasion.

As a consequence of considerations of this sort, Russell devised a theory in which definite descriptions were eliminated in favor of terms that referred only to objects of acquaintance. In developing his theory, Russell simultaneously solved a number of puzzles, perhaps the most important of which is the paradox of the name relation.

A related issue arises from the fact that many philosophers have assumed that meaning is always determinate. As has just been noted, in the work of Russell, this determinacy was characterized in epistemological terms, hence the famous distinction between acquaintance and description. It was only because descriptions could at some underlying level be analyzed into epistemologically primitive components, or so Russell thought, that such expressions had a determinate meaning.

The Wittgenstein of the *Tractatus* took a view similar to Russell's, although he was not motivated by epistemological considerations. Thus he secured determinacy of sense by arguing that descriptions could always be analyzed into simpler expressions standing for the ultimate substance of the world. Wittgenstein's views led to problems concerning the analysis of general sentences, problems, it seems, that were not properly resolved in the *Tractatus*.

In the course of our discussion of Russell's work, a brief excursion was made into Quine's account of the ontogenesis of reference. Quine suggests that, to a certain extent, Russell's theory of descriptions can be viewed as a reconstruction—in reverse—of the ontogenesis of reference.

7

Descriptions as Names

7.1. The Fregean Theory

7.1.1. Concepts and Objects

7.1.1.1. Introduction. In linguistics, Frege is well known for his sense-nominatum (Sinn-Bedeutung) distinction (see 4.3.1.1). Another key dichotomy was between object (Gegenstand) and concept (Begriff), and this division was examined at length in a paper called, not surprisingly, "Ueber Begriff und Gegenstand" (published 1892, which appears here as Frege 1960:42-55). Concepts, or the expressions designating them, were predicative in nature, whereas object words, which Frege called proper names, were incapable of occurring as predicates. We might be tempted to say that this view is incorrect because in each of, for example,

(1)   *A* is Alexander the Great

and

(2)   *B* is the morning star,

we appear to have an object expression in predicative position. But that analysis betrays a failure to distinguish between 'is' as a marker of predication (a mere copula) and 'is' as the identity sign, in which role it has the same function as the '=' of arithmetic. In (1) and (2), 'is' does not indicate predication but serves to express what Frege called 'an equation' (1960:44). On the other hand, in

(3)   *A* is green,

'is' is a copula and 'green' occurs predicatively; that is, as a concept word. Frege took '=' to mean 'no other than', 'the same as', or 'identical with' (1960, p. 44, footnote) and, accordingly, sentence (2) would mean

(4)   *B* is no other than the morning star.

Here, what is predicated of (ascribed to) *B* is not the object the morning star but the concept *no other than the morning star*. Thus, in Frege's theory, an object expression such as 'the morning star' could form part of a predicate, but it could never *be* one (Frege 1960:43-44).

7.1.1.2. Concepts and generality. A further aspect of the concept-object distinction concerned the quantifier words 'all', 'some', 'no', and so on. Such words are used to form existential and universal sentences, that is, sentences about 'something' and 'everything', respectively. For example,

(5)   All Brazilians like football

(6)   Some Spaniards are great time trialists

can be seen as meaning:

(7)   Everything that is a Brazilian likes soccer

(8)   Some things that are Spaniards are great time trialists,

respectively. The ideas of *something* and *everything,* together with the derived notion *nothing,* are collectively referred to under the heading *generality.* Frege had argued in *"Funktion und Begriff"* (published 1891, which appears here as Frege, 1960:21-41) that general sentences were fundamentally different than the type of sentence that was discussed in the previous section. This was because, in such sentences, we expressed 'relations between concepts' (1960:48), as opposed to predicating a concept of an object. Consequently, words such as 'some', 'all', 'any', and 'no', being signs for generality, could be prefixed only to concept expressions and not to object expressions (Frege 1960:48). To understand what Frege meant by a relation between concepts, we need to consider briefly Frege's treatment of generality. This can be illustrated by his handling of sentences containing the word 'some'. (Frege's theory is discussed in detail in Chapter 10 of this book.)

For Frege, a general sentence such as

(9)   Some flower is red

meant something like this:

(10)   For at least one thing x: x is a flower and x is red.

The quasi-sentences

(11) x is a flower

(12) x is red

that occur in (10) indicate what are called *functions.* The characteristic of a function is that it has a vacant position in its structure, normally represented by an arbitrary letter 'x', 'y', or 'z'. To get a determinate sentence from a function, that is, one that can be used to make an assertion, the arbitrary letter needs to be replaced by an expression designating a specific object. For example, the substitution of the name 'Mars' for 'x' in (12) yields (returns) the sentence

(13)   Mars is red,

which, if uttered in isolation, expresses a truth. The fact that (13) expresses a truth shows that at least one substitution instance of '*x* is red' is true. This circumstance can be indicated using the symbol '(∃*x*)':

(14)   (∃*x*) (*x* is red),

which can be read as

(15)   For at least one thing *x: x* is red.

The object designated by the expression used to replace *x* in a particular substitution instance is called the *argument* of the function. In (13), for example, Mars is the argument of the function indicated by (12). Frege also regarded what we have designated by '∃*x*' as a function—he, in fact, uses a different notation—but one that took a *function* and not an object as its argument (1960:38). Frege called functions of this sort *second-order* or *second-level* functions. Therefore, another way of phrasing things, according to Frege at least, would be to say that (14) represents the circumstance in which the second-level function (∃*x*) takes as its argument the first-level function indicated by (12). Similarly, in sentence (9), which can be rewritten as

(16)   (∃*x*) (*x* is a flower & *x* is red),

the second-level function (∃*x*) takes as its argument the first-level function

(17)   *x* is a flower & *x* is red.

Sentence (16) will be true only if at least one substitution instance of (17) is true; that is, if there is at least one thing that is a flower and is red.

So far, we have discussed only functions that can be represented as quasi-sentences. However, mathematical expressions such as '2*x*' indicate functions too. Now, if we apply the function 2*x* to a number—say, 3—the result is another number, in this case, 6. In technical terms, 6 is the *value* of the function 2*x* for the argument 3. According to Frege, when a function such as (12) or (17) was applied to an object, the value was not a number but a *truth-value,* that is, either True or False. Using this terminology, Frege defined a concept as "a function whose value is always a truth-value" (1960:30). We can now see what Frege meant when he said that general sentences expressed a relation between concepts; an alternative way of looking at (14) and (9)/(16) is to see them in terms of a relation between two *concepts;* that is, as asserting that the first-level concepts *red* and *red flower* '[fall] *within*' (1960:51) a second-level concept (which, following Kenny 1995:122, might be glossed as *is instantiated*).

We can also see why the quantifier words 'all', 'some', 'any', and so on cannot be prefixed to object expressions, for, in Frege's theory, all such determiners indicate "the special kind of relation" (1960:48) to which we have just referred, and this is a relation that holds exclusively between concepts.

7.1.1.3. Concepts converted into objects. One of the critics of the explanation given of object and concept in Frege's *Die Grundlagen der Arithmetik* (The Foundations of Arithmetic; it appears here as Frege 1953) had argued that the sentence

(18)   The concept *horse* is easily attained

would present a counterexample to Frege's thesis. Here, the expression

(19)   the concept *horse*

appears to be an object expression, with

(20)   is easily attained

an obvious predicate. However, in view of its content, (19) must surely designate a concept. Thus the distinction between concept and object appears to break down. Frege responded in "Ueber Begriff und Gegenstand" by saying that the expression "the concept *horse*" did indeed designate an object and, for that very reason, did not designate a concept

(1960:45). Frege justifies this apparent piece of double-talk by pointing out that although 'is red' is a grammatical predicate in the sentence

(21)   This rose is red,

the expression

(22)   the grammatical predicate 'is red'

is not itself a predicate but a subject, as is shown by the following sentence:

(23)   The grammatical predicate 'is red' occurs frequently in English.

To call a predicative expression a predicate, we have to *refer* to the expression in question, and, in so doing, we deprive it of its predicative nature. Similarly, by calling the concept *horse* a concept, so as to talk about it, we 'convert' it into an object (1960:46). Thus whatever else may be wrong with Frege's distinction between object and concept, sentences such as (18) do not appear to pose any real difficulty for his thesis.

7.1.2. Object Expressions

7.1.2.1. The definite article. In the early work of Russell and in Wittgenstein's *Tractatus* (see the previous chapter), there is a fundamental cleavage between simple expressions (names) and complex expressions (descriptions and propositions). In the work of Frege, on the other hand, descriptions are regarded as names (Frege 1949:86), despite their obvious complexity. In fact, in *Die Grundlagen der Arithmetik*, Frege actually stated that the definite article (used in singular noun phrases) was a sure indication of a name (object expression), while the indefinite article indicated a concept expression (see §§51, 66, 68). Thus apparent subjects such as 'a woman' in

(24)   A woman came to see me

and apparent objects such as 'a washing machine' in

(25)   Smith has just purchased a washing machine

were not object expressions at all. (24) and (25) are general sentences and, as we saw in 7.1.1.2 above, Frege thought that such sentences asserted a relation between concepts. Thus (24) and (25) would assert what can be represented as

(26)   ($\exists x$) (x is a woman & x came to see me)

and

(27)   ($\exists x$) (x is a washing machine & Smith has just purchased x),

respectively. Generic definite noun phrases such as 'the lion' in

(28)   The lion is a feline creature

were treated as easily recognizable exceptions to the general rule (Frege 1960:45). Thus (28) would be treated as being synonymous with

(29)   All lions are feline creatures.

(The symbolic notation for universal sentences such as (29) is discussed in 10.3.2 and 10.3.3.3.)

7.1.2.2. Value ranges and the function: \. In *Grundgesetze der Arithmetik* (Basic Laws of Arithmetic; published 1893-1903, which appears here as Frege 1964), Frege proposed a formal method for dealing with the definite article. In §11, he introduced a function, represented by the symbol '\', that could be applied to what Frege called the value range or the course-of-values of a concept. The value range of a concept was more or less identical with the class of objects that fell under the concept, that is, the class of objects for which the concept, considered as a function, returned the value True.

As we saw in the previous chapter, the appropriate use of a sentence such as

(30) The discoverer of the elliptical shape of the planetary orbits died in misery

presupposes that the definite description

(31) the discoverer of the elliptical shape of the planetary orbits

has one and only one referent, namely, Kepler. An alternative way of viewing this circumstance is to say that there is one and only one object in the value range of the concept *is a discoverer of the elliptical shape of the planetary orbits*. From this perspective, definite descriptions can be seen as being built up from the definite article plus a concept whose value range contains only one object.

Now Frege's function \ was defined in such a way that, when it was applied to a value range for a concept under which only one object fell, the value of the function was that object. Frege designated value ranges by replacing the arbitrary letter '*x*', '*y*', and so on in the sign for a function by a Greek vowel, enclosing the result in parentheses and then prefixing to the whole the same Greek letter with a smooth breathing symbol (1960:27). For example, the value range of the function $x^2 - 4x$ is

(32) $\grave{\varepsilon}\,(\varepsilon^2 - 4\varepsilon)$.

Obviously enough, the function $x^2 - 4x$ never has a truth-value as its value. On the other hand, $x + 3 = 5$ does. Thus the function $x + 3 = 5$ is also a concept, namely, *which when increased by 3 yields 5*. The value range of this concept is

(33) $\grave{\varepsilon}\,(\varepsilon + 3 = 5)$.

If we apply Frege's function \ to (33), we have

(34) $\backslash\grave{\varepsilon}\,(\varepsilon + 3 = 5)$,

which delivers as its value the number 2. Similarly,

(35) \ ἐ (ε is a discoverer of the elliptical shape of the planetary
        orbits)

has as its value the individual Kepler. In other words, (35) is equivalent
to (31).

In Frege's account, then, definite descriptions are built up as follows. First, we have a concept such as *is a discoverer of the elliptical
shape of the planetary orbits*, which has one and only one object in its
value range. The linguistic expression for the concept—in this case,
'discoverer of the elliptical shape of the planetary orbits'—stands for
the value range. Here, this is

(36) ἐ (ε is a discoverer of the elliptical shape of the planetary
        orbits).

The definite article is the ordinary-language counterpart for the function \, which, when applied to a value range, delivers the unique object
in the value range. It is in this way that description (31) picks out the
individual Kepler, the only object in the value range of *is a discoverer
of the elliptical shape of the planetary orbits.*

It might be asked why Frege did not simply identify the value range
of a concept with the object that fell under it. If he had made that
identification, (31) would have been equivalent not to (35) but to (36),
which on the surface seems less complicated. The reason Frege chose
not to follow that course is given in footnote 17 in the *Grundgesetze*.
There, Frege points out that a value range can be identified with an
object only when that object is not itself given as a value range (Frege
appears to have taken value ranges to be objects in their own right; Frege
1960:26) and so the identification does not hold generally. Why this is
so can be illustrated in the following way.

Let us use the symbol 'Δ' to designate a particular object. Then

(37) ἐ (ε = Δ)

is a value range containing one object only, namely, the thing that is
identical to Δ. Now, if the object falling under a concept is to be
identified with the concept's value range, we have the following equation:

(38) $\grave{\varepsilon} (\varepsilon = \Delta) = \Delta.$

Let us consider the case when the object Δ is itself a value range; for example,

(39) $\grave{\alpha} (\alpha \text{ is Spanish}).$

(Note that the fact that we have changed the Greek vowel from 'ε' to 'α' is unimportant.)

If Δ is imagined to be value range (39), we have

(40) $\grave{\varepsilon} (\varepsilon = \grave{\alpha} (\alpha \text{ is Spanish})) = \grave{\alpha} (\alpha \text{ is Spanish}),$

by substitution of (39) for 'Δ' in (38). Like (38), (40) asserts an identity between an object, namely, value range (39), and the value range of the concept under which that object falls, that is,

(41) $\grave{\varepsilon} (\varepsilon = \grave{\alpha} (\alpha \text{ is Spanish})).$

Earlier on in the *Grundgesetze* (§§8-10), Frege had shown that a sentence asserting an identity between two value ranges always had the same truth-value as the corresponding universal sentence (for universal quantification, see 6.1.3.1). Thus, if Φ and Ψ are arbitrary concepts or functions,

(42) $\grave{\varepsilon} (\Phi\varepsilon) = \grave{\alpha} (\Psi\alpha)$

always has the same truth-value as

(43) $(x) (\Phi x \leftrightarrow \Psi x),$

which can be read as

(44) For everything x: if Φx, then Ψx; and vice versa.

(For the symbol '$\leftrightarrow$', see Tables 1.3 and 1.8 in Chapter 1.) In other words, if the value range defined on the concept Φ is identical to that defined on the concept Ψ, everything that is a Φ is also a Ψ and vice versa.

Now, in our own sentence (40), we had an equation between the value ranges defined on the following two concepts: = $\grave{\alpha}$ (α *is Spanish*) and *is Spanish*. Given that (42) and (43) always have the same truth value, (40) must have the same truth value as

(45) (x) [x = $\grave{\alpha}$ (α is Spanish) $\leftrightarrow$ x is Spanish],

which can be read as

(46) For everything x: if x = $\grave{\alpha}$ (α is Spanish), then x is Spanish; and vice versa.

Now it is readily seen that (45)/(46) is not true. For example, if we write in the name 'Azaña' for x, we have

(47) Azaña = $\grave{\alpha}$ (α is Spanish) $\leftrightarrow$ Azaña is Spanish,

which can be read as

(48) If Azaña = $\grave{\alpha}$ (α is Spanish), Azaña is Spanish; and vice versa.

The connective '$\leftrightarrow$' (see 1.2.4) is defined in such a way that the two sentences it joins together must have the same truth-value for the overall sentence to be true. Now, while 'Azaña is Spanish' is true, 'Azaña = $\grave{\alpha}$ (α is Spanish)' is not true, because the expression '$\grave{\alpha}$ (α is Spanish)', if it designates anything, designates the class of all Spaniards and not the individual Spaniard Azaña. Therefore, (47)/(48) is false, and, if that is false, so is (45)/(46). By the same token, (40) also is false. In this way, it is shown that the identity between a value range and the unique object falling under a particular concept—which is exemplified in (38)—does not hold when that unique object is a value range itself.

7.1.2.3. Vacuous and improper descriptions. Definite descriptions purport to designate one and only one individual. On occasion, however, nothing or more than one object fits the description. As we saw above, Russell's analysis of sentences containing descriptions was devised so that sentences containing descriptions that no object or more than one object fitted would be treated as being false. Frege adopted a different approach to the descriptions contained in such sentences. He stipulated that, when the argument of the function represented by '\' was not a value range containing only one object—for example, when it was a value range that contained more than one object or none—the value delivered by the function was to be the argument itself (Frege 1964:50). For example, 'the square root of 64' designates two objects, namely, 8 and −8, and so the value of

(49) $\backslash \varepsilon \, (\varepsilon \times \varepsilon = 64)$

is the value range

(50) $\varepsilon \, (\varepsilon \times \varepsilon = 64).$

Similarly, the value of

(51) $\backslash \grave{\varepsilon} \, (\varepsilon \text{ is current king of France})$

is

(52) $\grave{\varepsilon} \, (\varepsilon \text{ is current king of France})$

because no object falls under the concept *is current king of France*. It is readily seen that Frege's provisions for improper and vacuous descriptions are somewhat artificial.

7.2. Referential Descriptions

7.2.1. Attributive and Referential Descriptions

As we saw in 4.3.1.1, Frege argued that a description determined its nominatum or reference through its sense. The apparatus discussed in 7.1.2.2 above can be seen as a formalization of the way in which a description's sense delivered its nominatum. In a much discussed paper, "Reference and Definite Descriptions" (1966), the American philosopher Keith Donnellan argued that the reference of a description was not always determined by its sense.

Donnellan builds up to this claim by considering the sentence

(53) Smith's murderer is insane,

which has now become a cliché in the literature. According to Donnellan, there are two quite different ways in which the definite description 'Smith's murderer' could be used in the making of a statement. In the first use, which Donnellan called the *attributive* use, sentence (53) would be roughly equivalent to

(54) Whoever murdered Smith is insane.

In the attributive use, a speaker "states something about whoever or whatever is the so-and-so" and "the attribute of being the so-and-so is all important" (Donnellan 1966:285).

Donnellan's account of attributively used descriptions seems to be compatible with both Russell's and Frege's theories. On a Russellian analysis (see 6.1.3.2), (53) would come out as

(55) $(\exists x)$ [x murdered Smith & (y) (y murdered Smith $\rightarrow y = x$) & x is insane]

and, on a Fregean analysis, it would be

(56) \ $\hat{\varepsilon}$ (ε murdered Smith) is insane.

It is true that, according to (55), sentence (53) is false if nothing or more than one thing fits the description 'Smith's murderer', and it is also true that, according to (56), (53) is very *probably* false if nothing or more than one thing fits the description—a value range is not likely to be a murderer. However, Donnellan offers no logical symbolism and does not say either way whether (53) would be false or neither true nor false if nothing or more than one thing fitted the description. Thus there is no explicit incompatibility with either Russell or Frege.

The second use of descriptions, which Donnellan called the *referential* use, is best illustrated by the following example (inspired by one of Donnellan's). A person called Cuitláhuac has been convicted of Smith's murder and everybody knows that Cuitláhuac is Smith's murderer. It is later discovered that Cuitláhuac is insane. Now I wish to convey this fact to somebody but I find it difficult to pronounce the name 'Cuitláhuac'. Therefore, I resort to the next best way of referring to Cuitláhuac, namely, using the description 'Smith's murderer', and I utter sentence (53) and my addressee recovers the fact that Cuitláhuac is insane. This would be a referential use of the description.

Again, Donnellan does not actually say what the logical form of a statement with a referentially used description would be, but the implication throughout is that what is envisaged is *something* along the lines of 'ϕa', that is, name plus predicate. We see this when, for example, Donnellan discusses the interrogative sentence

(57) Who is the man drinking a martini?

Here, an attributive use of the description might occur if the sentence was uttered by the president of the Teetotalers' Society, who, at one of the society's meetings, had just been informed that a man was drinking a martini, in breach of the rules. A referential use might occur if the sentence was uttered by someone who had noticed an interesting-looking man apparently drinking a martini and wished to refer specifically to that man. Donnellan says that, if the description 'the man drinking a martini' has been used referentially, then "we have asked a question about a particular person" (p. 287). This seems to imply that, in Russellian terms, a particular individual is a *constituent* of the proposition or propositional content.

It is interesting to note that, insofar as the describing condition in a definite description can be expressed using a relative clause, the referential-attributive distinction may be grammaticalized in some languages. For example, if we paraphrase sentence (53) as

(58) He who murdered Smith is insane,

we discover that Spanish has two possible nonsynonymous translations. First, we could use the subjunctive mood:

(59)   El que haya matado a Smith está loco ('He who killed
[subjunctive] Smith is insane').

This would give an indisputably attributive reading of the description
'Smith's murderer'. In other words, insanity would be predicated of the
murderer qua murderer and, if it turned out that no one had murdered
Smith, the whole statement would lose its point. On the other hand, we
could also use the indicative:

(60)   El que ha matado a Smith está loco.

Here, the Spanish description 'el que ha matado a Smith' could be given
either an attributive *or* a referential reading. If the description 'el que
ha matado a Smith' is used referentially—for example, if our wish is
simply to pick out Cuitláhuac by any means and the use of this particular
description is just one of several different tools available—then it is not
absolutely necessary that Sr. Cuitláhuac actually is a murderer. So it is
only when the indicative occurs that Donnellan's remarks (see 7.2.2
below) apply about the speaker being able to say something true of the
intended referent of the description even when this individual does not
actually fit the description. Thus we could say that, while the occurrence
of the subjunctive determines an unequivocally attributive reading, the
indicative is compatible with both the attributive and the referential
uses.

7.2.2. Obliteration of Descriptive Content

As we have just seen, statements containing referentially used
descriptions, in Donnellan's sense, appear to have a distinctly non-
Russellian logical form. On a Donnellan-style referential reading (53),
for example, would appear—given the circumstances imagined above—
to have the logical form '*Ic*' (where '*I*' translates 'insane' and '*c*' stands
for Cuitláhuac), whereas, for Russell, the logical form would be as in
(55).

Similarly, Donnellan's referentially used descriptions differ from
descriptions as they are envisaged by Frege, for, according to Donnellan,
it is *not necessary for the nominatum to be delivered by the sense.*
Donnellan states that "using a definite description referentially, a

speaker may say something true even though the description correctly applies to nothing" (p. 298). Thus, in the referential use of a description, "it is quite possible for the correct identification [of the referent] to be made even though no one fits the description," because the description is "merely one tool for doing a certain job—calling attention to a person or thing—and in general any other device for doing the same job, another description or a name, would do as well" (p. 285). What this implies is that a referentially used description can pick out something *x* even if *x* does not fit the description and *something else y* does, provided that *y* is not the thing to which reference was intended to be made. This possibility is illustrated by the following case. You see Jane Smith in the corner drinking what appears to be champagne (it is in fact Spanish wine). Jane Smith looks particularly happy and you say,

(61) The woman in the corner drinking champagne is happy tonight,

meaning to convey that Jane Smith is happy tonight. Unbeknown to you, some other, very unhappy, woman in the corner (Carmen Jiménez) is drinking genuine champagne and, in fact, is the only champagne drinker in the corner. According to Donnellan's view, provided that you were using the description referentially, you would be deemed to have 'said something true', despite the fact that, taken literally, your sentence would be false. In other words, in your assertion, happiness would be predicated not of the nominatum delivered by the Fregean sense of the description, namely, Carmen Jiménez, but of the person to whom you the speaker intended to refer, namely, Jane Smith. Therefore, in Donnellan's referential use, the content of a description (in Fregean terms, its sense) can be obliterated and, in this respect, Donnellan's account diverges both from Frege's treatment and from the decompositional approach favored by Russell and Wittgenstein (see the previous chapter).

7.2.3. The Status of Donnellan's Referential Descriptions

In a celebrated paper, Kripke (1979b) sought to rebut the view that the referential use of descriptions was at variance with Russell's theory of descriptions. His argument was based on a theory that has been pioneered by Grice (see, for example, Grice 1975). According to Grice, there is often a distinction between the meaning of a linguistic expression per se and the meaning with which a speaker uses the expression on a particular occasion. This distinction can be illustrated by the following examples (the first two are from Kripke 1979b).

One burglar says to another,

(62)   The cops are around the corner.

Obviously enough, (62) in itself means only that the cops are around the corner. But presumably, in uttering this sentence, the speaker would intend to convey something in addition to this bare fact, for example, that he or she and the other burglar should leave right away. This additional, context-determined, piece of meaning is not part of the bare meaning of the linguistic expression used but belongs to what can loosely be called the speaker's meaning. Similarly, someone recalling a conjuring trick in which a handkerchief is made to appear to change color might say,

(63)   The handkerchief looked red,

meaning to imply not just that the handkerchief *looked* red (this would be the bare meaning of the expression used) but also that perhaps it was not *really* red, that this was just an illusion. This additional component would be the speaker's meaning. Grice (1975) codified general principles of rational behavior that, he argued, could be used to account for the way in which in everyday conversation what we have been calling the speaker's meaning was overlaid on the bare meaning of linguistic expressions.

Now, Kripke applied this distinction between speaker's meaning and expression meaning to definite descriptions and ordinary proper names, which, together, he calls *designators*. He distinguished between the 'speaker's referent' of a designator and its 'semantic referent'. The speaker's reference is the referential counterpart of speaker meaning, while semantic reference is the counterpart of expression meaning. In our example (61), Carmen Jiménez would be the semantic referent of the description 'the woman in the corner drinking champagne', while Jane Smith would be the speaker's referent. According to Kripke, an analogous distinction holds for proper names, too. For example, two people see Smith in the distance and mistake him for Jones. They discuss what Smith is doing, namely, raking the leaves, but refer to Smith by using the name 'Jones'. The name 'Jones' has Jones as its semantic referent but, on this particular occasion, the speaker's referent is Smith.

Kripke argued that Donnellan's referential-attributive distinction should be regarded as an instance of the distinction between speaker's reference and semantic reference. Leaving aside the case in which deictic words ('this', 'that', and so on) occur, the semantic referent of a designator is determined by the rules of the language to which the designator belongs. These general rules translate into what Kripke (1979b:15) calls a "*general* intention of the speaker [of the language in question] to refer to a certain object whenever the designator is used." The speaker's referent, on the other hand, is determined by "a *specific* intention, on a given occasion, to refer to a certain object." Kripke distinguishes between two cases. First, the general intention may coincide with the specific intention, as when someone uses 'Smith' to refer to Smith or 'the 42nd president of the USA' to refer to Clinton. This Kripke calls the 'simple' case. Second, the specific intention may diverge from the general intention, as when we mistakenly use 'Jones' to refer to Smith or 'the 45th president of the USA' to refer to Clinton. When the possibility of divergence arises, we have what Kripke calls the 'complex' case. We assume that, in the complex case, the speaker believes that the two intentions coincide; that is, the speaker believes that the object to which reference is intended to be made is indeed the object that fits the description or is the true bearer of the proper name. (In fact, it is not strictly necessary that the speaker believe this, because it is also possible for a description to pick out something when everybody knows that this something does not fit the description. This happens all the time when we use descriptions ironically, for example, when we inquire about 'the great explorer' to the friend of someone who has done a bit of tourism in Peru. Compare Donnellan 1966:290-291.) Kripke argues that Donnellan's attributive use is the simple case and that the referential use is the complex case, specialized to definite descriptions.

Given the above way of looking at Donnellan's distinction, Kripke goes on to make the following point. He asks us (1979b:16-18) to imagine three "Russellian" languages of differing Russellianness, that is, versions of English for which the Russellian analysis of descriptions is stipulated to be correct to varying degrees. I discuss only the fully Russellian language, which Kripke calls the "strong" Russell language, because this is the one for which Kripke's result tells most forcefully against Donnellan's account. Moreover, any conclusions that we can draw about the strong Russell language apply a fortiori to the weaker versions. In the strong Russell language, definite descriptions are banned and are replaced by Russell-style paraphrases. For example,

(64)   The king of France is bald

becomes

(65)   There is one and only one king of France and he is bald.

So, in fully fledged Russellian English, to pick out someone whose name is not known, a speaker is always forced to employ an existential circumlocution. As Kripke points out, it is not unheard of for speakers of normal English to pick out individuals through the use of such a turn of phrase, especially in so-called arch conversation:

(66)   There is exactly one person drinking champagne in that corner, and I hear that he is romantically linked with Jane Smith.

In fact, whether this is a common way of talking about people is not strictly relevant, because it is clear that we *could in principle* get by using existential circumlocutions in place of definite descriptions, cumbersome though it would be.

Now Kripke's point is that the use of circumlocutions such as (65) and (66), instead of descriptions, would give rise to something wholly analogous to the distinction between the complex and simple occurrences of designators highlighted above and under which he wanted to subsume Donnellan's referential-attributive distinction. This can be demonstrated using the "arch" example just given, which is definitely a piece of Russellian English and, as was observed, is possibly a piece of normal English too.

Imagine that the man in question is Jon West and that, in fact, he is not drinking champagne but water. There seems to be no reason not to generalize the distinction between speaker's referent and semantic referent to include the more limited referential apparatus of Russellian English, and, if we do that, we see immediately that Jon West is a *speaker's referent*. Moreover, if there happened by chance to be one and only one (other) person in the corner drinking real champagne, that person would be a *semantic referent* (Russell, of course, would prefer the term 'denotation'; see 6.3.3). This shows that, like a description in normal English, a Russell-style circumlocution would do its job in Russellian English even when the intended referent did not quite fit the words used by the speaker. By the same token, in Russellian English there will also be counterparts to the complex and simple occurrences of the descriptions of normal English. The Jon West example would be an instance of the complex case, because the general intention of the speaker—which would be a function of the rules of Russellian English— would be divergent from the specific intention to say something about Jon West.

The moral of all this is that if, as Kripke argues, Donnellan's distinction between the attributive and referential uses of descriptions is really an instance of the more general distinction between the simple and the complex occurrences of a wider class of expressions, then the phenomenon of which Donnellan's distinction is merely one specific manifestation *would actually occur in Russellian English*. This would mean that Donnellan's referentially used descriptions did *not* tell against Russell's theory of definite descriptions, for that theory, if it says anything at all about English, says that English as we know it is really a form of Russellian English. (The discussion has been couched in terms suggesting that the only language in question is English. Obviously, of course, the whole argument could be generalized to include other, if not all, natural languages. Russell would not have wished to imply that his theory was limited to English alone.)

Speaking more generally, we see that the assimilation of referential-attributive to the broader distinction between the complex and simple occurrences of designators provides a comprehensive rebuttal of the view that the descriptive content of a description can be obliterated. From this perspective, the specific device whereby 'the woman in the corner drinking champagne' is used to refer to someone not actually drinking champagne can be regarded as part of a more general mechanism whereby we, as speakers, can mean something different than what our words mean. Linguists and philosophers typically treat utterance meaning as being determined by two factors, the literal meaning of the words used (the semantic factor) and some sort of pragmatic overlay (the pragmatic factor). In example (62), the semantic factor delivers the literal meaning 'The cops are around the corner', while the pragmatic overlay would consist in additional implications such as 'Let's get out of here' and so on.

Such additional implications are 'worked out' by the addressee from the literal meaning plus knowledge of the context of utterance, in accordance with more or less universal principles governing rational behavior and interaction. Thus we can interpret Kripke's argument as the claim that Donnellan's referentially used descriptions are to be handled by a theory of pragmatics rather than by a theory of semantics.

Kripke's argument, as outlined above, appears to be conclusive. But— someone might be tempted to object—to explain away Donnellan's phenomenon, Kripke has invoked a general dichotomy between literal meaning and meaning-in-use, and surely literal meaning is simply an abstraction from recurrent patterns of use, a mere descriptive convenience. It is true that the literal meaning of an expression does not subsist independently (unless we follow Chomsky and say that meaning is somehow represented in the brain)—but think what happens if we eliminate this notion. Consider the case of example (62). That sentence could be used to imply a vast number of different things:

(67)   Have you finished cleaning out the safe?

(68)   Stop and keep quiet

and on and on. The force or import that such a sentence would have in practice would be determined by the exact details of the context of utterance, together with the universal principles governing rational interaction just alluded to. Now, if we were to conflate the two notions of utterance meaning (the force the sentence has in practice on a particular occasion) and literal sentence meaning, the consequences would be absurd. Every sentence would have a potential infinitude of meanings and so there could be no algorithm by which the meaning of a sentence was calculated from the meaning of its component parts. There thus would be no compositionality, hence no accounting for speakers' ability to understand new sentences. How linguistic communication would work in such circumstances seems to be unimaginable. In other words, to account for language use at all, we need some fixed point of reference, which we can call literal meaning, and this in principle must be describable in terms of 'rules' (in a broad sense of the term).

Surely, someone else might object, there is an obvious difference between saying of *A* (Smith's murderer) that he is insane and asserting that Smith's murderer (whoever that may be) is insane, and so there must be a genuine semantic ambiguity (a duality of literal meanings). But this is rather like arguing that the obvious difference between

(69)   Can you pass the salt?

qua question and qua request reflects a semantic ambiguity. It is true that the distinction between the two uses of the description in the Smith's murderer case is perceived with particular clarity but, on the other hand, clear-cut cases of this sort seem to shade off into other cases in which the attributive-referential distinction becomes less and less obvious. Consider the circumstance in which a would-be Sherlock Holmes looks at the crime scene and says in a rather self-satisfied way,

(70)   Smith's murderer has a florid complexion.

The use made of the description here bears the hallmark of an attributive use; namely, the speaker does not have any individual in mind. On the other hand, if it turned out that Smith's supposed murderer was not in fact a murderer (for example, if the crime was manslaughter) but did indeed have a florid complexion, our would-be Sherlock Holmes might have a case for claiming that what he or she had said was in some sense true, and this possibility of saying something true even when nothing fits the description is supposed to be a property of *referentially* used descriptions. Thus the attributive-referential distinction is more clear-cut in some cases than in others. The temptation is to focus on the very clear-cut cases and to infer from those that the phenomenon under discussion is a genuine case of semantic ambiguity.

7.3. Summary

Unlike Russell, Wittgenstein, and many contemporary philosophers such as Kripke (see Chapter 5), Frege regarded definite descriptions as a type of name. This is because, having drawn a fundamental distinction between concept expressions and object expressions, he identified names with object expressions. Concept expressions, on the other hand, he took to be predicative in nature, and, in ordinary language, one of their principal characteristics was that they were capable of being introduced by the indefinite determiners 'some', 'every', 'no', and so on.

In *Grundgesetze der Arithmetik,* Frege proposed treating the definite article as indicating a function that, when a value range containing a unique object was its argument, returned that object as its value. Frege did not identify the value range of a concept under which only one object fell with that object, because this identity does not hold in the case in which the object in question is itself given as a value range.

Like Frege, Donnellan thought that descriptions could function as names. However, in distinction to Frege, he appears to have believed that the content of a description was not always relevant to the determination of its reference. Such a view would also be at variance with Russell's theory of descriptions. More recently, Kripke has shown that Donnellan's argument rests on a failure to distinguish clearly between what a speaker means on a given occasion and what his or her words mean.

Part III: Further Reading

For Russell's theory of descriptions, start with Russell 1959 (chapter 5). This gives a highly readable account of the distinction between acquaintance and description. For the actual theory, read Russell 1905 and Russell 1919a (chapter 17). The text of these two is deceptively easy, and remarks of great philosophical importance can be easily missed. See also Russell 1937 and Kaplan 1972.

To find out more about Quine's thinking in relation to reference, one can do no better than read *Word and Object* (especially pp. 80-124). More than anyone else, Quine is the linguist's philosopher.

Wittgenstein's account of descriptions and generality in the *Tractatus* is almost impossible to understand from the bare text, so concise is the exposition. However, Black 1964 is an admirable tool for getting at the hidden treasures and Kenny 1973 (especially pp. 78-93) is also extremely useful. *Philosophical Investigations,* §§1-80 (especially §60), contains much that makes clear what Wittgenstein's thinking was when he wrote the *Tractatus*. Waismann 1965 (pp. 304-322) contains an excellent discussion of Wittgenstein's pictorial conception of language and the associated program of analysis.

Frege subsumed ordinary proper names and descriptions within the same category—object expressions—and so what he says about the one type of expression applies equally to the other. For Frege's views on object expressions and the distinction vis-à-vis concept expressions, see Frege 1960:21-55; see also Kenny 1995:100-125. For the sense-nominatum distinction, see Frege 1949:85-102; the French translation in Frege 1971 (pp. 102-126) is recommended to readers who know French.

For the special function '\', see §11 of the *Grundgesetze* (Frege 1964), together with §§8-10 to understand the symbolism employed in §11. Kenny (1995:152-154) gives invaluable help.

Donnellan 1966 can be read without help. Much the same goes for Kripke 1979b, which is the best possible commentary on Donnellan's paper. It is worth cross-referencing the ideas and methods employed in Kripke 1979b with Kripke's best-known work on names, namely, Kripke 1980.

PART IV

NONEXTENSIONAL CONTEXTS

8

Modality

8.1. What Is Logical Modality?

In linguistics, the term 'modality' applies to a range of phenomena. In particular, a 'modal system' is a grammatical system in which the speaker's attitude or relation to the truth-conditional content expressed in his or her utterance is regularly indicated by some grammatical device, such as verbal inflection or the agglutination of a modal affix. Consider the following sentences from Aymara (spoken in the Lake Titicaca area of Bolivia and Peru):

(1)   Um wara-tay-ta

       Water you-poured-away-(but-I-didn't-witness-this)

and

(2)   Um wara-ta

Water you-poured-away.

Both sentences come into English as 'You poured away water', but only (2) can be used to make an unqualified assertion. Sentence (1), on the other hand, which incorporates the modal affix 'tay', indicates in addition that the speaker did not personally witness the pouring away of the water.

In logic and philosophy, the term 'modality' has a rather different sense. In the first place, while linguistic modality is essentially speaker- or subject-oriented, its logical counterpart is wholly impersonal. Thus the ordinary-language correlates of the logical modalities are taken to be sentences of the form 'Necessarily . . .' and 'Possibly . . .' (or alternatively, 'It is necessary/possible that . . .') and their translation equivalents in other languages.

In ordinary conversation, 'possibly' is often used as an informal alternative to such speaker-oriented expressions as 'I have an inkling that . . .' or 'I think, but am not sure, that . . .'. Likewise, the word 'necessarily' is customarily used to indicate that a sentence follows from some background assumption. In addition, both adjuncts can be used with an indefinite noun phrase as alternatives to the quantifiers (see Chapter 10). For example,

(3)   A swan is necessarily white

and

(4)   A swan is possibly white

approximate more or less to 'All swans are white' and 'Some swans are white', respectively. However, when taken to express *logical modalities,* the expressions in question have a quite different meaning. Thus an assertion of the form 'necessarily p' is understood as stating that the contained sentence 'p' is true *unconditionally.* When taken in the same spirit, 'possibly' indicates that the sentence to which it is appended does not express a necessary (in the favored sense) falsehood; that is to say,

(5)   'Possibly p' is an abbreviation for 'Not necessarily not-p'.

Note that what is possibly true is not thereby *factually* true. For example, it is possible that there is intelligent life on Mars, in that it is not necessarily false that there is intelligent life on Mars; however, at the present moment, it appears that it is not a fact that there is intelligent life on Mars.

8.2. Interchangeability and Existential Generalization

As we saw in Chapter 4, a distinction is normally drawn between occurrences of expressions that are purely referential and occurrences that are not. Of referential occurrences, Quine writes: "I call an occurrence of a singular term in a statement *purely referential* (Frege: *gerade*), if, roughly speaking, the term serves in that particular context simply to refer to its object" (Quine 1953:66).

It is generally thought that, when an expression has a referential occurrence in a sentence, it can be exchanged *salva veritate*—that is, with truth preserved—for any expression that designates the same object. Carnap calls this the principle of interchangeability (see 4.1).

It is also thought that, from a sentence in which an expression occurs referentially, for example,

(6)   The Eiffel Tower is in Paris,

an existential sentence (see 6.1.3.1) can be derived such as

(7) $(\exists x)$ (the Eiffel Tower is in x).

Sentence (7) can be roughly paraphrased as

(8)   For at least one thing x: the Eiffel Tower is in x.

The move whereby (7) was derived from (6) is called *existential generalization* (see Quine 1949:49).

Now, as Quine points out (1960:197), modal sentences exhibit a type of context in which the principle of interchangeability fails. For example, although most people might be prepared to accept that

(9)   Necessarily 9 is greater than 7

expresses a truth, many would be reluctant to say the same of

(10)   Necessarily the number of planets is greater than 7,

despite the fact that 'the number of planets' and '9' designate the same object, namely, the number 9. Obviously enough, the reason for (9)'s apparent truth and (10)'s apparent falsity is this: Nine's greaterness than seven does not depend on any fact, whereas the circumstance that there are more than seven planets is an accident in the history of the solar system.

Possibility sentences are in the same boat as necessity sentences. For example, given (5), sentence (11) below must be false:

(11)   Possibly 9 is less than 7.

If we attempt to apply the principle of interchangeability, in the same way as before, to the expression '9' in (11), we have

(12)   Possibly the number of planets is less than 7,

which is true, for although there *are* more than seven planets, this circumstance, as we have said, is an accident of history.

Thus we see that modal sentences in general do not allow the free interchange of coreferential expressions. According to some, such sentences do not permit existential generalization either.

If we attempt to existentially generalize on the numeral '9' in sentence (9), for example, we have

(13)   ($\exists x$) (necessarily x is greater than 7),

which can be paraphrased as

(14)   For at least one thing x: necessarily x is greater than 7.

Now, (13), unlike sentence (7), involves what is called *quantifying into* a modal context from outside. Quine (1953:80-81, 1960:199) and others have flatly denied the legitimacy of such a move. In particular, Quine argues that it commits us to what he calls *Aristotelian essential-*

ism, namely, "the doctrine that some attributes of a thing (quite independently of the language in which the thing is referred to, if at all) may be essential to the thing and others accidental" (1953:80). Thus, if we countenance (13), we must also countenance, for example,

(15) ($\exists x$) (x is Jones's favorite number & $\sim$necessarily x is Jones's favorite number & necessarily x is greater than 7),

which asserts that there is at least one object x that has a certain property (greaterness than 7) essentially and another (a privileged position in Jones's affections) only accidentally (for the symbol '$\sim$', see Table 1.3). Such an object is a number variously known as 9 and Jones's favorite number.

Quine rejects what he takes to be the underlying Aristotelian view behind formulations such as (15) and (13) on the grounds that "necessity resides in the way in which we say things, and not in the things we talk about" (1953:81). In a later work (1960:199), Quine illustrates the point with an argument that can be summarized as follows.

Mathematicians *qua mathematicians* might conceivably be said to be necessarily rational and accidentally two-legged, and cyclists *qua cyclists* accidentally rational and necessarily two-legged. But what do we say of the concrete *individual* who happens to be both a cyclist and a mathematician? As long as we speak of the individual, without favoring any secondary classification as a mathematician or as a cyclist, it makes no sense to regard some properties as essential and others as accidental.

In traditional philosophical terms, Quine's position is that modalities are *de dicto* ('about the saying') rather than *de re* ('about the thing'), and what Quine sees as the problem with the sort of quantification exemplified by (13) and (15) is that it implies that there is such a thing as *de re* modality. Quine himself does not use the terms *de re* and *de dicto.*

It should be noted that in the ideal symbolism of many philosophers, particularly in Quine's "regimented" notation (1960, §§37-38), proper names and definite descriptions are eliminated through the use of Russell-style contextual definitions (see 6.1.3.2). Such contextual definitions result in the replacement of a proper name or a description with a quantificational circumlocution whose only expressions of individual

172 ■ NONEXTENSIONAL CONTEXTS

type are variables such as 'x' and 'y'. For example, in Quine's regimented notation, the sentence

(16)   Socrates is wise

becomes

(17)   ($\exists x$) (x is Socrates and x is wise).

Therefore, for thinkers like Quine, it is existential generalizability rather than interchangeability that is the fundamental criterion for the referential occurrence of an expression (see Quine 1953:79). Indeed, Quine prefers to state the principle of interchangeability in the following way:

(18)   (x) (y) [($x = y$) → ($Fx \leftrightarrow Fy$)],

which can be read as

(19)   For any objects x and y: if x is identical to y, then Fx is equivalent to Fy.

(For the universal quantifier (x), see 6.1.3.1. For the truth-functional connectives → and ↔, see 1.2.4.)

8.3. Necessity as a Semantic Predicate

In keeping with the position just outlined, Quine (1953) recommends treating 'necessity' as a semantic predicate, that is, as a predicative expression that is attachable to names for sentences. Quine represents this semantic predicate using the symbol 'Nec'. For example, our sentence (9) would be rewritten as

(20)   Nec '9 is greater than 7',

in which the expression ' "9 is greater than 7" ' is a quotation name for the English sentence

(21)   9 is greater than 7. (Compare Quine 1953:65.)

Sentence (20) makes a statement about sentence (21), namely, that it expresses an unconditional truth. Therefore, sentence (20) belongs to a 'higher' language than sentence (21). The difference between two such linguistic levels is normally expressed in terms of a distinction between a *metalanguage* and an *object language,* according to which the former treats of the latter (see 2.2.2.2).

Now, Quine treats quotations as single unstructured units. Thus the occurrence of '9' inside the quotation name ' "9 is greater than 7" ' is to be regarded as being like the occurrence of 'cat' inside the word 'cattle': Both occur as what Quine calls "orthographic accidents" and not as independent expressions (1953:67). On account of the mono-lithic nature of quotations, (20) does not lend itself to the sort of quantification exemplified in (13) and (15), which Quine regarded as leading to "the metaphysical jungle of Aristotelian essentialism" (1953:81).

What Quine regarded as the illegitimate quantification exhibited in (13) and (15) involved a cross-reference from a quantifier ($\exists x$) outside a necessity context to a variable 'x' inside. Now, if 'necessarily' is assimilated to Quine's semantic predicate 'Nec', such a cross-reference becomes impossible. We can see why this is so if we rewrite (13) using the semantic predicate

(22)   ($\exists x$) (Nec 'x is greater than 7').

Given that quotations are to be viewed as internally unstructured, the 'x' that occurs inside ' "x is greater than 7" ' is simply a *fixed letter* and not a variable. Therefore, it cannot be reached (bound) by the quantifier ($\exists x$). In other words, (22) fails in just the same way as, for example, '($\exists x$) (Smith is mortal)' fails, namely, because the would-be scope (see 6.1.3.1) of the quantifier does not contain a variable (see Quine 1953:77).

By the same token, treating necessity as a semantic predicate blocks what, for Quine, is a highly undesirable inference from (18). This can be shown in the following way: 'F' in (18) can be replaced by any predicative expression we care to imagine: 'is happy', 'is identical to Bill Clinton', 'is a camel', or whatever. In particular, we might try replacing

'F' with 'is necessarily identical to x', that is, with 'necessarily x = . . .'.
This move results in

(23) (x) (y) {(x = y) → [(necessarily x = x) ↔ (necessarily
x = y)]}.

Now, there is a logical law that says, if a sentence 'p' is true, the
formulation 'p ↔ q' can be reduced to just 'q'. (The reason for this is
that 'p ↔ q' is true only if 'p' and 'q' have the same truth-value [see
Table 1.8]. So, if we have 'p ↔ q' and 'p', we also have 'q'.) Therefore,
and because 'necessarily x = x' is obviously true whatever x is, we can
simplify (23) to

(24) (x) (y) [(x = y) → (necessarily x = y)],

that is, the assertion that where identity holds, it holds necessarily (see
Quine 1953:80). (24) is of a piece with essentialism, because it implies
that necessity resides in things and not in the way we talk about them.
Thus it is highly undesirable, in Quine's eyes at least, that (24) should
be derivable from (18).

Now Quine's semantic predicate 'Nec' is incompatible with formulations such as (23) and (24). This is readily seen if an attempt is made
to substitute 'Nec' for 'necessarily' in (23) and (24), for such a move
converts the variables 'x' and 'y' that are in the scope of 'necessarily'
into fixed letters that cannot be reached by the universal quantifiers (x)
and (y). Therefore, if necessity is construed as a semantic predicate, as
Quine recommends, the unwanted inference from (18) to (24) is
blocked.

8.4. Kripke: Essentialism

8.4.1. Interchangeability

In contrast to Quine, Kripke openly embraces the principle enshrined in (24) (see Kripke 1980:3). He also espouses the view that
ordinary proper names are what he calls *rigid designators* (see 5.1.2). A
rigid designator is an expression that designates the same thing regard-

less of what state of affairs we entertain, assuming language is held constant. For example, the description 'the author of *Waverley*' is *not* a rigid designator, because we can entertain a possible state of affairs in which someone other than Walter Scott had written *Waverley*. On the other hand, the numeral '7' *is* a rigid designator, because it names the number seven whatever state of affairs we care to imagine (assuming language is held constant).

As we saw in 5.2, Kripke thinks that, in modal sentences, the principle of interchangeability always holds for proper names, on account of their status as rigid designators, and sometimes for definite descriptions. Therefore, in his terms, modal contexts are *Shakespearean* (1979a:267; see also note 41 for the origin of this term) but not *referentially transparent*. (A Shakespearean context is one in which coreferential proper names are interchangeable; a referentially transparent context—in Kripke's particular usage—is one in which both coreferential proper names and coreferential definite descriptions are interchangeable.)

Now, although Kripke regards modal contexts as not being referentially transparent, he appears to think that, in such contexts, coreferential definite descriptions can be exchanged salva veritate when the modality is understood to be *de re* (see 1979a:241-242). Consider the following sentence:

(25) Necessarily Beijing is the capital of China.

This can be read in two ways. First, it can be seen as asserting the necessity of Beijing's being the capital of China. Under that reading—the *de dicto* reading—(25) expresses a manifest falsehood, for it can easily be imagined that Shanghai, for example, rather than Beijing was the Chinese capital. On the other hand, construed *de re*, (25) asserts the necessity of an identity between Beijing and the object that, in the actual state of affairs, is the capital of China, namely, Beijing.

The difference between the two readings of (25) can be captured using Russell's device of scope (see 6.4). Thus, on the *de dicto* reading, we have (leaving aside extraneous details)

(26) Necessarily: $(\exists x)$ (x is the capital of China & x = Beijing)

and on the *de re* reading:

(27) (∃x) (x is the capital of China & necessarily x = Beijing).

Kripke would regard (25) as true, if read de re. What is more, he thinks that "a *de re* reading, if it makes sense at all, by definition must be subject to a principle of substitution *salva veritate*" (1979a:242).

8.4.2. Essential Properties

When we entertain a nonactual state of affairs concerning some particular thing x from the actual state of affairs, some facts about x are different from the way they are in the actual state of affairs. For example, we can imagine what it would be like if Clinton had not been the 42nd U.S. president, had never married Hillary, had not inaugurated the 1996 Olympic Games, and so on. Similarly, we can imagine that gold was the least valued of all metals, that it occurred in abundance in mines in the middle of New York, that it had never been used as an international monetary standard, and so on. Such properties can vary and we still feel we are talking about Clinton or about gold.

Now, Kripke argues (1980, pp. 39-53, 123-126) that some of the properties that a thing x has in the actual state of affairs must, as it were, be retained by x in any nonactual state of affairs. In other words, Kripke subscribes to the doctrine that some of a thing's properties are essential. For example, if we take Kripke's line, there is no possible state of affairs in which Clinton is not human or in which gold has the molecular structure of pyrite (fool's gold). If we entertain such states of affairs, we cease to be talking about either Clinton or gold in any intuitively appreciable sense (assuming that Clinton is indeed human and that scientists are not making a mistake when they say gold has a different molecular structure than pyrite).

Analogous remarks apply in the case of things like tigers or heat and, indeed, in the case of anything that we care to regard as a thing or a kind. Thus basketball, electricity, cows, lightning, units of measurement, and so on all have essential properties, which they cannot *not* have in any imagined state of affairs (see 5.4).

Although, according to Kripke, some of a thing's properties are essential, that the thing has these properties need not be known by us a priori, that is, prior to experience. For example, most people have never met Clinton personally and so cannot be said to *know*—let alone know a priori—that he is not, for example, some perfect android. But as it happens that Clinton *is* human (let us assume that he is, for the sake of argument), he could not possibly—if we follow Kripke's line—*not* be human. Thus there can be a divergence between what one knows about a thing, which is an *epistemological* matter, and what is necessarily the case concerning a thing, which is a *metaphysical* matter (see 5.1.1 and 5.4.4).

We can characterize Kripke's views about essential properties in the following way: Sentences such as

(28) Gold's atomic number is 79

and

(29) Clinton is human

express necessary truths. By the same token,

(30) Necessarily gold's atomic number is 79

and

(31) Necessarily Clinton is human

express truths. Nevertheless, the truth of sentences such as (28) and (29) need not be known a priori.

8.5. Frege-Kaplan: The Middle Way

We have seen, in 8.3 and 8.4 above, that there are two poles to the debate concerning modal contexts. On the one hand, Quine (1953) repudiates what he takes to be the Aristotelian conception of (meta-physical) essence and treats modal contexts as being sealed off. On the other hand, Kripke (and like-minded thinkers) espouses a fully fledged essentialism, with its attendant *de re* modalities and unrestricted quan-tification into modal environments. Within these two poles, a middle way was proposed by Kaplan in "Quantifying In" (1968-1969).

Kaplan's method is based on Frege's treatment of quotation contexts. Frege argued that expressions occurring in a quotation referred to themselves (Frege 1949:87). For example, the expression 'the author of *Waverley*' in

(32) Smith said, 'The author of *Waverley* is English'

would refer to the definite description 'the author of *Waverley*'.
It is readily seen that this treatment of quotation differs from Quine's: According to Quine, the entire quotation alone refers and not any individual piece of it. The difference between Fregean quotation and the Quinean variety is important. For one of the supposed merits of the latter is that it flaunts a visible barrier to quantifying in, whereas the former permits quantifying in but only when the quantification is *over* expressions. For example, using '<' and '>' to indicate Fregean quotation and 'α' as a variable referring to expressions, we can write (following Kaplan 1968-1969:186):

(33) (∃α) (<α is greater than 7> is a truth of arithmetic),

which can be read as

(34) For some expression α: 'α is greater than 7' is a truth of arithmetic.

Now, what Kaplan does is to combine Quine's treatment of necessity as a semantic predicate with the Fregean idea that quotation contexts can be quantified into. Kaplan designates his own version of the semantic predicate using the symbol 'N'. Thus we have, for example,

(35) (∃α) (N <α is greater than 7>).

Now, although the method exhibited in (35) enables us to quantify into a modal context without thereby committing ourselves to essentialism, it is obvious that, in some sense, the variable 'α' lacks a genuine grip on the extralinguistic. According to the essentialist treatment, a quantifier can simultaneously bind (cross-refer to) one variable outside and another inside a modal context, as in our earlier sentence (15).

However, if we try to achieve the same effect along the lines implied by (35), we get

(36) ($\exists\alpha$) (α is Jones's favorite number & $\sim$(N <α is Jones's favorite number>) & N <α is greater than 7>),

which is false (Jones's favorite number is a number and not an expression for a number) and is not the intended result (compare Kaplan 1968-1969:189).

To remedy this defect, Kaplan (1968-1969:194) introduces a necessary-designation relation, symbolized by 'Δ_N', which holds between an expression and an object. (In fact, Kaplan talks of an expression's necessarily *denoting* an object. The form of words 'necessarily *designates*' is preferred here, to avoid confusion with Russell's theory of descriptions, in which 'denotes' has a specific technical meaning.) If the relation Δ_N holds between an expression and the object it designates, that expression *always* designates that object, assuming that language is held constant. Thus we have, for instance,

(37) Δ_N ('9', 9),

which is to be read as

(38) '9' necessarily designates 9.

On the other hand,

(39) Δ_N ('the number of planets', 9)

is not true, because the description 'the number of planets' does not necessarily designate 9. Obvious paradigms for necessary designation are numerals and quotation names.

Using the 'Δ_N' symbol, Kaplan's nonessentialist version of the essentialist sentence (15) becomes

(40) ($\exists x$) ($\exists\alpha$) [x is Jones's favorite number & Δ_N (α, x) & $\sim$(N <α is Jones's favorite number>) & N <α is greater than 7>].

This rather forbidding piece of symbolism can be roughly paraphrased as

(41)   For some object x and some expression α: x is Jones's
       favorite number & α necessarily designates x & 'α is
       Jones's favorite number' is not necessarily true & 'α is
       greater than 7' is necessarily true.

In a way then, Kaplan manages to have his cake and eat it. He
quantifies into modal contexts but avoids essentialism. Using his technique, we can even come up with a nonessentialist counterpart to what,
for Quine, would be an inadmissible *de re* reading of sentence (9):

(42) $(\exists\alpha)$ $[\Delta_N (\alpha, 9)$ & N $<\alpha$ is greater than 7$>$]. (Compare
       Kaplan, 1968-1969:196.)

8.6. The Method of Extension and Intension

Carnap (1956) argues that expressions have what he calls an *extension*
and an *intension*. An expression's extension corresponds more or less
to an expression's Fregean nominatum (see 4.3.1.1), although Carnap
stresses (1956:143) that an expression is not to be viewed as a name of
its extension. Concerning an expression's intension, it suffices to point
out that any two expressions ϕ and ψ only have the same intension if
their identity sentence '$\phi = \psi$' is necessarily true (see Carnap 1956,
pp. 10, 14, 23).

Carnap lays down certain principles that determine when expressions can be interchanged. Thus he stipulates that any two expressions
with the same extension, but not the same intension, are interchangeable
only in extensional contexts (see 4.2), while any two expressions with
the same intension are interchangeable in both extensional and modal
contexts. Given the condition for identity of intension just mentioned,
this stipulation forestalls, in Quine's eyes, the illegitimate substitution
that took us from sentence (9) to (10).

Another interesting result of Carnap's concerns quantified modal
sentences. As we have seen, Quine thought that the very use of a
quantified modal sentence such as our earlier example (13)

(13) $(\exists x)$ (necessarily x is greater than 7)

committed one to essentialism. This is because he regarded a variable 'x' as referring, albeit indefinitely, to extralinguistic objects. On the other hand, Carnap, who thought of linguistic expressions (including variables) not as designating extralinguistic objects, but as merely *having* an extension and an intension, is not obliged to regard the use of (13) as committing him to essentialism.

Accordingly, if we follow Carnap's method, (13) will be true if at least one substitution instance of its scope

(43) necessarily *x* is greater than 7

is true, that is, if one substitution instance of

(44) *x* is greater than 7

expresses a necessary truth.

Now, as we saw in 3.2.4, Carnap reconstructs the concept of necessary truth in terms of state descriptions. A state description in a given language can be construed as an exhaustive assignment of truth-values to all the sentences of that language. A sentence that expresses a necessary truth is one that comes out true under every state description (see 3.2.4.3). Accordingly, for a substitution instance of (44) to express a necessary truth, there must be some sentence that (i) comes out true under every state description and (ii) can be derived from (44) by replacing the variable 'x' with a specific expression. One such sentence is our earlier sentence (21):

(21) 9 is greater than 7.

On the other hand,

(45) The number of planets is greater than 7

will not come out true under every state description and therefore is not a substitution instance of (44) that expresses a necessary truth.

Thus we see that Carnap's way of regarding expressions not as names but merely as *having* an extension and an intension enables him to quantify freely into modal contexts without thereby committing himself to essentialism (see also Carnap 1956, §44).

8.7. Summary

Quine thinks that the principle of interchangeability is suspended in modal sentences, because he flatly rejects the idea that necessity resides in things, as opposed to the way we talk about things. By the same token, he regards quantifying into modal contexts as illegitimate. He represents these views notationally by treating modal contexts as being on a par with quotations, which, in his opinion, have no logically relevant internal structure. Thus, for example, a quantifier that is prefixed to a modal context is unable to reach or bind any of the expressions inside the context because such expressions do not really occur as expressions at all but, instead, as orthographic accidents.

Kripke, on the other hand, espouses a fully fledged essentialism and consequently accepts unrestricted quantifying into modal contexts. He also thinks that coreferential proper names are always interchangeable salva veritate in such contexts and that coreferential descriptions sometimes are, depending on whether the containing sentence is read *de re* or *de dicto*.

Kaplan adopts a middle way. Using Frege's conception of quotation, according to which quoted expressions refer to themselves, together with the idea of a necessary-designation relation, he develops a notation in which quantification into modal contexts is permissible but only when the quantification is over linguistic expressions and not extralinguistic objects.

Carnap declines to regard linguistic expressions as names of extralinguistic objects. As a consequence, in his method, the variables of quantification do not refer to extralinguistic objects. Instead, they stand in place of linguistic expressions. By looking at matters in this way, he is able to permit unrestricted quantification into modal contexts without thereby committing himself to essentialism.

9

Propositional Attitudes

9.1. What Are Propositional Attitudes?

The term 'propositional attitude' refers to what is expressed by such forms as 'believes that', 'says that', 'is surprised that', 'wishes that', and 'urges that' (and their equivalents in other languages). What characterizes a propositional-attitude sentence is the assertion of a relation between an agent (a believer, an urger, a fearer, and so on) and a proposition. (We use the term 'proposition' informally, without commitment to any philosophical doctrine of propositions.)

Propositional attitudes are apt to create contexts in which coreferential expressions are not necessarily interchangeable *salva veritate* (with truth preserved) and, in addition, they are subject-oriented rather than impersonal like the modalities (see the previous chapter). On both these scores, propositional-attitude expressions are similar to such verbs as 'looks for', 'wants', 'hunts', and 'is frightened of', which superficially have a quite different grammatical form (compare examples (1) and (2) below). For the purposes of logical analysis, however, the latter can be *paraphrased into* the idiom of propositional attitude. For example, we might rewrite 'Ernest is hunting lions' as something like 'Ernest strives that Ernest finds a lion' (see Quine 1956:178), with 'strives that' an explicit propositional-attitude expression.

The following remarks are intended to apply both to the overt propositional-attitude expressions and to those expressions ('looks for' and the like) that can be paraphrased into propositional-attitude expressions, although the phraseology may occasionally suggest that only the former are under consideration.

9.2. Interchangeability and Quantifying In

Consider the following sentences:

(1)   Jones believes that the Tagus flows into the Atlantic.

(2)   Jones is looking for the Head of Department.

The name 'Tagus' in (1) is coreferential with the description 'the longest river in the Iberian Peninsula'. However, it is readily apparent that there is a way of reading (1)—the *de dicto* reading (see 8.2)—according to which, although (1) itself may be true, the following sentence is not:

(3)   Jones believes that the longest river in the Iberian Peninsula flows into the Atlantic.

For example, Jones's knowledge of Iberian geography might be sufficient for him to place the Tagus's estuary but not its length relative to other rivers in Spain and Portugal.

We see also that interchangeability fails in the *de dicto* reading of (2). An appropriate scenario would be one in which the Head of Department happens to be the Dean of Faculty but Jones is unaware of this fact. In such circumstances, the expressions 'the Head of Department' and 'the Dean of Faculty', although coreferential, would not be interchangeable salva veritate.

These results illustrate a failure of interchangeability that involves replacing a proper name with a description (example (1)) or replacing one description with another (2). Thus it seems that, on the *de dicto* reading at least, propositional-attitude contexts are *referentially opaque;*

that is, they do not admit exchanges involving definite descriptions *salva veritate*. Quine and most other philosophers have assumed that, in addition, propositional-attitude contexts are not *Shakespearean*; that is to say, they hold that such contexts do not allow the exchange of even coreferential *proper names* (see 8.4.1). Quine's famous example apparently illustrating this point is the sentence

(4)   Tom believes that Cicero denounced Catiline.
      (Quine 1960:145)

From the facts that (i) Cicero and Tully were the same person and (ii) Tom assents to 'Cicero denounced Catiline' but denies 'Tully denounced Catiline', Quine concludes that, on what we have been calling the *de dicto* reading, (4) will be true, while 'Tom believes that Tully denounced Catiline' will be false. Accordingly, the principle of interchangeability would fail even for proper names. Therefore, when construed *de dicto*, propositional-attitude contexts would be non-Shakespearean.

In 8.2, we saw that some philosophers think that quantifying into a modal context is not legitimate. The same philosophers also reject quantification into propositional-attitude contexts when these are construed *de dicto*. Consider sentence (2), for example. That sentence may be read *de dicto* if, for instance, Jones, a new student, is not personally acquainted with the Head of Department but simply intends to observe the rule that all new students report for an interview with their respective Heads of Department. In such circumstances, if we try to quantify into the 'is looking for' construction from outside, we get

(5)   ($\exists x$) (Jones is looking for x),

which can be read as

(6)   For some thing x: Jones is looking for x.

Given the stipulated *de dicto* reading of 'is looking for', (5) appears to be nonsensical (for the existential quantifier ($\exists x$) and its use in the representation of *de re* and *de dicto* readings, see 6.1.3.1 and 6.4, respectively). Indeed, (5) would imply that there was some particular individual (albeit someone not mentioned by name) whom Jones was seeking and this is just what we have said is ruled out by the *de dicto* reading.

Similarly, it appears that, on what we are calling the *de dicto* reading, there can be no quantifying into the 'believes that' construction exemplified in (4) (see Quine 1960, §31). Thus, if 'believes that' is understood in such a way that Tom's belief is not about the *individual* Cicero, then, by the same token, there is no particular (although unspecified) someone whom Tom can be said to believe to be a Catiline denouncer.

9.3. Quine

9.3.1. Relational and Notional Senses

Propositional attitudes are like the logical modalities 'Necessarily . . .' and 'Possibly . . .' in that both types of construction create nonextensional contexts (see 4.2). Now, we saw in 8.2 that Quine rejects the idea that a modal sentence such as

(7)   Necessarily 9 is greater than 7

is to be construed as ascribing to a certain nonlinguistic object, namely, the number nine, the necessary possession of the property *greater than 7*. To make this clear in his notation, Quine rewrites sentences such as (7) in the following way:

(8)   Nec '9 is greater than 7',

which can be read as

(9)   '9 is greater than 7' is necessarily true.

Quine considers direct quotations, as in (8)/(9), to have no logically relevant internal structure. Thus the forms '9' and '7', as they occur in (8)/(9), are not independent expressions at all but mere notational accidents like the form 'cat' in the word 'cattle'.

Because of this circumstance, attempted quantification into (8)

(10)   ($\exists x$) (Nec 'x is greater than 7')

is doomed to failure, for the 'x' in (10)'s would-be scope (see 6.1.3.1) is not a variable at all but a fixed letter.

In some respects, Quine's view concerning propositional-attitude contexts is different than his view concerning modality, for he accepts that beliefs, wishes, and so on can be about nonlinguistic objects. In our terms, he accepts that propositional attitudes can be de re.

In a well-known paper, "Quantifiers and Propositional Attitudes" (1956), he distinguishes between what he calls the *notional* and the *relational* senses of propositional-attitude expressions (p. 177). These correspond more or less to what we have been calling the *de dicto* and *de re* readings.

9.3.2. The Semantic Technique

9.3.2.1. The technique. The distinction mentioned above, between the notional and the relational senses of propositional-attitude expressions, is only provisional, for Quine (1956:180-187, also 1960:149) later dispenses with it.

Take the case of belief. The notional or *de dicto* sense gives way to a relation between an attitude agent (a believer, a searcher, or whatever) and a linguistic expression (Quine 1956, pp. 180, 185; 1960:212-213). Thus, when read notionally, the sentence

(11)   Ralph believes that Ortcutt is a spy

becomes

(12)   Ralph believes-true 'Ortcutt is a spy',

which can be read as

(13)   Ralph believes the sentence 'Ortcutt is a spy' to be true.

Notice that, like ' "9 is greater than 7" ' in (8)/(9), ' "Ortcutt is a spy" ' is a quotation name (see 2.2.2.1) for an English sentence.

The method employed in (12) is semantic in spirit, for (12) asserts something about another sentence, namely, that Ralph believes it to be true, and so belongs to a metalanguage (see 2.2.2.2). Many people might argue that (11) says something not about a sentence but about a *proposition*. Quine's view, however, is that propositions are essentially an analytical fiction (1960:206-209). He argues that the notion of language-transcendent sentence meanings, of which propositions are traditionally regarded as the repository, should, on the whole, be discarded. Also, he finds the appeal to propositions as vehicles of truth (much loved by linguists) unconvincing, for there seems to be no reason not to assign the job of having truth-values to what he calls 'eternal sentences,' that is, sentences in which there are no context-dependent expressions and whose truth-values thus stay fixed through time and from speaker to speaker (1960:193).

According to the notional *(de dicto)* reading of (11), the expression 'Ortcutt' is not interchangeable salva veritate with coreferential expressions. For example, read notionally, (11) does not permit us to infer

(14)   Ralph believes that the man seen at the beach is a spy,

despite the fact that, unbeknown to Ralph, Ortcutt and the man seen at the beach are one and the same. Similarly, given the stipulated notional or *de dicto* reading of 'believes', any attempt to quantify into (11)

(15)   ($\exists x$) (Ralph believes x to be a spy)

must be deemed meaningless.

Thus we see that, on the favored reading, the 'Ortcutt' position in (11) is not subject to the principle of interchangeability and cannot be quantified into.

Now, the technique used in (12), Quine's version of the notional reading of (11), has the effect of making both of these circumstances explicit, for, given Quine's understanding of quotation (see 9.3.1 above), the form 'Ortcutt' occurs in (12) as a notational accident and not as an independent expression.

Formulation (12) gives us a characterization of the notional reading of (11). But what about the relational (de re) reading of a sentence?

Quine reconstructs this in terms of a relation holding between a believer, a propositional function (see 6.1.3.1), *and* an object:

(16) Tom believes-true 'y denounced Catiline' of Cicero
(Quine 1960:212; see also 1956:185),

which can be read as

(17) Tom believes of Cicero that 'y denounced Catiline' is true of him;

that is,

(18) Tom believes Cicero to be a Catiline denouncer.

The point about (16) is that, in addition to 'Tom', we have a name *outside* the quotation and, accordingly, one of the positions *inside*, namely, the denouncer's position, has been made vacant; hence the presence of the variable 'y'. In other words, 'Cicero'—like 'Tom'—may be exchanged salva veritate for any coreferential name. Thus if (16) is true, so, for example, is

(19) Tom believes-true 'y denounced Catiline' of Antony's denouncer in the *Philippics*,

because 'Antony's denouncer in the *Philippics*' and 'Cicero' both designate Cicero. By the same token, we can quantify into the 'Cicero' position in (16):

(20) $(\exists x)$ (Tom believes-true 'y denounced Catiline' of x).

It is also possible for Tom to have a relational (de re) belief about both Cicero and Catiline, namely, that they are related as denouncer and denounced:

(21) Tom believes-true 'y denounced z' of Cicero and Catiline.

Here, we have a four-way relation involving Tom, Cicero, Catiline, and the linguistic expression '*y* denounced *z*'. Again, the positions outside the quotation are subject to the principle of interchangeability and we are free to quantify into them, as in, for example,

(22) $(\exists w)$ $(\exists x)$ (Tom believes-true '*y* denounced z' of *w* and *x*).

Note that the above semantic formulations are not intended to imply that the belief agent (the subject of the belief construction) speaks the language used in the quotation name. Thus, as Quine puts it (1956:186), "we may take a mouse's fear of a cat as his fearing true a certain English sentence." The semantic technique does, however, involve a relativity to specific languages, for a quotation name is a name of a phonetic or an orthographic form, and it is not impossible for a given form to exist, and be understood differently, in two different languages (Quine 1960:213). Thus (12) should perhaps be rewritten as

(23) Ralph believes-true in English 'Ortcutt is a spy'

and similarly for (16) and (21).

In fact, (23) and so on do not give quite the final analysis, for Quine has certain qualms about the concept of a language. Thus he suggests (1960:214) that, instead of relativizing quotation names to *a language*, we should relativize them to a speaker's idiolect. Such a move would not, of course, alter the fundamentals of his approach outlined above.

9.3.2.2. A possible problem. Church (1950:97-99) sees a difficulty with the semantic treatment of belief. The nub of the matter is that (23), for example, does not convey quite the same information as (11), even when the latter is restricted to the notional reading of 'believes that'. This can be seen if we translate both sentences into another language, say, Spanish. Sentence (11) becomes

(24) Ralph cree que Ortcutt es un espía

and (23) comes out as

(25) Ralph cree-verdadero en inglés 'Ortcutt is a spy'.

It is readily seen that a Spaniard ignorant of English would not get the same information concerning Ralph from (25) as he or she would from (24) (read notionally). If it is assumed that the pair (25) and (23) and the pair (24) and notional (11) are pairs of translation synonyms, the two sentences in each pair have an identical meaning. Therefore, just as (25) fails to capture exactly the meaning of (24), so, it seems, (23) must miss the meaning of (11).

As was mentioned earlier, Quine feels that on the whole the concept of language-transcendent sentence meanings should be rejected. Now the above objection to his semantic treatment of the attitudes turns on just that notion. Specifically, some such concept is implicit in the assumption that the bilingual pairs (25) and (23) and (24) and (11) are pairs of synonyms. Thus the foregoing objection is based on a premise to which Quine would not subscribe in the first place (see Quine 1960:214, also 1956:187).

9.3.2.3. Attitudes other than belief. A final point to note is that Quine's proposed treatment of belief can be extended to other propositional attitudes and also to the 'looks for' and 'wants' types of construction. For example, the notional reading of

(26) Tom says that Cicero denounced Catiline

becomes

(27) Tom says-true 'Cicero denounced Catiline'.
      (Quine 1960:213)

The above expression 'says-true' should not be confused with the 'says' of direct speech, for 'says-true' is meant to retain the latitude associated with reported speech. Thus we might accept as evidence for the truth of (27) the utterance by Tom of some sentence other than 'Cicero denounced Catiline', for example, 'Catiline was denounced by Cicero'.

Verbs such as 'looks for' and 'wants' require a little more work, because, at first sight, these contain no propositional-attitude expression, hence no subordinate clause that can be made into a quotation name. Such constructions can, however, be expanded so as to include propositional-attitude expressions. For example, sentence (2) might be paraphrased as

(28)   Jones is endeavoring that Jones finds the Head of
        Department

in which we have the propositional-attitude expression 'endeavors that' (compare Quine 1960:152). The notional reading of (28) might, in the semantic notation, be rendered as

(29)   Jones endeavors-to-make-true 'Jones finds the Head of
        Department'.

The *de re* reading would then come out as

(30)   Jones endeavors-to-make-true 'Jones finds x' of the Head
        of Department.

Other expressions that are similar to 'is looking for' can be rewritten in analogous ways, which I leave to the reader—for example, wanting can be construed as wishing to have.

9.3.2.4. Exportation. Although Quine recognizes the utility of being able to quantify into propositional-attitude contexts, he accepts that the attendant relational (de re) readings involve a certain oddity (1960:148, 1956:182). This oddity can be illustrated in the following way.

Read *de dicto,* our earlier sentence (14)

(14)   Ralph believes that the man seen at the beach is a spy

seems to imply

(31)   Ralph believes-true in English 'x is a spy' of the man seen
        at the beach,

for we cannot imagine Ralph simultaneously (i) believing-true in English 'the man seen at the beach is a spy' and (ii) not believing-true in English 'x is a spy' *of* the man seen at the beach. Quine calls the move whereby we go from a sentence such as (14) to a sentence such as (31) *exportation* (1956:182).

Now, in exporting from (14) to (31), we pass from a *de dicto* to a *de re* construal of 'the man seen at the beach' and so this expression becomes subject to the principle of interchangeability. Therefore, if Ortcutt is the man at the beach, (14) implies not just (31) but also

(32) Ralph believes-true in English 'x is a spy' of Ortcutt.

However, taken *de dicto,* (14) is not logically inconsistent with

(33) Ralph believes that Ortcutt is not a spy.

Now, if we export on the name 'Ortcutt' in (33), we have

(34) Ralph believes-true in English 'x is not a spy' of Ortcutt.

Thus if we take (14) and (33) as factual premises, as we are entitled to do, we end up deriving *both* (32) and (34).

Quine's response to this odd result is robust. He argues that a distinction can be reserved between, on the one hand, the conjunction of (31) and (34), and, on the other,

(35) Ralph believes-true in English 'x is a spy & x is not a spy' of Ortcutt.

Only (35), Quine contends, and not the conjunction of (32) and (34), ascribes contradictory beliefs to Ralph (1956:182). Note that our *own* judgments are not in question at all, for the contradiction in (35) affects only Ralph's beliefs and not our reporting of them.

9.4. Kaplan: Cognitive Fixes

9.4.1. Representation

In 8.3, we saw that, on account of his opposition to Aristotelian essentialism, Quine (1953) urged a semantic treatment of modal environments.

It will be recalled that the modal equivalent of 'believes-true'—namely, 'Nec'—was attachable only to quotation names for complete sentences and that, owing to that restriction, there was no question of quantifying into modal contexts.

Kaplan (1968-1969) found Quine's position defeatist but, like Quine, he was opposed to Aristotelian essentialism (p. 193). Kaplan thus steered a middle course, by using the Fregean conception of quotation. Unlike their Quinean counterparts, Fregean quotations can be quantified into, although we are only at liberty to quantify over expressions (see 8.5).

A Kaplan-style version (see 1968-1969:196) of the illicit *de re* reading of our earlier sentence (7), for example, would be

(36) $(\exists \alpha) \, [\Delta_N \, (\alpha, 9) \, \& \, \mathbf{N} <\alpha$ is greater than $7>]$,

which can be read as

(37) For some expression α: α necessarily designates 9 and 'α is greater than 7' is necessarily true.

It will be recalled from 8.5 that 'Δ_N' symbolizes a necessary-designation relation and also that '$<$' and '$>$' are intended to indicate Fregean quotation.

Now, Kaplan adopts the same sort of strategy for propositional-attitude contexts. However, he thinks that only expressions for abstract objects, such as numerals, can ever be said to necessarily designate their referents. Thus Kaplan's necessary-designation relation Δ_N can never be said to hold between, for example, a proper name and a person (1968-69:196-197). Furthermore, Δ_N is a relation between an expression and its referent, which is satisfactory for the analysis of impersonal modality but not, according to Kaplan, for the analysis of *subject-oriented* pro-positional-attitude constructions. What is required, according to Kaplan, is a three-place relation, linking a belief agent (Kaplan confines matters to belief), an expression, and an object. Kaplan (pp. 197-204) introduces such a relation and calls it *representation,* symbolized by '$\mathbf{R}$'.

According to Kaplan's definition of this relation (p. 203), an expression α represents an object x to a person if and only if (i) α

designates x; (ii) α is a name *of x* for that person, in Kaplan's special sense (see below); and (iii) α is sufficiently vivid (see below).

Kaplan's notion of a designator's being a name *of* something *for* someone can be characterized as follows. In the first place, the term 'name' is being used in a broad sense that includes definite descriptions. In fact, it is descriptive content that, in Kaplan's view, determines what a name *designates*, but it is what he calls the 'genetic character' of a name that determines what it is a name *of* for some particular person (p. 200). Kaplan's notion of 'genetic character' is not immediately clear. However, he says that the relation between a photograph and the person it is of depends entirely on genetic character: The person is involved in the causal chain leading to the production of the photograph and, also, he or she is the object of the photograph (p. 198).

Concerning linguistic expressions, Kaplan gives the impression that, for example, the definite description 'the murderer' is to be understood as a name *of* the murderer for Holmes after he has observed the victim (p. 204). Similarly, if Wyman is introduced to Ralph as 'Ortcutt', then 'Ortcutt' is a name *of* Wyman for Ralph (p. 201).

What is meant by a *vivid* name, in Kaplan's sense, is not immediately clear either. However, Kaplan says (p. 201) that, in the case in which Ralph actually knows x, the "conglomeration of images, names, and partial descriptions which Ralph employs to bring x before his mind . . . when suitably arranged and regimented" is a vivid name. For example, the description 'the murderer' in the previous paragraph would not be a vivid name for Holmes.

From the above brief characterization, it should be clear that Kaplan's relation of representation is designed to capture what he takes to be a cognitive aspect of belief reports. Using the new relation, Kaplan proposes the following as his own version of the Quinean formulation that occurred as our (32):

(38) $(\exists\alpha)$ [R $(\alpha,$ Ortcutt, Ralph) & Ralph B $<\alpha$ is a spy$>$].

This can be roughly paraphrased as

(39) For some expression α: α represents Ortcutt to Ralph and Ralph believes 'α is a spy',

in which **B,** Kaplan's doxastic counterpart to **N,** expresses a relation between a believer and a linguistic expression.

Given the definition of **R,** the only substitution instances (see 6.1.3.1) of (38)'s scope, namely,

(40)   R (α, Ortcutt, Ralph) & Ralph B <α is a spy>,

that will be true are those in which the variable α is replaced by an expression that, in addition to *designating* Ortcutt and being, historically speaking, a name *of* Ortcutt for Ralph, reflects Ralph's *cognitive purchase* on Ortcutt. In Kaplan's words (p. 197), the relation **R** indicates "a special intimacy between name and object which allows the former to go proxy for the latter in Ralph's cognitive state." Thus there is a fundamental difference between (38) and its Quinean counterpart (32); namely, in Quine's formulation it suffices that the individual in question simply *be* Ortcutt, whereas Kaplan requires, in addition, that Ralph must have this individual "in mind" (p. 204).

9.4.2. The Blocking of Certain Exportations

We saw earlier that Quine envisaged a principle of exportation, whereby relational belief sentences could be derived from notional belief sentences. One of the advantages Kaplan claims for his method is that it apparently rules out (what he takes to be) certain unforeseen and undesirable exportation possibilities (p. 204). These can be illustrated by the following example (p. 192).

Ralph believes that there are such things as spies and, in addition, that among all the spies there is one who is the shortest. Thus, using Quine's semantic notation, we write,

(41)   Ralph believes-true in English 'the shortest spy is a spy'.

By exportation, this yields

(42)   Ralph believes-true in English 'x is a spy' of the shortest spy,

from which we conclude

(43) (∃y) (Ralph believes-true in English '*x* is a spy' of *y*),

which can be read as

(44) For some thing *y*: Ralph believes-true in English '*x* is a spy' of *y*.

Kaplan argues that, intuitively, there is a "vast difference" (p. 193) between the sort of belief embodied in (41) and that embodied in (43). For example, what is expressed by the latter, but not what is expressed by the former, is something that would be of interest to the FBI. (Note that this is different than the earlier case of exportation from (14) to (31), for, in that case, although we passed from notional to relational belief, both sentences expressed facts that would be of interest to the agencies of law enforcement.) Therefore, according to Kaplan, it is not right that (43) should be derivable from (41).

Kaplan argues that his own method would rule out the undesirable exportation from (41) to (42). Presumably, his version of (41) would be

(45) Ralph **B** <the shortest spy is a spy>

and his version of (42):

(46) (∃α) [**R** (α, the shortest spy, Ralph) & Ralph **B** <α is a spy>].

Now, according to the definition of the relation **R**, the expression α in (46) has to be (among other things) a name *of* the shortest spy *for* Ralph. Therefore, any exportation from (45) to (46) is blocked, for, whoever the shortest spy is, the expression 'the shortest spy' is not a name of that individual for Ralph (nor, a fortiori, is it a vivid name).

We see then that the effect of Kaplan's method is to put certain requirements on what Quine called the relational sense of belief. Thus, according to Kaplan's analysis, "Ralph must have quite a solid conception of *x* before we can say that Ralph believes [in the relational sense] *x* to be a spy" (p. 204).

9.5. Individuating Attitude Objects

Generally speaking, the syntax of natural languages encourages us to treat the propositional attitudes as relations between an agent and an object such as a belief or a desire. Thus English complement clauses of the form 'that . . .' have traditionally been regarded as being on a par with noun phrases and, in many of the less familiar languages, the tendency toward nominalization in propositional-attitude sentences is even more marked. Consider, for example, this sentence from the South American language Aymara:

> (47) Nayax aymar yatiqañam munta. (Sáenz and Yapita Moya
> 1994:140)
>
> I + Aymara + your-learning + want.
> I want you to learn Aymara.

Here, the expression that indicates what the speaker wants is a noun phrase, consisting in the verbal noun 'yatiqaña', the possessive suffix 'm', and the complement 'aymar'.

Moreover, we often encounter sentences in which we appear to be quantifying over things like beliefs and wishes:

> (48) Paul believes something that Elmer does not.
> (Quine 1960:215)

The fact that ordinary language throws up phenomena such as (47) and (48) encourages us to try to define a criterion of identity for things like beliefs. Quine's treatment of propositional attitudes, as outlined earlier, can be seen as setting the highest possible standard for such identity, namely, notational identity, but many have argued that notational identity is too narrow a gauge, that a single belief, desire, and so on can be portrayed in more than one way.

One influential technique for widening the criterion of identity is to analyze belief (and other propositional attitudes) as a relation between an agent and some sort of syntactic object. In the work of Carnap (1956, pp. 53-64, 230-232), the syntactic object in question is still a sentence in a particular language. However, Carnap lays down a convention according to which the quotation name of any sentence that is taken to be the object of a belief can be replaced, salva veritate, by the quotation name of any other sentence (from any language) that has an identical *intensional structure* (Carnap 1956:231-232).

As we have seen ((13) in 4.3.1.2), Carnap thought that any two expressions ϕ and ψ have the same intension if their identity sentence '$\phi = \psi$' is L-true (true in all possible states of affairs; see 3.2.4.3). Two sentences or formulae can then be said to have the same intensional structure if (i) they are L-equivalent (have the same truth-value in all possible states of affairs); (ii) both sentences have the same number of parts and each part x of one sentence corresponds to a part x_1 from the other sentence such that '$x = x_1$' is L-true; and (iii) the parts of both sentences are *to be taken* in an identical order (see Carnap 1956:59). For instance,

(49) $2 + 3 = 5$

and

(50) $2 + 2 + 1 = 5$

do *not* have the same intensional structure. On the other hand,

(51) $2 + 3 = 5$

and

(52) $[\text{Sum (II, III)}] = V$

do have the same intensional structure. (Compare Carnap, 1956:59.)
Accordingly, the English sentence

(53) Ortcutt is a spy

and the Spanish sentence

(54) Ortcutt es un espía

have the same intensional structure. Therefore, given Carnap's convention according to which one quoted sentence can be replaced by another
with the same intensional structure, the truth of our earlier sentence
(12) guarantees the truth of

> (55) Ralph believes-true 'Ortcutt es un espía'. (Compare
> Carnap, 1956:232.)

On the other hand, we could not infer

> (56) Ralph believes-true 'Ortcutt is a practitioner of espionage'

from (12), because, although the sentences

> (57) Ortcutt is a spy

and

> (58) Ortcutt is a practitioner of espionage

are L-equivalent, they are not composed of an identical number of
semantically relevant parts.

We see from the foregoing remarks that Carnap's criterion for
identity between beliefs is less restrictive than Quine's. Many thinkers,
particularly those working in linguistic semantics, have found this to
be an advantage of Carnap's method, and there have been several
attempts to develop the concept of intensional structure (for a survey,
see Chierchia and McConnell-Ginet 1990:258-261).

A currently popular approach involves projecting the syntactic-
structures-as-attitude-objects into people's minds or brains. This technique is very much in keeping with the modern Chomskyian view that
knowledge of language is represented in the neural structure of the
brain (see 1.1.2.4) but, in fact, it is a very traditional method. For
example, in *Tractatus Logico-Philosophicus* (first published 1921),
Wittgenstein espoused the view that "these concepts: proposition, language, thought, world, stand in line one behind the other, each equivalent to each" (quoted from *Philosophical Investigations,* §96). Applied
to expressions of propositional attitude, this meant that a sentence of

the form 'X believes that *p*' was to be analyzed as describing a state of affairs in which what was going on in X's mind had the same logical structure as the proposition *p*. Thus, according to the view enshrined in the *Tractatus,* someone looking into the mind of a believer would see not just *that* this person believed something but also *what* he or she believed.

The *later* Wittgenstein was highly critical of the psychologism of the *Tractatus* and an idea of why he repudiated this aspect of his earlier work can be gleaned from his remarks concerning belief, hope, and expectation (see *Philosophical Investigations,* I, §§571-587).

His essential point was that beliefs and so on have no objective correlate in people's mental behavior. For example, if someone believes Goldbach's theorem (the hypothesis that every even number can be given as a sum of prime numbers), the belief cannot be identified with some feeling that is experienced when the theorem is heard or thought about, for there is no constant psychological state that accompanies things like beliefs (§578). By the same token (§584), a single minute extracted from my sitting in my room hoping for someone to bring me some money cannot necessarily be said to be an instance of hoping, for there may be nothing that I do or experience in that minute that is such that you could look at it (even assuming that you had access to my mind) and say, "Ah yes, he is hoping." As Wittgenstein put it (§583), "the word 'hope' refers to a phenomenon of human life" and not to an objective psychological state.

In saying that words such as 'hope' and so on refer to "a phenomenon of human life," Wittgenstein means that attributions of supposed psychological states are not to be taken literally but are to be seen as being "embedded," to use one of his favorite words, in customs and institutions. Thus, for example, it is not *because* someone expects an explosion that that person behaves in certain way; rather, it is because people behave in a certain way that we *say* they expect an explosion (§§581-582).

It is natural to think that, if one could obtain a cross section of a believer's (hoper's, expecter's, and so on's) mind, one would see something that corresponded to the belief (hope, expectation, and so on). However, according to Wittgenstein, if we scrutinize what is involved in ascribing such things as beliefs, hopes, and so on, we are forced to relinquish this idea.

9.6. Summary

Quine draws a distinction between the notional and the relational senses of propositional-attitude constructions. Only the relational sense is compatible with the principle of interchangeability and existential generalization.

Quine captures the difference between the two senses by treating the attitudes as relations between agents and *either* complete sentences *or* propositional functions plus one or more individuals. In the Quinean notation, such sentences and propositional functions are designated by quotation names. Now, Quine regards direct quotations as single unstructured units. Therefore, any form appearing inside the quotation name of an object of a propositional attitude is not subject to the principle of interchangeability. By the same token, we cannot quantify into the position that such a form occupies.

It is possible, in Quine's account, to infer a relational belief sentence from a notional belief sentence. Quine calls this process *exportation*.

Kaplan, too, treats propositional attitudes as relations between agents and linguistic expressions. However, unlike Quine, Kaplan allows quantification into the quotation names for these linguistic expressions. He also stipulates that, for someone x to be said to believe something *of* somebody y—in the relational sense—it must be the case that the name used to refer to y in the belief ascription satisfies certain criteria. Together, these criteria determine that the name in question *represents* its referent to the belief agent. In this way, Kaplan argues, he blocks some unwanted inferences that arise from Quine's notion of exportation.

In the closing section of the chapter, different criteria were considered for identity between beliefs. Quine's semantic treatment of belief sets the most rigorous possible standard for such identity, namely, notational identity. Thus it is never possible to replace one quotation name for a belief with another, unless the two names are formally identical. Carnap, on the other hand, proposes that one quotation name for a belief can be exchanged for another as long as the two have an identical intensional structure.

The chapter ends with an outline of the later Wittgenstein's scepticism concerning the psychologistic approach to propositional attitudes.

Part IV: Further Reading

For an explanation of the simple logical principles behind existential generalization and similar moves, see Quine 1949; also Quine 1960, §§34-35.

The best introductions to both propositional attitudes and modality are to be found in Quine 1956 and Quine 1953. Both can be tricky, but the difficulties of the first can be offset by simultaneously reading Quine 1960, §§30-32, 42-44, and those of the second by first consulting some of Quine's writings on quantification and validity in general; see Quine 1950. Carnap's "Quine on Modalities" (§44 of Carnap 1956) gives some useful insights into Quine's views on modality.

Quine's discussion of propositional attitudes in Quine 1960 (pp. 191-221) is outstanding. It demystifies the topic, and there are affinities between some of his remarks (pp. 216-221) and the antipsychologism of Wittgenstein's *Philosophical Investigations*.

Kaplan 1968-1969 should be attempted only once Quine 1956 and 1953 have been properly understood.

Kripke's work is quite easy to read and both Kripke 1980 and 1979a are accessible and largely self-contained. There are some quite interesting remarks in Putnam 1979 (immediately following Kripke's puzzle); see also Marcus 1981.

Carnap's discussion of modal logic (1956:173-202) is very explicit, but understanding it requires some technical knowledge, which can be gained from Carnap 1956, pp. 1-52, 145-172, plus, if necessary, any general logic textbook such as Quine 1950. Carnap's treatment of belief, together with his development of the concept of intensional structure, is concisely explained in §§13-15 of Carnap 1956, but his remarks there have to be counterbalanced by a reading of his "Reply to Alonzo Church," which is included in Carnap 1956 (pp. 230-232).

Modern developments along the lines of Carnap's intensional structure are briefly discussed in Chierchia and McConnell-Ginet 1990 (pp. 252-261). See also, for example, Cresswell 1985. For a good survey of related work, see Richard 1990 (chapter 1).

Wittgenstein's comments on propositional attitudes in the *Tractatus* (5.542) are compressed, to put it mildly. Russell's introduction clarifies matters a little, as do pp. 298-302 of Black 1964. For the view of propositional attitudes expounded in *Philosophical Investigations,* which is quite opposed to the psychologism of the *Tractatus,* see, in addition to the text itself, Kenny 1973 (chapters 7 and 8) and Hallett 1977 (use index).

PART V

GENERALITY

10

Indefinite Noun Phrases, Fregean Quantifiers, and Class Theory

10.1. Indefinite Noun Phrases

In Parts I to IV of this book, we have taken for granted a distinction between, on the one hand, grammatical subjects and objects and, on the other, predicative and relational locutions. Among the expressions belonging to the first category, we have considered, in addition to proper names, *definite* noun phrases such as 'the largest of the Canary Islands' and 'Jones's favorite number'. Much discourse depends, however, on *indefinite* noun phrases, plural and singular, such as 'a Spaniard', 'some Spaniard(s)', 'all/every/any Spaniard(s)', and just 'Spaniards'.

Indefinite noun phrases do not even purport to refer to things. Thus, while the definite description 'the student' in

(1)   I spoke to the student this morning

is presumed to refer to some particular individual (whose exact specification is determined in part by the context of utterance), the use of the corresponding indefinite noun phrase

(2)   I spoke to a student this morning

involves no such supposition. Sentence (2) will be true if one student, any student, was spoken to by me.

The conditions under which sentence (2) will be true illustrate a further aspect of indefinite noun phrases, namely, that whether they are grammatically in the singular or in the plural is often not relevant at a deeper level of analysis. Thus (2) counts as true even if *more than one* student was spoken to by me, for it would be mendacious or inconsistent on my part to deny (2) if (3) below, for example, was true:

(3)   I spoke to three students this morning.

Regarding plurality, *definite* noun phrases are not in the same boat as their indefinite counterparts. For example, while the expression 'the book you sent me' in

(4)   I enjoyed reading the book you sent me

is a straightforward singular definite description, of the sort discussed in Chapters 6 and 7 of this book, its plural form in

(5)   I enjoyed reading the books you sent me

is more readily treated as a vaguer or more noncommittal version of 'every book you sent me'. The affinity between, on the one hand, *plural* definite noun phrases and, on the other, indefinite noun phrases is clearer in the Romance languages, in which generic assertions habitually feature the plural definite article. For example, the Spanish sentence

(6)   Los leones comen sólo carne,

in which a plural definite noun phrase occurs as the subject of the verb, comes into English as

(7)   Lions eat only meat.

(7), of course, is to be understood as a vaguer or less categorical version of

(8)   Every lion eats only meat. (Compare Quine 1960:134.)

Sentences (5) and (6) were interpreted *distributively;* however, certain predicative and relational expressions demand a *collective* interpretation of the plural noun phrases with which they combine. Such is the case in

(9)   The rioters outnumbered the police,

which describes a situation in which the rioters *as a group* outnumbered the police. Those definite noun phrases that, like 'the rioters' in (9), call for a collective interpretation can be assimilated to the model of singular definite descriptions, although they have to be treated as designating abstract objects, namely, *classes* of concrete objects. From that perspective, the subject noun phrase in (9) is seen as being short for

(10)   the class α such that if anything is a rioter, it is a member
       of α, and vice versa,

which could, in turn, be eliminated in favor of a Russell-style contextual definition (see 6.1.3.2).

Unlike definite descriptions and proper names, indefinite noun phrases affirm existence rather than presuppose it. For example, while there is a case for saying that

(11)   Jones didn't see *the* griffin

would be neither true nor false but simply uncalled for, the sentence

(12)   Jones didn't see *a* griffin

would count as true. The reason (11) and (12) differ in this way is that, as has already been observed, indefinite noun phrases just do not refer, or even purport to refer, a circumstance that is further illustrated in cases of repetition. Compare, for example,

(13)   Jones spoke to the student and Smith spoke to the student

with

(14)   Jones spoke to a student and Smith spoke to a student.

Both occurrences of the definite description 'the student' in (13) have to be correlated with the same object but this is not the case for the indefinite noun phrase 'a student' in (14).

One interesting consequence of the mutual independence of each occurrence of a repeated indefinite noun phrase is that the suppression of one occurrence can affect the truth or falsity of the containing sentence. For instance,

(15)   Every human being is female or every human being is male

goes from false to true if we delete the second occurrence of 'every human being'. In this respect, definite descriptions and proper names are quite different. Thus

(16)   Smith is female or Smith is male

stays true if the second occurrence of 'Smith' is deleted.

10.2. Scope Ambiguities Concerning Indefinite Noun Phrases

Consider this sentence (adapted from Kripke 1979b:9):

(17)   Jones believes he will marry a debutante from Dubuque.

This can be taken to assert either (i) that Jones's belief has a certain content, namely, that he will marry a debutante from Dubuque, or (ii) that Jones has a belief concerning a particular individual, who happens to be a debutante from Dubuque, namely, that he will marry her. This duality of interpretations can be put down to a *scope ambiguity* (see 6.4) attaching to the expression 'a debutante from Dubuque'.

Although the English indefinite article 'a(n)', together with its translation equivalents in other languages, is ambiguous regarding scope, other indefinite determiners have a fixed scope. Consider the following pair of examples from Quine (1960:138):

(18) If any member contributes, he gets a poppy.

(19) If every member contributes, I'll be surprised.

Sentence (18) says this of each member *x:* If *x* contributes, *x* gets a poppy. Therefore, in (18), both the antecedent and the consequent clauses are in the scope of the indefinite noun phrase. Sentence (19), on the other hand, says this: If, for each member *x: x* contributes, then I'll be surprised. Thus the scope of 'every member' includes only the antecedent clause. (Notice that, when we explain (18) and (19), we can replace 'any' and 'every' with the neutral—regarding scope—expression 'each'.)

Neither (18) nor (19) is *ambiguous* with respect to scope, for owing, as Quine puts it (1960:139), to "simple and irreducible trait[s] of English usage," the determiners 'any' and 'every' always call for the longer and the shorter of two possible scopes, respectively. The long-scope reading of (18) is reinforced by the presence of the pronoun 'he' in the consequent clause; however, this is incidental, as can be shown if we remove the anaphoric link back to the antecedent clause:

(20) If any member contributes, I'll be surprised.

Here, as in (18), what applies to each member *x* is the whole of what is asserted, namely, that I'll be surprised if *x* contributes. It is for this reason that, unlike (19), which suggests that some contributions are expected but not the maximum possible number, (20) implies that no contributions are expected.

The contrast between the respective scopes associated with 'any' and 'every' is even more striking in negative sentences. Consider these two examples:

(21) I haven't met anyone.

(22) I haven't met everyone.

Sentence (21) says this: For each person *x:* It is not the case that I have met *x.* Sentence (22), on the other hand, says this: It is not the case that, for each person *x:* I have met *x.* In other words, what applies to each person *x* in (21) is the whole of the rest of the sentence, namely, 'I haven't met *x*', while what applies in (22) is only the subsentence 'I have met *x*'. It is for this reason that (22) but not (21) leaves open the possibility that I have met at least some persons.

10.3. Logical Analysis of Indefinite Noun Phrases

10.3.1. Functions

Sentences whose subject or object expressions are indefinite noun phrases are called *general sentences.* The basic technique for the logical analysis of generality or *quantification,* to use the more modern term, was devised by Frege and presented in his *Begriffsschrift* (Conceptual Notation), which was published in 1879 (and appears here as Frege 1972).

Frege's whole logical apparatus is based on the concept of a *function,* which is considered at length in "Funktion und Begriff" (Function and Concept), although Frege had already introduced the idea in *Begriffsschrift.* Consider the following mathematical expressions (Frege 1960:24):

(23a) $2 \times 1^3 + 1$.

(23b) $2 \times 4^3 + 4$.

(23c) $2 \times 5^3 + 5$.

Frege says that a common element can be discerned in these expressions, and we can bring this to light by replacing the part that is not common with an arbitrary letter:

(24) $2 \times x^3 + x.$

The common part highlighted in (24)—not the actual symbol '$2 \times x^3 + x$'—is an example of a function in Frege's sense. The arbitrary letter 'x' (or 'y' and so on) is called a *variable* and, obviously enough, the function of a variable is to refer to a number *indefinitely*.

Notice that a function cannot be identified with a number. The reason for this is illustrated by the following two facts. First, although we recognize the same function in (23a) to (23c), those expressions nevertheless stand for different numbers. Second, as Frege points out (1960:24), we do *not* recognize the same function in '$2 \times 1^3 + 1$' and '$4 - 1$', although these two expressions designate the *same* number.

Now, given the presence of the variable 'x', a function expression such as (24) is clearly indeterminate; indeed, it is in the nature of a function to be incomplete or, to use Frege's term, 'unsaturated' (ungesättigt). Frege argues (1960:24) that, in this respect, functions are fundamentally different from numbers and that it is just this difference that explains *why* a function cannot be identified with a number.

To supplement (24), we have to replace the 'x', at all its places of occurrence, with an expression for a specific number, as in each of (23a) to (23c). This specific number—for instance, 4 in (23b)—is called an *argument* of the function (Frege 1960:24). The result of applying the function to a particular argument is called the *value* of the function for that argument. For example, 3 is the value of the function represented in (24) for the argument 1.

In the preceding examples, we have considered only functions requiring a single argument, hence a single variable in their symbolic representation. However, it is perfectly possible to have a function that takes two or more arguments:

(25) $x^2 + y^2.$

The value of this for the arguments 2 and 3 is 13. Notice that when there are two or more arguments, we use two or more *distinct* letters or variables in the symbolic notation. This is why the earlier example (24) represents a function with only *one* argument, despite the fact that there are two occurrences of the letter 'x'.

Prior to Frege's investigations, the only things functions were considered to take as arguments were numbers and, possibly, other functions (see below). Similarly, values of functions were always conceived of as numbers. Frege went further in both directions. First, he introduced the method of treating *truth* and *falsity* as values for certain types of function. For example, the value of

(26) $x^2 = 1$

can, in Frege's theory, be said to be the truth-value True when the argument is 1 or -1 and the truth-value False when the argument is any other number (Frege 1960:28). Similarly,

(27) $4x > x^2$

returns the value True for, say, 3 but False for 10.

So far, what Frege says appears to be more or less intuitive. However, he goes on to say that, for example, '$2^2 = 4$' *designates* (the) True, just as '2^2' can be said to designate '4' (1960:28-29). The ontological suppositions implied by this additional claim, which appear to involve reifying truth (hence falsity also), have to many people seemed unpalatable. Nevertheless, we can embrace the essence of what Frege says without having to accept that truth and falsity are somehow 'out there'. In other words, we can regard (26) and (27) as indicating functions that return either True or False as values for given arguments, without thereby committing ourselves to a Fregean ontology.

Thus Frege developed the concept of a function by admitting truth-values as values of functions. He also widened the concept in the other direction, namely, in terms of what could occur as an argument. He thought that statements in general, and not just mathematical equations and inequalities, could be split up into function and argument(s). Consider this example (1960:31):

(28) Caesar conquered Gaul.

We can regard this as a function of Caesar, of Gaul, or of both. In the last case, the function could be represented in the following way:

(29) *x* conquered *y*.

Here, the function would be one that took two arguments; moreover, it would be one that returned the value True only when its arguments were *concrete things*.

10.3.2. Second-Level Functions

So far, we have considered only functions that take numbers or things as arguments, but it is also possible for a function to take *another function* as its argument (see 7.1.1.2). Frege called functions that took other functions as arguments *second-level functions,* and the modern logical analysis of generality is based wholly on this concept. Take, for example, the idea of *every(thing)*. Frege treats this in terms of a second-level function, which, using a modern equivalent of Frege's now obsolete notation, we can represent as

(30) (x) (Φx),

in which the Greek letter 'Φ' is a variable referring to functions. The '(x) $(\ldots x \ldots)$' part of (30) says that the function Φ returns the value True for every argument *x*. For example, if Φ is $x^2 = 1$, we have

(31) (x) $(x^2 = 1)$,

which returns the value False, because, if *x* is anything other than 1 or −1, $x^2 = 1$ does not return the value True. In ordinary language, (31) says the same thing as

(32) Every number, when squared, equals 1.

Now, in paraphrasing (31) as (32), we tacitly assumed that the only things that could be the argument of $x^2 = 1$ were numbers. If, however, we interpret $x^2 = 1$ as a general logical function, as opposed to a purely numerical function, (31) then says,

(33) Everything, when squared, equals 1,

which is plainly false.

As we have observed, Frege called functions such as (x) (Φx) second-level functions. Frege regarded such functions as "fundamentally different from functions whose arguments are objects and cannot be anything else" (1960:38); furthermore, he regarded the distinction as being "not made arbitrarily, but founded deep in the nature of things" (p. 41).

10.3.3. Application of Frege's Technique to Ordinary Language

10.3.3.1. 'Everything'. We can now show how virtually all the indefinite noun phrase constructions of ordinary language can be analyzed in terms of the concept enshrined in the generality function (x) (Φx), which is now called the *universal quantifier.*

As we saw (in 10.3.2), the idea of *everything* is explained directly in terms of (x) (Φx). Thus, if Φ is taken to be the function *x has mass,* for example, we have

(34) (x) $(x$ has mass$)$,

which gives us a Fregean paraphrase of 'Everything has mass'.

10.3.3.2. 'Something' and existence. To get a paraphrase for 'Something has mass', we simply insert the negation sign '$\smallfrown$' at two different places in (34):

(35) $\smallfrown(x)$ $(\smallfrown x$ has mass$)$.

This can be read as: Not everything doesn't have mass.

Notice that the scope of the first negation is '(x) $(\smallfrown x$ has mass$)$', whereas the scope of the second negation is just 'x has mass'. Frege, together with most logicians since, regarded the second-level function that occurs in (35), namely, $\smallfrown(x)$ $(\smallfrown\Phi x)$, as indicating existence (1960:37-38). For example, the assertion that at least one positive number exists can be analyzed in terms of the application of $\smallfrown(x)$ $(\smallfrown\Phi x)$ to the argument $x \geq 0$:

(36) $\backsim(x)$ ($\backsim x \geq 0$). (Frege 1960:37)

Similarly, an ordinary-language sentence such as 'There are immortals' can be represented as

(37) $\backsim(x)$ ($\backsim x$ is immortal).

Notice that, as was remarked in connection with the earlier example (2), the grammatical distinction between plural and singular is often not relevant in the case of indefinite noun phrases at deeper levels of analysis.

10.3.3.3. *'Every'*. Sentences (34) to (37) are much more general than the general sentences that normally occur in everyday language, for we tend, in ordinary general sentences, to use full indefinite noun phrases, such as 'some women' or 'every man', rather than the indefinite pronouns 'something' and 'everything'. Sentences involving full indefinite noun phrases can easily be accommodated in Frege's method. Consider the sentence

(38) Every human is mortal,

which is equivalent in meaning to 'All humans are mortal'. Intuitively, and as Russell observed in "On Denoting" (p. 481), sentences like (38) are really hypothetical, for what (38) really asserts is that *if* anything is a human being, it is mortal. We can factor this out into two Fregean functions, namely, (x) (Φx) and *if x is human, x is mortal*—the latter serving as the argument of the former. In other words, (38) can be analyzed as saying that the function *if x is human, x is mortal*, that is, *x is human* → *x is mortal* (for '→', see Table 1.3), always returns the value True. Therefore, following the model of (34), we replace 'Φ' in '(x) (Φx)' with '*x* is human → *x* is mortal', a move that gives us

(39) (x) (x is human → x is mortal).

Now the schema (see 3.2.1) '$p \rightarrow q$' can be treated as an abbreviation for '$\backsim(p \ \& \ \backsim q)$'. We see why this is so when we consider a sentence such as

(40)   If Clinton is president, then Clinton won the election.

What (40) does is exclude the case in which, on the one hand, Clinton is president and, on the other, Clinton did not win the election. Thus what (40) really says is this:

(41)   ⌐(Clinton is president & ⌐Clinton won the election).

Therefore '. . . → . . .' and '⌐(. . . & ⌐ . . .)' are notational variants of each other. In Fregean terms, they represent the same function (see 1.2.4; see also Frege 1972, pp. 115, 123). To return to example (38), we now see that that sentence can be expanded to

(42)   (x) ⌐(x is human & ⌐x is mortal),

which is an instance of the schema

(43)   (x) ⌐(Φx & ⌐Ψx).

In what follows, sentences conforming to the schema '(x) (Φx → Ψx)' can be understood as being abbreviations for sentences conforming to schema (43). In this way, it will be seen that the whole complex phenomenon of generality can be reduced to just a handful of primitive concepts.

   10.3.3.4. 'Some' and 'no'. We can now explain sentences such as 'Some humans are mortal' (which is normally taken to say the same thing as 'Some human is mortal') and their negation, as in 'No human is mortal'. The sentence 'Some humans are mortal' asserts that not every human is not mortal, while 'No humans are mortal' denies this. Thus we have

(44)   ⌐(x) (x is human → ⌐x is mortal)

and

(45)   ⌐⌐(x) (x is human → ⌐x is mortal),

of which the latter, with its initial double negation, becomes '(x) (x is human → ⌐x is mortal)'. Generally speaking, it is convenient to convert the '→' of formulations such as (44) and (45) into combinations of '⌐' and '&'. Thus 'Some humans are mortal' becomes

(46) ⌐(x) ⌐(x is human & x is mortal),

for which the abbreviated form

(47) (∃x) (x is human & x is mortal)

is normally used. 'No humans are mortal' becomes (47) with the negation sign prefixed.

10.3.3.5. Scope: 'Every' versus 'any'. We mentioned scope informally in connection with the earlier examples (18) and (19). As was pointed out then, 'any' and 'every' have the same meaning, except that the former demands a long-scope reading, while the latter calls for a short-scope reading. The determiner 'each', it will be recalled, is neutral with regard to scope.

The idea of scope in this informal sense gives way, in the Fregean notation, to the more precise notion of the scope (*Gebiet*) of the generality sign, which we write as '(x)'. Frege illustrates the concept of scope with a comparison between three schemata (1972:130-131), of which we instantiate two below:

(48) (x) (x floats).

(49) (x) (x floats) → this lead ball floats.

Sentence (48) is a Frege-inspired paraphrase of 'Everything floats' and (49) does duty for 'If everything floats, this lead ball floats'. It is easily seen that, if (48) is true (in fact, it is false), so is any less general sentence that can be derived by deleting the generality notation '(x) (. . . x . . .)' and arbitrarily replacing it with a symbol for something definite, as in

(50) Smith's yacht floats.

On the other hand, this move is not open to us in the case of (49), because the truth of that sentence does not secure the truth of, for example,

(51) Smith's yacht floats → this lead ball floats

(for the truth-table for '→', see Table 1.6). Thus in (49) we cannot, as Frege puts it (1972:131), "arbitrarily substitute for [the generality notation] without jeopardizing the truth of the judgement [i.e., the assertion]."

Following Frege, we can say that the reason for this difference between (48) and (49) is that in the former, but not in the latter, the scope of the generality sign '(x)' is the *whole* of the rest of the sentence; arbitrary substitutions, Frege contends, are possible only if the scope of the generality sign is "the content of the whole judgement" (1972:131).

In the modern version of Frege's symbolism, the scope of the generality sign is marked out through the use of brackets. For example, the scope of the generality sign in (49) is just 'x floats'. And that sentence contrasts with

(52) (x) (x floats → this lead ball floats),

which gives a paraphrase for the English sentence 'If anything floats, this lead ball floats'. Sentence (52) is false, but

(53) (x) (x floats → Smith's yacht floats)

is true (provided that Smith's yacht is not damaged in some way). Given that '(x)' has maximum possible scope in (53), we are free, unlike in (49), to substitute arbitrarily for the generality notation '(x) (. . . x . . .)'. For example, if (53) is true, so is 'Wood floats → Smith's yacht floats'.

We can now employ the Fregean technique to bring out the difference between Quine's sentences (18) and (19)

(18) If any member contributes, he gets a poppy.

(19) If every member contributes, I'll be surprised.

As was observed, 'any' always calls for long scope. Therefore, (18) becomes

(54) (x) [(x is a member & x contributes)→ x gets a poppy].

On the other hand, we render (19) as

(55) [(x) (x is a member → x contributes)] → I'll be surprised,

in which the generality sign '(x)', together with its scope, is contained within the antecedent clause '(x) (x is a member → x contributes)'—the square brackets '[' and ']' merely indicate how (54) and (55) are to be read.

Similarly, the difference between the two readings of (17) now finds explicit expression in the contrast between

(56) Jones believes $(\exists x)$ (x is a debutante from Dubuque & Jones will marry x)

and

(57) $(\exists x)$ (x is a debutante from Dubuque & Jones believes Jones will marry x).

However, note that (56) and (57) are only provisional, pending a more rigorous treatment of 'believes that' (see 9.3).

10.4. Numerically Definite Quantifiers

It is readily seen from the foregoing that the delicate phenomenon of indefinite noun phrases, which involves a plethora of determiners and different scopes, can be reduced to just three logical primitives: the generality function (x) (Φx), negation, and conjunction. This reduction, however, still leaves us with a large class of noun phrases in need of analysis, namely, those in which the determiner is a fixed numerical expression.

Numerically definite noun phrases, such as 'five gold rings', can in fact be brought within the scope of the Fregean technique through the simple addition to the notation of the identity sign '='. What follows is based on Quine (1950, pp. 211, 231-236, 1960:118).

Before looking at numerically definite noun phrases, we need to see how identity enters into quantification theory. Therefore, consider the following sentence:

(58)   Jones hears people.

As was remarked earlier, grammatical plurality is often not relevant in the logical analysis of indefinite noun phrases. On the other hand, there is a case for saying that if (58) is true, there must be at least two people whom Jones hears. If this is correct, what (58) amounts to is this:

(59)   Jones hears a person other than a person that he hears,

which, in symbolic notation, with '$x \neq y$' an abbreviation for '$\backsim x = y$', becomes

(60) $(\exists x)$ $(\exists y)$ (x is a person & y is a person & Jones hears x & Jones hears y & $x \neq y$).

We can extend the above technique to numerically definite expressions in the following way, starting with 'zero'. We have seen that a sentence such as 'No humans are mortal' (see (45) above) becomes

(61) $\backsim (\exists x)$ (x is human & x is mortal).

Obviously, 'No humans are mortal' says the same thing as 'Zero humans are mortal'. Thus 'Jones hears zero people' becomes

(62) $\backsim (\exists x)$ (x is a person & Jones hears x),

which we can abbreviate to

(63) $(\exists x)_0$ (x is a person & Jones hears x).

Speaking generally, we can say that '$(\exists x)_0(\Phi x)$' is an abbreviation for '$\backsim (\exists x)(\Phi x)$'. Each succeeding quantifier $(\exists x)_1$, $(\exists x)_2$, and so on can then be explained in terms of its predecessor. Thus, using the symbol '≠' as in (60), we have

(64) $(\exists x)_1\ (\Phi x)$ for $(\exists x)\ [\Phi x\ \&\ (\exists y)_0\ (\Phi y\ \&\ y \neq x)]$

(65) $(\exists x)_2\ (\Phi x)$ for $(\exists x)\ [\Phi x\ \&\ (\exists y)_1\ (\Phi y\ \&\ y \neq x)]$

(66) $(\exists x)_3\ (\Phi x)$ for $(\exists x)\ [\Phi x\ \&\ (\exists y)_2\ (\Phi y\ \&\ y \neq x)]$

(67) $(\exists x)_4\ (\Phi x)$ for $(\exists x)\ [\Phi x\ \&\ (\exists y)_3\ (\Phi y\ \&\ y \neq x)]$

and so on. The general pattern, as Quine puts it (1950:232), is this: "For anything to be true of $n + 1$ things is for it to be true of something other than which it is true of n things." (The astute reader will have noticed that (64) is logically equivalent to '$(\exists x)\ [\Phi x\ \&\ (y)(\Phi y \rightarrow y = x)]$', that is, the schema of the existential and uniqueness-securing clauses of a Russell-style contextual definition of a definite description [see 6.1.3.2].)

By three steps of expansion according to the above definitions, the logical structure of, for example,

(68)   Jones has visited exactly three cities

can be reduced to a combination of generality, conjunction, negation, and identity (the letter '*F*' is to be understood as meaning '. . . is a city & Jones has visited . . .'):

(69) $(\exists w)\ [Fw\ \&\ (\exists x)\ [Fx\ \&\ (\exists y)\ [Fy\ \&\ \sim(\exists z)\ (Fz\ \&\ z \neq w\ \&$
         $z \neq x\ \&\ z \neq y)]]]$.

Formulation (69) obviously differs greatly from its ordinary-language counterpart (68). This, however, should not be looked upon as a defect, because the whole point of (69) is to get underneath the superficial grammatical form of (68). If the logical structure of (68) is constrained beforehand to look like its superficial grammatical structure, there is hardly any point in undertaking the logical analysis in the first place.

10.5. Expanding the Theory

10.5.1. Limits of Numerically Definite Quantifiers

A different type of sentence than those that we have considered so far is exemplified by

(70)   More students play football than lecturers.

Using the sort of technique introduced in the previous section, we might attempt to render this as

(71) $(\exists m)$ $(\exists n)$ $[(\exists x)_m$ (x is a student & x plays football) & $(\exists x)_n$ (x is a lecturer & x plays football) & $m > n]$.

But such a move fails, because no definitions are available for expanding '$(\exists x)_m$ (Φx)' and '$(\exists x)_n$ (Φx)', with unspecified m and n, along the lines suggested by (69).

10.5.2. Definition of the Concept of a Number

To solve the problem, we need to see how numbers can be defined. First, we need to consider the predicative use of numerical expressions, which is illustrated by

(72)   We are four (in number),

as opposed to

(73)   4 is Jones's favorite number.

(I use letters, as in 'four', when the numerical expression occurs predicatively, and the Arabic numeral otherwise.) Note that, although the construction exemplified in (72) sounds rather archaic in English, it is very common in Romance languages, thus 'Somos cuatro' ('There are four of us'). Notice too that, used predicatively, a numerical expression is true of a class of objects rather than of an individual object: It is we as a group who are four in (72) and not any individual one of us. So we can treat (72) as saying that the class of us has four members; that is,

(74) $(\exists x)_4$ ($x \in$ the class of us).

Therefore, if 'α' is a variable referring to classes, the predicative expression 'four' can be defined as

(75) $(\exists x)_4$ ($x \in \alpha$)

(compare Quine 1950:232) because any class for which function (75) returns the value True will be a class that has exactly four members; that is, any such class will be a class of which the predicate 'four' is true.

Now, it is natural to think of nonpredicative '4' as designating that which predicative 'four' is true of, namely, every class that has exactly four members. Thus, following Frege's classic development of the theme in *Grundlagen der Arithmetik* (first published in 1884, which appears here as Frege 1953), we can treat any *numeral* 'κ' as designating the class of all and only those classes that have κ members. For example, '2' designates the class of pairs, '3' the class of trios, and so on. This means that identity between any *numbers* κ and λ can be expressed as

(76) (α) ([$\alpha \in \kappa \to \alpha \in \lambda$] & [$\alpha \in \lambda \to \alpha \in \kappa$]),

which we can abbreviate to

(77) (α) ($\alpha \in \kappa \leftrightarrow \alpha \in \lambda$). (Quine 1950:233)

We then need to define what the individual numerals '0', '1', '2', and so on designate without making use of the corresponding concepts *zero, one, two,* and so on. To do this, we can make use of the notation '$\hat{\alpha} \, \Phi\alpha$' as an abbreviation for 'the class of all classes α such that $\Phi\alpha$'. Then we can define 0 (i.e., the designatum of '0') as

(78) $\hat{\alpha} \frown (\exists x)$ ($x \in \alpha$),

that is, as the class of empty classes (in fact, because classes with the same members are the same class, there is only one empty class). Now, in explaining the determiner '(exactly) one', that is, '$(\exists x)_1 (\Phi x)$', in section 10.4, use was made of the concept of identity. We can avail ourselves of the same strategy to define the number 1, which can be treated as

(79) $\hat{\alpha} (\exists x) [x \in \alpha \ \& \ \frown(\exists y)(y \in \alpha \ \& \ y \neq x)]$,

that is, the class of all and only those classes α such that α has exactly one member.

Given the above definition of 1, the numbers 2, 3, and so on can be defined as $1 + 1$, $1 + 2$, and so on. The sum of two numbers $\kappa + \lambda$ can be defined as the class of every class α such that α can be broken down into two mutually exclusive classes β and γ, where $\beta \in \kappa$ and $\gamma \in \lambda$:

(80) $\hat{\alpha} (\exists \beta) (\exists \gamma) [\beta \in \kappa \ \& \ \gamma \in \lambda \ \& \ (x) \frown(x \in \beta \ \& \ x \in \gamma) \ \&$
        $(x) (x \in \alpha \leftrightarrow x \in \beta \lor x \in \gamma)]$

(for the symbol '$\lor$', see Table 1.3).

We can now, finally, define the concept of a number. To be a number is to be either 0, or $1 + 0$, or $1 + (1 + 0)$, or $1 + (1 + (1 + 0))$ . . . . In other words, the expression 'κ is a number' says that κ belongs to every class (of classes of classes) to which 0 belongs and to which $1 +$ each member belongs. Therefore, using 'ϕ' as a variable that refers to classes of classes of classes, we can rewrite 'κ is a number' as

(81) $(\phi) [[0 \in \phi \ \& \ (\lambda) (\lambda \in \phi \rightarrow 1 + \lambda \in \phi)] \rightarrow \kappa \in \phi]$.

(This is based on Quine 1950:235 but the technique stems from Frege 1953.)

10.5.3. 'More Than', 'Half as Many', 'Few'

Using '$N\kappa$' for 'κ is a number'—technically speaking, we are dealing only with the natural numbers 0, 1, 2, 3, 4, and so on—and 'α' and 'β' as names for the classes of students and lecturers, respectively, we can explain

(82) There are (exactly) as many students as lecturers

as

(83) (∃κ) (Nκ & α ∈ κ & β ∈ κ).

In other words, we treat (82) as saying that the class of students and the class of lecturers belong to the same number. Taking α and β now to be the classes of football-playing students and football-playing lecturers, respectively, we can explain sentence (70) as

(84) (∃μ) (∃κ) (∃λ) [Nμ & Nκ & Nλ & κ = μ + λ & μ ≠ 0 & α ∈ κ & β ∈ λ];

that is,

(85) The number of football-playing students is equal to at least 1 + the number of football-playing lecturers.

It will be noted that, in (83) and (84), we used 'α' and 'β' as names of specific classes (and not as variables, as previously). Now, these names are really abbreviations for such definite descriptions as 'the class α such that for everything x: $x ∈ α ↔ x$ is a student' or 'the class β such that for everything x: $x ∈ β ↔ x$ plays football & x is a lecturer'. And these can be eliminated using the method introduced in 6.1.3.2. For example, (83) can be expanded to

(86) (∃α) (∃β) (∃κ) [(x) [(x is a student ↔ $x ∈ α$) & (x is a lecturer ↔ $x ∈ β$)] & Nκ & α ∈ κ & β ∈ κ].

Given a definition of multiplication (see Quine 1950:234), we can apply the above technique to sentences such as the following:

(87) Twice as many students as lecturers play football.

(88) Half as many students as lecturers play football.

(89) Half the students play football.

Sentence (87) can be treated as saying that the number of football-playing students is identical to 2 × the number of football-playing lecturers; (88) says the converse of (87); and sentence (89) says that the number of students is identical to 2 × the number of football-playing students.

Determiners such as 'few' and 'many' are dependent in their interpretation on some host term. For instance, the *few* Americans who vote for a third party outnumber the *many* British university students who play some sort of sport. If we are prepared to be legalistic, we can stipulate fixed proportions as boundaries below and above which a given number of Xs are to count as few Xs and many Xs, respectively. From that perspective, a sentence such as

(90)   Few students play football

becomes, say,

(91)   The number of students is greater than 10 × the number of football-playing students,

which can then be translated into the symbolic apparatus described above.

10.5.4. Generalized Quantifiers

In sections 10.1 to 10.4 above, our quantifiers (x) and $\exists x$ applied only to functions whose arguments could be individual objects or numbers viewed as individual objects; that is, we quantified only over individuals. In 10.5, however, we have ascended to a level at which we quantify over *classes of classes* of individuals and even, in the case of '$(\phi) (\ldots \phi \ldots)$', over *classes of classes of classes* of individuals. This ascent appears to be unavoidable if the objective is to represent the logical structure of sentences involving constructions such as 'more than' and 'as many as', which force us into class theory and into defining numbers.

In recent years, some logicians (see Barwise and Cooper 1984) have gone the other way and generalized the use of classes of classes to *all* the sentences of ordinary language. Accordingly, all noun phrases and proper names are taken to designate what are called *generalized quantifiers,* that is, classes of classes. For example,

(92)   Some students are cyclists

becomes what, in ordinary English, amounts to

(93)   The class of cyclists is a member of the class of every class whose intersection with the class of students is not empty,

and

(94)   Smith runs fast

becomes

(95)   The class of fast runners is a member of the class of every class to which Smith belongs.

10.6. Summary

Indefinite noun phrases are used to express general propositions, as opposed to propositions about specific things. The technique for analyzing the sentences that express such propositions was introduced by Frege in *Begriffsschrift*. This technique consists in factoring out a general sentence into a (first-level) function expression and a quantifier expression '$(\exists x)$' or '(x)'; the quantifier expression indicates a function too, but one belonging to a higher level. The function expression contains a variable and, on account of this circumstance, is indeterminate or 'unsaturated'. The quantifier expressions '$(\exists x)$' and '(x)' express the fact that the function indicated by the function expression returns the value True for some or for every argument, respectively. By representing generality in this way, Frege is able, systematically, to capture differences in the scope of indefinite noun phrases.

Owing to the circumstances that (i) the schema '$(x) (\Phi x \rightarrow \Psi x)$' can be expanded to '$(x) \smallsmile (\Phi x \ \& \ \smallsmile \Psi x)$' and (ii) '$(\exists x)$' is an abbreviation for '$\smallsmile (x) \smallsmile$', it can be shown that Frege's theory reduces the whole complex business of indefinite noun phrases to just the generality function (x) (Φx), plus negation and conjunction.

To analyze numerically definite quantifiers, the concept of identity must be introduced into the theory. Accordingly, 'Exactly one thing is a Φ' becomes '$(\exists x)\ [(\Phi x)\ \&\ \frown(\exists y)\ (\Phi y\ \&\ y \neq x)]$'. Each successively higher numerically definite quantifier is then defined in terms of its predecessor.

To deal with constructions such as 'as many as' and 'more than', it becomes necessary to quantify over classes, classes of classes, and even classes of classes of classes.

Part V: Further Reading

Quine 1960 (§§23, 24, 29) gives a self-contained and perceptive overview of how indefinite noun phrases function in ordinary language. §34 shows how matters can be 'regimented' using the standard notation of quantification.

A suggested program for reading about Frege's treatment of generality is this: Frege 1972:111-135 (there is an alternative translation, with some deletions, in Frege 1960:1-20), followed by Frege 1960:21-41. Kenny (1995:12-49, 100-125) provides an excellent introduction or, alternatively, can be read as a kind of running commentary.

For the numerically definite quantifiers, see Quine 1950, §39, and possibly having read §35 beforehand.

Quine 1950:232-236 is a concise and (relatively) easy-to-read account of how to use class theory to go beyond the numerically definite quantifiers, although it may be advisable to look at pp. 225-231 beforehand.

For the Fregean view of numbers, see Kenny 1995 (use index) and also Kenny 1973 (pp. 39-42).

For a thorough introduction to generalized quantifiers, see Barwise and Cooper 1984. That paper does not make easy reading, however, and a good place to start is Cann 1993 (pp. 187-195) or Chierchia and McConnell-Ginet 1990 (pp. 406-430).

References

Baker, G. P., and Hacker, P. M. S. 1985. *Wittgenstein: Rules, Grammar and Necessity. Volume 2: An Analytical Commentary on the Philosophical Investigations*. Oxford: Basil Blackwell.

Barwise, J., and Cooper, R. 1984. Generalized quantifiers and natural language. *Linguistics and Philosophy* 4:159-219.

Black, M. 1964. *A Companion to Wittgenstein's 'Tractatus'*. Cambridge: Cambridge University Press.

Cann, R. 1993. *Formal Semantics*. Cambridge: Cambridge University Press.

Carnap, R. 1956. *Meaning and Necessity*. 2nd edition. Chicago: University of Chicago Press.

Carnap, R. 1958. *Introduction to Semantics and Formalization of Logic* (2 volumes in one). Cambridge, Mass.: Harvard University Press.

Chierchia, G., and McConnell-Ginet, S. 1990. *Meaning and Grammar: An Introduction to Semantics*. Cambridge: MIT Press.

Chomsky, N. 1986. *Knowledge of Language: Its Nature, Origin, and Use*. Convergence, N.Y.: Praeger.

Chomsky, N. 1990. Language and problems of knowledge. Lecture delivered in Madrid, April 28, 1986. Printed in *The Philosophy of Language*, edited by A. P. Martinich (pp. 509-527). 2nd edition. Oxford: Oxford University Press.

Church, A. 1936. A note on the Entscheidungsproblem. *Journal of Symbolic Logic* 1:40-41, 101-102.

Church, A. 1950. On Carnap's analysis of statements of assertion and belief. *Analysis* 10:97-99.

231

Cole, P., and Morgan, J. L., eds. 1975. *Syntax and Semantics.* Volume 3. New York: Academic Press.

Cresswell, M. J. 1985. *Structured Meanings.* Cambridge: MIT Press.

Crimmins, M. 1992. Context in the attitudes. *Linguistics and Philosophy* 15:185-198.

Davidson, D. 1967. Truth and Meaning. *Synthèse* 17:304-323.

Donnellan, K. 1966. Reference and definite descriptions. *Philosophical Review* 75:281-304.

Evans, G. 1973. The causal theory of names. *Proceedings of the Aristotelian Society,* Supplementary Volume 47:187-208.

Feigl, H., and Sellars, W., eds. 1949. *Readings in Philosophical Analysis.* New York: Appleton-Century-Crofts.

Frege, G. 1949. On sense and nominatum. In *Readings in Philosophical Analysis,* edited by H. Feigl and W. Sellars (pp. 85-102). New York: Appleton-Century-Crofts.

Frege, G. 1953. *The Foundations of Arithmetic: A Logico-Mathematical Inquiry into the Concept of Number.* Translated by J. L. Austin. 2nd edition. Oxford: Basil Blackwell.

Frege, G. 1960. *Translations from the Philosophical Writings of Gottlob Frege.* Edited by P. Geach and M. Black. 2nd edition. Oxford: Basil Blackwell.

Frege, G. 1964. *The Basic Laws of Arithmetic.* Translated by Montgomery Furth. Berkeley: University of California Press.

Frege, G. 1971. *Ecrits logiques et philosophiques.* Translated by C. Imbert. Paris: Points.

Frege, G. 1972. *Conceptual Notation and Related Articles.* Translated by Terrell Ward Bynum. Oxford: Clarendon.

French, P. A., Uehling, T. E., and Wettstein, H. K., eds. 1979. *Contemporary Perspectives in the Philosophy of Language.* Minneapolis: University of Minnesota Press.

French, P. A., Uehling, T. E., and Wettstein, H. K., eds. 1981. *Midwest Studies in Philosophy.* Minneapolis: University of Minnesota Press.

Grice, H. P. 1975. Logic and conversation. In *Syntax and Semantics,* edited by P. Cole and J. L. Morgan (pp. 41-58). New York: Academic Press.

Grice, H. P., and Strawson, P. F. 1956. In defense of a dogma. *Philosophical Review* 65:141-158.

Hallett, Garth. 1977. *A Companion to Wittgenstein's 'Philosophical Investigations'.* Ithaca, New York: Cornell University Press.

Kaplan, D. 1968-1969. Quantifying in. *Synthèse* 19:178-214.

Kaplan, D. 1972. What is Russell's Theory of Descriptions? In *Bertrand Russell,* edited by D. F. Pears (pp. 227-244). Garden City, N.Y.: Anchor Books.

Kenny, Anthony. 1973. *Wittgenstein.* London: Penguin.

Kenny, Antony. 1995. *Frege.* London: Penguin.

Kripke, Saul. 1979a. A puzzle about belief. In *Meaning and Use. Papers Presented at the Second Jerusalem Philosophical Encounter, April 1976,* edited by A. Margalit (pp. 239-283). Dordrecht: D. Reidel.

Kripke, Saul. 1979b. Speaker's reference and semantic reference. In *Contemporary Perspectives in the Philosophy of Language,* edited by P. A. French, T. E. Uehling and H. K. Wettstein (pp. 6-27).

Kripke, Saul. 1980. *Naming and Necessity.* 2nd edition. Oxford: Basil Blackwell.

Kripke, Saul A. 1982. *Wittgenstein on Rules and Private Language. An Elementary Exposition.* Oxford: Basil Blackwell.

Lyons, J. 1977. *Semantics.* Cambridge: Cambridge University Press.

Lyons, J. 1995. *Lingusitic Semantics: An Introduction.* Cambridge, UK: Cambridge University Press.

Marcus, Ruth Barcan. 1981. A proposed solution to a puzzle about belief. In *Midwest Studies in Philosophy,* edited by P. A. French, T. E. Uehling and H. K. Wettstein (pp. 501-510). Minneapolis: University of Minnesota Press.

Margalit, Avishai, ed. 1979. *Meaning and Use. Papers Presented at the Second Jerusalem Philosophical Encounter, April 1976.* Dordrecht: D. Reidel.

Martinich, A. P., ed. 1990. *The Philosophy of Language.* 2nd edition. Oxford: Oxford University Press.

Mill, John Stuart. 1967. *A System of Logic.* 8th edition. London: Longman.

Pears, D. F., ed. 1972. *Bertrand Russell.* Garden City, N.Y.: Anchor.

Putnam, Hilary. 1962. It ain't necessarily so. *Journal of Philosophy* 59:658-671.

Putnam, Hilary. 1973. Meaning and reference. *Journal of Philosophy* 70:699-711.

Putnam, Hilary. 1979. Comments on Kripke's 'Puzzle About Belief'. In *Meaning and Use. Papers Presented at the Second Jerusalem Philosophical Encounter, April 1976,* edited by A. Margalit (pp. 284-288). Dordrecht: D. Reidel.

Quine, W. V. O. 1943. Notes on existence and necessity. *Journal of Philosophy* 40:113-127.

Quine, W. V. O. 1949. Designation and existence. In *Readings in Philosophical Analysis,* edited by H. Feigl and W. Sellars (pp. 44-51). New York: Appleton-Century-Crofts.

Quine, W. V. O. 1950. *Methods of Logic.* New York: Holt.

Quine, W. V. O. 1951. Two dogmas of empiricism. *Philosophical Review* 60:20-43.

Quine, W. V. O. 1953. Three grades of modal involvement. *Proceedings of the XIth International Congress of Philosophy,* Volume 14 (pp. 65-81), Brussels, August.

Quine, W. V. O. 1956. Quantifiers and propositional attitudes. *Journal of Philosophy* 53:177-187.

Quine, W. V. O. 1960. *Word and Object.* Cambridge: MIT Press.

Richard, M. 1990. *Propositional Attitudes: An Essay on Thoughts and How We Ascribe Them.* Cambridge, UK: Cambridge University Press.

Russell, B. 1905. On denoting. *Mind* 14:479-493.

Russell, B. 1919a. *Introduction to Mathematical Philosophy.* London: George Allen and Unwin.

Russell, B. 1919b. Propositions: What they are and how they mean. *Proceedings of the Aristotelian Society,* Supplement II, 1-43.

Russell, B. 1921. *Analysis of Mind.* London: George Allen and Unwin Ltd.

Russell, B. 1937. Denoting. In *Principles of Mathematics* (pp. 53-65). 2nd edition. New York: Norton.

Russell, B. 1959. *The Problems of Philosophy.* Oxford Paperbacks University Series. Oxford: Oxford University Press. (First published 1912)

Sáenz, S. D., and Yapita Moya, J. 1994. Las oraciones compuestas en Aymara. In *Language in the Andes,* edited by P. Cole, G. Hermon, and M. D. Martin (pp. 126-150). Newark, Del.: Latin American Studies.

Schlick, M. 1938. *Gesammelte Aufsätze 1926-36.* Vienna: Gerold.

Searle, J. R. 1958. Proper names. *Mind* 67:166-173.

Searle, J. R. 1983. *Intentionality.* Cambridge, UK: Cambridge University Press.

Tarski, A. 1949. The semantic conception of truth. In *Readings in Philosophical Analysis,* edited by H. Feigl and W. Sellars (pp. 52-84). New York: Appleton-Century-Crofts.

Tarski, A. 1983. *Logic, Semantics and Metamathematics.* Translated by J. H. Woodger. 2nd edition. Oxford: Clarendon.

Waismann, F. 1965. *The Principles of Linguistic Philosophy.* Edited by R. Harré. London: Macmillan.

Wittgenstein, Ludwig. 1953. *Philosophical Investigations.* Translated by G. E. M. Anscombe. Oxford: Basil Blackwell.

Wittgenstein, Ludwig. 1961. *Notebooks 1914-1916.* Edited by G. H. von Wright and G. E. M. Anscombe. Oxford: Basil Blackwell.

Wittgenstein, Ludwig. 1961 (first published 1921). *Tractatus Logico-Philosophicus.* Translated by D. F. Pears and B. F. McGuinness. London: Routledge.

Index

Acquaintance, 105-107, 114-115
Acquisition:
  of language, 13
  of referential function, 115-120
Adjectives, in ontogenesis of reference, 118
"All," as logical expression, 59
Analysis, of definite descriptions:
  Frege and, 108-112
  Quine and, 115-119
  Russell and, 105-115, 119-127
Analysis, of indefinite noun phrases, Fregean technique, 212-221
Analyticity, 61-66
"And," in Carnap's method, 41
Arguments, of functions, 213
Aristotelian essentialism, 170-171
Arithmetic operations, 4
Articles:
  definite, 117, 145-148
  indefinite, 145-146, 211
Attitudes, semantic treatment of, 187-193. *See also* Propositional attitudes
Attributive descriptions, 151-154, 157-159, 161. *See also* Adjectives
Axioms, of truth-functional logic, 54-57

Belief:
  cognitive fixes and, 195-197
  identity criteria for, 198-201
  semantic treatment of, 187-191
  See also Propositional attitudes

Calculus of classes, 48
Carnap, R.:
  on definition of truth, 40-45
  on extension and intension, 180-182, 199-200
  on name relation method, 71-73
  on rules of ranges, 60
  on state descriptions, 58-61, 181
Causal chain, and rule following, 8-10
Causal theory of names, 88-100
Chomsky:
  I-language of, 12-14
  on species-specific properties, 13, 16
Circumlocution, 158, 171
Classes of classes, 226
Class theory, 48, 225-229
Cognition, genuine, 75
Cognitive fixes, 193-197
Cognitive purchase, 196

Common structure, 17. *See also* Language-reality isomorphism; Structure, of language and reality
Concept-object distinction, 140-145. *See also* Object expressions
Connectives, truth functional, 22-26, 41-42
Constants, 40, 137
Coreferential expressions:
　modality and, 170, 175
　propositional attitudes and, 183, 185, 189
Course-of-values, 146

Decision procedures, for truth-functional logic, 53
Decomposition. *See* Analysis
De dicto readings, 126-127
　modality and, 171, 175
　propositional attitudes and, 184-186, 187, 188, 192-193
Definite articles, 117, 145-148
Definite descriptions:
　according to Frege, 108-112
　according to Quine, 115-119
　according to Russell, 105-115, 119-127
　according to Wittgenstein, 127-138
　acquaintance and, 105-107, 114-115
　as names, Donnellan on, 152-155, 157, 158, 159, 160
　as names, Fregean theory of, 140-151
　as names, Kripke on, 155-160
　attributive, 151-154, 157-159, 161
　compared to indefinite noun phrases, 207-210
　complex versus simple symbols and, 107-108, 145
　concept-object distinction and, 140-145
　content obliterated in, 154-155
　epistemological basis of theory on, 106, 128
　generality and, 108-115, 119, 132-138, 141-144
　improper, 150-151
　meaning lacking in, 114
　modality and, 175

numerically definite quantifiers and, 221-223
object expressions and, 145-151
plurality of, 208-209
propositional attitudes and, 185, 195
referential, 151-161
referential function acquisition and, 115-120
scope and, 109, 125-127
truth-value gaps and, 105-106, 120
vacuous, 150-151
value ranges and, 146-151
would-be subjects and, 123-125
Deictic features, and definition of truth, 48-49
Demonstrative modifiers, 116-117
Demonstrative singular terms, 117
Denoting expressions, 179
Denoting phrases, 108, 125
De re readings, 126-127
　modality and, 171, 175-176
　propositional attitudes and, 187, 188, 189, 192-193
Descriptions:
　concept of, and Wittgenstein, 129-131
　definite. *See* Definite descriptions
Designating:
　functions and, 214
　modality and, 179
　propositional attitudes and, 196
Designation, rules of, 42-43
Designators, 156, 158. *See also* Rigid designators
Dispositional account, of language use, 9-10
Disquotational principle, 92-95
Divided reference, 115-116
Donnellan, on attributive-referential distinction, 152-155, 157, 158, 159, 160

Epimenides' Liar Paradox, 37-38
Epistemic necessity, 88-89, 99
Epistemic sentences, 92-95
Epistemological basis:
　of definite description theory, 106, 128

of essential properties, 177
Essentialism, 170-171, 174-177
Essential properties, and modality, 176-177
"Every," in Frege's technique, 217-218
"Everything," in Frege's technique, 215, 216
Excluded middle, law of, 120
Existence, in Frege's technique, 216-217
Existential circumlocution, 158
Existential generalization, and modality, 169-172
Existential quantifier, 112, 125-127
  general propositions and, 135-136
  See also Generality; Quantification theory
Exportations, and propositional attitudes, 192-193, 196-197
Expression versus speaker meaning, 156-160
Extension, and modality, 180-182
Extensional contexts, xii, 84-85

Facts:
  atomic, 20
  common structure of, 18-19
  complex, 20, 22-26
  correspondence of, to rules, 8-14
  Satzzeichen as representation of, 18-19, 20
  simple, 20, 25
  See also Propositions; Sentences
"Few," and class theory, 228
Formal correctness, 37, 44
Form of an object, 20-21
Form of life, 15
Frege, G.:
  on analysis of general sentences, 108-112, 212-216
  on descriptions as names, 140-151
  on functions, 212-216
  on generality, 142-144, 212-216
  on name relation paradox, 76-83, 121-123
  on quotations, 178, 194
  on sense-nominatum distinction, 74-76, 121
Fregean quantifiers, 212-221

Functions:
  "\," 146-151
  definite descriptions and, 142-144
  indefinite noun phrases and, 212-216
  levels of, 143, 215-216
  propositional, 109
  sentential, 40
  See also Truth functions

Gegenstände (objects), 19-22, 26-27, 128-131
Generality:
  concept-object distinction and, 141-144
  definite descriptions and, 108-115, 119, 132-138, 141-144
  indefinite noun phrases and, 212-229
  modality and, 169-172
  See also Quantification theory
Generalized quantifiers, 228-229
Genetic character, 195
Grice, H. P., on speaker versus expression meaning, 156

"Half as many," and class theory, 227-228
Historical chain of reference-transference, 90-91

Identity:
  criteria of, and belief, 198-201
  intension and, 77, 78
  numerically definite quantifiers and, 222
  rigid designators and, 89-90
  sign of, 127, 141
  substitutivity of, 84
  theoretical, 98-99
"If and only if," 36, 41
"If...then," 24-25, 41
I-language, 12-14
Indefinite articles, 145-146, 211
Indefinite noun phrases:
  class theory and, 225-229
  compared to definite noun phrases, 207-210

Fregean technique for, 212-221
functions and, 212-216
generality and, 212-229
logical analysis of, 212-221
number concept and, 224-226
numerically definite quantifiers and,
    221-223
plurality of, 208
scope ambiguities and, 210-212
scope of generality sign and, 219-221
Individual constants, 40
Intension:
    identity of, 77, 78
    modality and, 180-182
    propositional attitudes and, 199-200
Interchangeability, principle of, 72, 73,
    80, 84, 86, 123
    disquotational principle and, 92-95
    epistemic sentences and, 92-95
    modal sentences and, 91, 169-172,
        174-176, 180. *See also* Modality
    propositional attitudes and, 183-186,
        188-193
    See also Name relation, paradox of
Interpretations. *See De dicto* readings;
    De re readings
"Is," roles of, 141

Kaplan, D.:
    on modality, 177-180
    on necessary-designation relation, 179
    on propositional attitudes, 193-197
Kripke, S.:
    on causal theory of names, 88-99
    on designators, 89-90, 98, 156, 158,
        174-175, 195
    on Donnellan's referential
        descriptions, 155-160
    on modality, 174-177
    on paradigms for natural-kind terms,
        96-97

Language acquisition, 13
Language-reality isomorphism:
    Gegenstände in, 19-22, 26-27,
        129-131
    mathematical multiplicity and, 18-19

reality structure and, 16-29
Satzzeichen in, 18-19, 20
truth and, 31-34
truth functions and, 22-26
Wittgenstein's theory on, 16-22,
    25-29
See also Definite descriptions
Learning, and ontogenesis of reference,
    115-120
Liar Paradox, 37-38
Linguistic philosophy, definition of, ix
Linguistics, definition of, ix
Logical connectives, 22-26, 41-42
Logical contradictions, 54, 61
Logical structure, 17, 27-29, 52
Logico-syntactical employment, 20-21
L-truth, 61. *See also* Truth, logical

Machine-as-symbol, 10
Material adequacy, 35-37, 39, 44
Mathematical functions, 212-214
Mathematical multiplicity, 18-19
Mathematical operations, 4
Mathematical series, 5-6
Meaning:
    causal chain and, 8-10
    dispositional accounts and, 9-10
    I-language and, 12-14
    postulates for, 61-63
    qualitative mental states and, 10-12
    regularity of use and, 16
    rules and, 3-16
    Wittgenstein's paradox and, 3-8
Mental states, and rule following, 10-12
Mention, compared to use, xi
Metalanguages:
    compared to object languages, xi,
        38-40, 173
    definition of, xii
    propositional attitudes and, 188
Metalinguistic sentences, xii
Metaphysical aspect, of essential
    properties, 177
Metaphysical necessity, 88-89, 99
Modality:
    Carnap on, 180-182
    de dicto versus *de re* readings in, 171,
        175-176

essentialism and, 170-171, 174-177
essential properties and, 176-177
existential generalization and,
    169-172
extension, intension, and, 180-182
Fregean quotations and, 178
interchangeability and, 91, 169-172,
    174-176, 180
Kaplan on, 177-180
Kripke on, 174-177
linguistic versus logical, 167-169
necessary-designation relation in, 179
necessity and, 168-171, 172-174
possibility and, 168-170
quantifying into, 170-182
Quine on, 169-174, 178
quotations and, 173-174, 178
state descriptions and, 181
Modal system, definition of, 167
"More than," and class theory, 226-228

Name relation:
    oblique occurrence and, 80-83
    paradox of, 73-74
    paradox of, Frege's solution, 76-83
    paradox of, Quine's solution, 83-85
    paradox of, Russell's solution, 85-86,
        121-123
    principles of, 71-73
Names:
    causal theory of, 88-100
    common structure and, 19-22
    complex, 76-77
    historical chain with referents, 90-91
    nominata of. See Nominata
    of natural kinds, 95-100
    proper. See Proper names
    quotation, 37
    sense of. See Sense, of a name
    sociolinguistic hypothesis and, 100
    structural-descriptive, 39
    vivid, 195
    See also Definite descriptions;
        Gegenstände
Natural-kind terms, 95-100
Necessary-designation relation, 179, 194
Necessity:
    modality and, 168-171, 172-174

naming and, 88-89, 99
"Nec" symbol, and semantic predicates,
    172-174, 194
Negation, and indefinite noun phrases,
    221
"No," in Frege's technique, 218-219
Nominata, 71-73
    extension related to, 180
    oblique versus customary, 81
    sense and, 74-83, 90, 121-123
Nonextensional contexts, xii, 74, 80.
    See also Modality; Propositional
    attitudes
"Not," in Carnap's method, 41
Notional sense, and propositional
    attitudes, 187-192. See also De
    dicto readings
Noun phrases, 49. See also Definite
    descriptions; Indefinite noun
    phrases
Nouns, count versus mass, 115-116
Number concept, 224-226
Numerically definite quantifiers, 221-
    223

Object expressions, 145-151. See also
    Concept-object distinction
Object languages:
    compared to metalanguages, xi,
        38-40, 173
    definition of, xi
Objects (Gegenstände), 19-22, 26-27,
    128-131
Oblique contexts, 80-83, 84-85
Observational terms, 64
Ontogenesis of reference, 115-120
"Or," in Carnap's method, 41

Paradigms, for natural-kind terms, 96-98
Paradoxes:
    Liar, 37-38
    name relation, 73-86, 121-123
    Wittgenstein's, 3-8
Philosophical Investigations
    (Wittgenstein), ix
    central problem of, 14
Philosophy of language, definition of, ix

Picture theory, 16-22, 27-29, 128-134. *See also* Language-reality isomorphism
Possibility, and modality, 168-170
Possible worlds, 58. *See also* State descriptions
Predicates:
  concept-object distinction and, 140-145
  definition of, 40-41
  degree of, 45-48
  modality and, 172-174, 178-179
  types of, and analyticity, 64-65
Primary occurrence, and the existential quantifier, 126
Proper names:
  concept-object distinction and, 140
  generalized quantifiers and, 229
  modality and, 174-175
  name relation paradox and, 83
  necessary truths and, 88-89
  ontogenesis of reference and, 116, 117
  ordinary, 76, 83, 88-91, 98
  propositional attitudes and, 184-185
  reference-transference and, 90-91
  rigid designators and, 89-90, 98, 174-175
  sense and, 76
  See also Definite descriptions; Names
Propositional attitudes:
  belief-identity criteria and, 198-201
  de dicto readings and, 184-186, 187, 188, 192-193
  definition of, 183
  de re readings and, 187, 188, 189, 192-193
  exportations and, 192-193, 196-197
  Fregean quotations and, 194
  intensional structure and, 199-200
  interchangeability and, 183-186, 188-193
  Kaplan on, 193-197
  notional sense and, 187-192
  psychologistic approach to, 200-201
  quantifying into, 185, 186-187, 188, 190, 194

Quine on, 185-193
  quotations and, 186-187, 189-200
  relational sense and, 187-192
  representation relation and, 194-196
  semantic technique for, 187-193
Propositional functions, 40, 109
Propositional prototypes, 132-138
Propositions:
  analytic, 51, 54
  atomic, 131, 132-138
  definition of, xi
  factual, 51
  general, 133-138
  Satzzeichen as formal expression of, 18
  synthetic, 51
  truth, fitting with, 34
  See also Facts; Propositional attitudes; Sentences
Prototype (*Urbild*), propositional, 132-138
Psychologistic approach, to propositional attitudes, 200-201

Qualitative mental states, 10-12
Quantification theory, 57-61, 112
  concept-object distinction and, 141-144
  See also Generality
Quantifiers, 112, 125-127, 135-137
Quantifying into:
  for modal contexts, 170-182
  for propositional-attitude contexts, 185, 186-187, 188, 190, 194
Quine, W. V. O.:
  on epistemic sentences, 92-95
  on modality, 169-174, 178
  on name relation paradox, 83-85
  on notional and relational senses, 187-192
  on propositional attitudes, 185-193
  on quotations, 173-174, 178
  on referential function, acquisition of, 115-119
  on referential occurrence, pure versus opaque, 84-85, 169
Quotation names, 37

Quotations:
modality and, 173-174, 178
propositional attitudes and, 186-187, 189-200

Ranges, rules of, 59-61
Readings, *de dicto* and *de re*. *See De dicto* readings; *De re* readings
Reality structure. *See* Language-reality isomorphism
Reference:
failures of, 118
ontogenesis of, 115-120
See also Nominata
Reference-transference chain, 90-91
Referential-attributive distinction, 152-155, 157, 158, 159, 160
Referential descriptions, 151-161. *See also* Nominata
Referential function, acquisition of, 115-120
Referentially opaque contexts, 84
Referential occurrence, pure versus opaque, 84-85, 169, 184-185. *See also* Modality
Relational sense, and propositional attitudes, 187-192. *See also De re* readings
Relational terms, 118-119, 226-228
Relative clauses, 118-119, 153
Representation relation, 194-196
Rigid designators, 89-90
modality and, 174-175
propositional attitudes and, 195
theoretical identities as, 98
Rules:
causal chain and, 8-10
correspondence of, to concrete facts, 8-14
explicitness of, 4-5
form of life and, 15
inherent in society, 16
interpretations of, 4-8, 16
mental experience and, 10-12
of designation, 42-43
of ranges, 59-61
of truth, 42-45, 47

Wittgenstein's paradox and, 3-8, 14-16
Russell, B.:
Donnellan's referential descriptions and, 155, 157, 158, 159
on name relation paradox, 85-86, 121-123
on subjects that name nothing, 123-125
on theory of descriptions, 105-115, 119-127
on truth-value gaps, 120

Sachverhalten (facts), 20, 22. *See also* Facts
Satisfaction, and definition of truth, 40
Satzzeichen (sign for a fact), 18-19, 20
Saying, of information, 29
Schemata, and logical truth, 52-57
Scope:
definite descriptions and, 109, 125-127
indefinite noun phrases and, 210-212, 219-221
modality and, 175
of the generality sign, 219-221
Secondary occurrence, and the existential quantifier, 126
Self-reference, and Liar Paradox, 38
Semantic conception of truth, 34-49
Semantic predicates, and modality, 172-174, 178-179. *See also* Predicates
Semantic treatment, and propositional attitudes, 187-193
Semantic versus speaker referent, 156-160
Sense, of a name:
determinacy of, 128-129
essential properties and, 96
natural-kind terms and, 95-96
nominata and, 74-83, 90, 121-123
referential-attributive distinction and, 152, 154
Sense, of propositional attitude constructions, 186-192
Sense impressions, acquaintance with, 106-107

Sentences:
  analytic, 63-65
  atomic, and definition of truth, 42-45
  atomic, and state descriptions, 59-61
  atomic, definition of, 59
  complex, and definition of truth,
    42-45
  definition of, x
  epistemic, 92-95
  general, 61, 108-112, 132-138,
    212-216
  identity, 61, 77, 78, 89-90
  modal, 74, 91, 167-182. *See also*
    Modality
  necessity, 168-171
  observation, 64-65
  possibility, 168-170
  range of, 59-61
  universal, 62
  See also Facts; Propositions
Sentential functions, 40. *See also*
  Propositional functions
Sequence of objects, 46-47
Shakespearean context, 175, 185
Sociolinguistic hypothesis, 100
"Some," in Frege's technique, 218-219
"Something," in Frege's technique,
  216-217
Speaker versus expression meaning,
  156-160
Speaker versus semantic referent,
  156-160
State descriptions, 58-61, 181
Structural-descriptive names, 39
Structure:
  logical, 17, 27-29, 52
  of language and reality, 16-29, 31-34
  See also Definite descriptions
Subject matter, principle of, 72-73, 82,
  84
Subordinate clauses, 49. *See also*
  Propositional attitudes
Substitutivity of identity, 84. *See also*
  Interchangeability, principle of
Syncategorematic expressions, 118

Tarski, A., and semantic conception of
  truth, 35-49

Tractatus Logico-Philosophicus
  (Wittgenstein), 17
Transformation rules, for
  truth-functional logic, 55-56
Truth:
  analytic, 61-66
  a posteriori, 99
  a priori, 89, 99
  as property of sentences, 48
  as relation between sentence, person,
    and time, 48-49
  causal theory of names and, 88-100
  contingent, 50-51
  definitions of, and material adequacy,
    35-37, 39, 44
  definitions of, and meta- and object
    languages, 37-40
  definitions of, and satisfaction, 40
  definitions of, Carnap's method,
    40-45
  definitions of, extensions of, 45-49
  definitions of, for atomic sentences,
    43, 47
  definitions of, for complex sentences,
    44
  epistemic versus metaphysical
    necessity of, 88-89
  logical, and quantification theory,
    57-61
  logical, and schemata, 52-57
  logical, and state descriptions, 58-61
  logical, and truth-functional theory,
    52-57
  logical, and validity, 52-61
  logical, definition of, 61
  not absolute, 31-34
  role of, 31
  rules of, 42-45
  semantic conception of, 34-49
  unconditional, 50-51
Truth functions, 22-26
  general propositions and, 134-137
  logical truth and, 52-57
  validity and, 53-54
Truth tables, 22-25, 53-54
Truth-values:
  functions and, 144, 214
  gaps in, 105-106, 120

Uniqueness, securing of, 112-113, 125, 127-128
Universal quantifier, 112, 136-137, 216. *See also* Generality; Quantification theory
Univocality, principle of, 72
Urbild (prototype), propositional, 132-138
Use, of language:
by rule versus by causal chain, 8-10
mention and, xi
Utterance, x

Validity:
in quantification theory, 57-61
in truth-functional theory, 53-57
logical truth and, 52-61
proof of, 54-57
truth tables and, 53-54
Value ranges, 146-151
Values, of functions, 213
Variables, 109, 213

Verbs, and propositional attitudes, 183-184
Vivid names, 195

Wittgenstein, L.:
of *Tractatus* versus Wittgenstein of *Investigations*, 17
on definite descriptions, 127-138
on language-reality isomorphism, 16-22, 25-29
on language use, ix
on machine-as-symbol, 10
on paradigms for natural-kind terms, 97-98
on propositional attitudes, 200-201
on qualitative mental states, 11-13
paradox of, 3-8, 14-16
truth tables and, 53
Word order, 18-19
World structure. *See* Language-reality isomorphism

About the Author

I. E. Mackenzie is currently Lecturer (Assistant Professor) in the School of Modern Languages at the University of Newcastle upon Tyne. He was educated at the universities of Oxford and Cambridge. His doctoral dissertation was on the semantics of Spanish verbal categories and was supervised by John Lyons. His research interests are diverse, ranging from the philosophy of language to Spanish and Latin American linguistics. He has published articles and reports on the philosophy of language, Spanish semantics, and language contact in the Andes.